Inuit Education and Schools in the Eastern Arctic

Inuit Education and Schools in the Eastern Arctic

Heather E. McGregor

UBCPress · Vancouver · Toronto

20 19 18 17 16 15 14 13 12 11 10   5 4 3 2 1

Printed in Canada on FSC-certified ancient-forest-free paper (100% post-consumer recycled) that is processed chlorine- and acid-free.

Printed in Canada on acid-free paper

Library and Archives Canada Cataloguing in Publication

McGregor, Heather E., 1983-
Inuit education and schools in the Eastern Arctic / Heather E. McGregor.

Includes bibliographical references and index.
ISBN 978-0-7748-1744-8 (bound); ISBN 978-0-7748-1745-5 (pbk.)

1. Inuit – Education – Nunavut – History. 2. Education and state – Nunavut – History. I. Title.

E99.E7M343 2010   371.829'7107195   C2010-901053-1

e-book ISBNs: 978-0-7748-1746-2 (pdf); 978-0-7748-5936-3 (epub)

Canadä

UBC Press gratefully acknowledges the financial support for our publishing program of the Government of Canada (through the Canada Book Fund), the Canada Council for the Arts, and the British Columbia Arts Council.

This book has been published with the help of a grant from the Canadian Federation for the Humanities and Social Sciences, through the Aid to Scholarly Publications Programme, using funds provided by the Social Sciences and Humanities Research Council of Canada.

UBC Press
The University of British Columbia
2029 West Mall
Vancouver, BC V6T 1Z2
www.ubcpress.ca

Contents

Illustrations

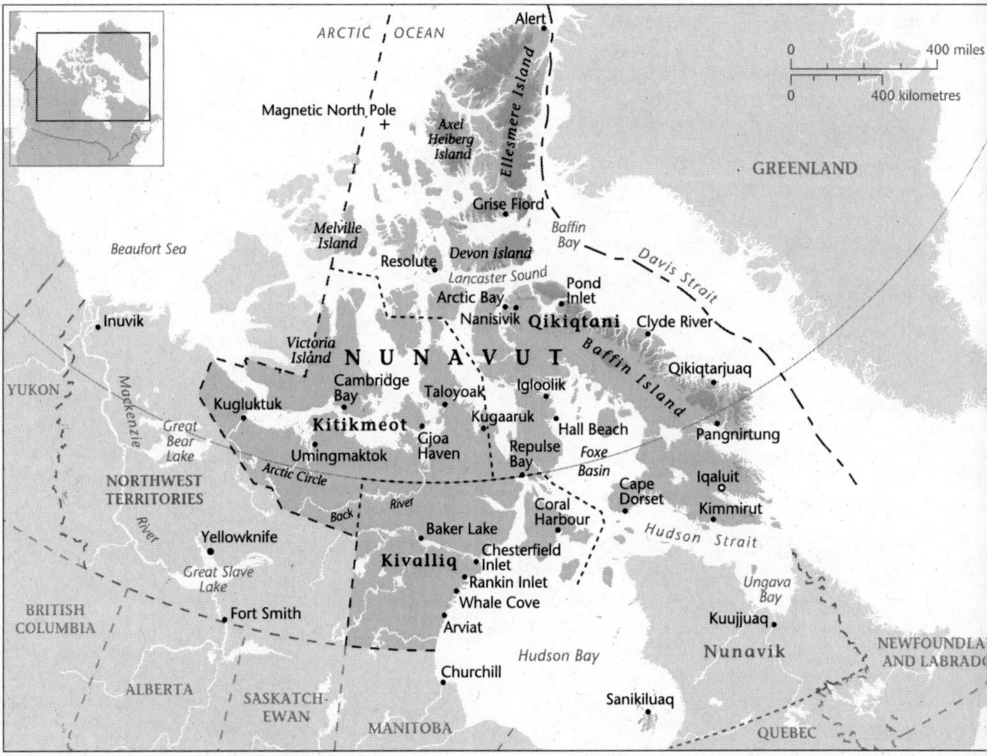

Figure 1 Map of Canada's northern territories, featuring Nunavut. Adapted from a map by Natural Resources Canada, 2009 and reproduced with permission, courtesy of the Atlas of Canada.

Preface

THIS HISTORY IS ABOUT how education unfolded in the Eastern Arctic during the twentieth century. In keeping with the view that history is a living process, it should be read not only as a collection of historical evidence but also as a contribution to the dialogue about where we have come from and what we have learned about Inuit education. It is intended not as a definitive narrative but as an invitation to examine more closely the factors that have influenced the purpose and practice of education in the Eastern Arctic.

What qualifies me to use the term "we" with regard to Inuit education? The debate as to the proper role for Euro-Canadian academics in Aboriginal or Inuit historiography is important, and cultural sensitivity is equally imperative. In her comments on Inuit historiography, historian Shelagh D. Grant argues that an Inuk would be best suited to capture and interpret the cultural nuances of his or her people's history.[1] Those familiar with research in Aboriginal communities and cultures know that scholar Linda Tuhiwai Smith has also led the call for Aboriginal peoples to write their own histories: "Indigenous peoples want to tell our own stories, write our own versions, in our own ways, for our own purposes."[2] I strongly concur with Grant and Smith, particularly because this history is relatively recent and focused on the experiences of people who are still living, the majority of whom are Inuit. The early chapters of the book have been informed by Elders and older Inuit who remember the traditional period of their youth, and the latter chapters refer to the experiences of nearly everyone in Nunavut – all those who had contact with the formal education system. However, a written history of Inuit education or schooling in the Eastern Arctic, authored by an Inuk, has not yet come about. In the meantime, Grant argues, non-Aboriginal historians, such as myself, "Must ask themselves whether they have a responsibility to help bridge the cultural divide by adding an Inuit voice to their writing."[3] To this question I respond with a resounding "yes." One of my goals is to incorporate the perspectives of Inuit to the greatest extent possible. I hope to bridge the gap between the work of scholars who contribute to a body of knowledge about the past, and the experiences of Inuit who continue to be influenced by the legacy of their Elders.[4]

The relationship between research and social, economic, and political power, especially in cross-cultural and postcolonial societies, compels authors to be transparent about their own position and perspective.[5] In writing a history that deals in large part with Inuit culture, I do not pretend to offer or to replace the insight of an Inuit perspective. My personal position in this history, however, is more complex and therefore due explanation. It is my first-hand experience and my own contact with the formal education system in the Eastern Arctic that have informed my conviction about this subject and the shape of this book.

I am the child of two "northerners," a term which I define as Euro-Canadians who have chosen to live almost their entire adult lives in the Arctic rather than where they came from or elsewhere. My parents have spent their careers in the territories, and have become part of the communities in which they have lived, including Yellowknife, where I was born. My parents later chose to live and raise me in Iqaluit, partially because of the unique experience we could have by participating in the birth of Nunavut Territory. The children of long-term northerners – such as myself – are some of the only Euro-Canadian children in Canada who grow up as minorities to an Aboriginal population. This is a unique experience that has undoubtedly shaped my perspective on this history, a perspective of liminality.[6]

I use the term "liminality" because I am a Qallunaaq[7] who speaks English as a first (and only fluent) language, who calls Iqaluit home, and who has had a deep respect for Inuit culture since the age of seven. This position of liminality results from a number of multifaceted particularities, which, taken together, illustrate the complexity of relationships in this cross-cultural context and cannot be simplified into two opposing categories such as insider versus outsider or powerful versus powerless.

Qallunaat have historically been a powerful and privileged minority in the Arctic who brought with them the inequities of colonialism. This legacy, not yet extinguished, is discussed in greater detail throughout this book. However, since 1993 the exercise of, and access to, social, economic, and cultural power has been shifting in the Eastern Arctic. The Nunavut Land Claims Agreement, which led to the creation of Nunavut and formed the basis of the public territorial government, brought with it cultural and linguistic initiatives. More important, it brought about entitlements for the Inuit residing in Nunavut, now called "beneficiaries." For example, beneficiaries receive preferable consideration for employment in the Government of Nunavut, whereas few provisions are made for Qallunaat, even if they were born and raised in the Arctic. The status of the Qallunaat minority has become much more nuanced since the creation of Nunavut, and what might be viewed as the privileges of my

Qallunaat identity are not as straightforward and powerful as might be assumed at first glance.

Broadly speaking, this complex situation demands that I define myself in relation to Inuit culture and the Arctic and, by extension, to this history. Even if I choose to label myself a "northerner" and wish to be viewed as an "insider," I could easily be mistaken by both southerners and northerners as an "outsider." In the eyes of most Inuit, and the provisions of the Nunavut Land Claims Agreement, I am a Qallunaaq, no matter how many years I live in the Arctic or how much I understand about Inuit culture. I am from the Arctic and call it my home on the basis of my experience there and my respect for the people and land. I feel very close to the traditions, values, priorities, and visions of Inuit as I have encountered them in my life. However, I cannot claim them as my own, and I am aware that my white face brings with it some remnants of the colonial past, my personal intentions, beliefs, and actions notwithstanding. Therefore, I occupy a position of liminality in the discussion of culture, ethnicity, and place herein.

My challenge, then, is to find ways to feature the Inuit perspective on the events represented in this history both as accurately as possible and as a means to balance out the many strong Qallunaat voices that are available through the historical record. Before undertaking this research, I anticipated difficulty writing about traditional Inuit education because of the limited documentary evidence from the Inuit perspective prior to the 1960s. On another level, I faced the difficulty of disentangling "education" as a Western idea from its more integrated role in Inuit society. Because Inuit education did not traditionally comprise a separate set of practices, supervised and documented by an administrative body, this topic necessitated input from Elders who were raised and educated by their parents on the land. I was further challenged by my intention to include evidence that spans a fairly long period (the entire twentieth century), that is also geographically representative (covering the entire Eastern Arctic and, in some cases, beyond), and that reflects some gender parity. Due to the breadth of my intended study, I felt that conducting interviews with Elders or other individuals might unduly limit the survey approach that I was hoping to employ in researching these issues of education through time and across the regions.

There are a number of other reasons why conducting interviews was not ideal in the context of this research. One reason was that I gained access to an important set of documents: the meeting minutes of the Elders' Advisory Committee, maintained by the Nunavut Department of Education. These numerous verbatim meeting transcripts reflect discussion facilitated by the department but structured as open-ended conversations between Elders. They talk about their experiences with education as children in a traditional context and about how those experiences may relate to the modern education system. This group of Elders is made up of men and women from throughout Nunavut who were asked to participate in such discussions because of their interest in education. Their discussions take place in Inuktitut and are later translated into English.[8] I also opted to use these documents because the cost, time, and logistical challenges involved in conducting comparable interviews or discussion groups would have been beyond my means, particularly as the resulting information might inform only a portion of my research.

The use of excerpts from these meeting minutes did, however, present a logistical challenge, one that allowed me insight into the difficulties of conducting primary research in Nunavut. This experience is worth describing here for the benefit of future researchers and historians working in Nunavut. Conducting research in this context is highly demanding, particularly in terms of communication barriers, cost, cultural expectations, and the participant-driven research imperative.

It is the prerogative of anyone participating in research to establish the conditions of their involvement. As Linda Tuhiwai Smith has commented, taking on the role of researcher, especially in small cross-cultural communities, involves an ongoing negotiation of relationships, especially because of the legacy of pain that inappropriate and invasive research methods have caused Aboriginal communities. Smith is unforgiving in her explanation of the role that research has played in the colonial experience: "The ways in which scientific research is implicated in the worst excesses of colonialism remains a powerful remembered history for many of the world's colonized peoples. It is a history that still offends the deepest sense of our humanity."[9] Her warning refers to scientific research, but that legacy equally applies to history and the humanities. Research must be participant-driven, and researchers must seriously investigate how to meet the expectations of participants and how to approach them appropriately.

However, meeting the above-mentioned expectations in Nunavut is not simple. A multiplicity of demands, which are sometimes contradictory, must be taken into consideration. In addition to meeting the criteria of the ethics review board at one's home institution, researchers are required to obtain a Nunavut Research Institute (NRI) licence. NRI licences are issued only if the researcher has demonstrated consultation and gained permission from all local or interested organizations, such as Government of Nunavut departments, municipalities, and Inuit organizations. This stipulation means in practice that researchers usually have to gain ethics approval simply to conduct preliminary consultations in order to determine whether the research is possible. While the NRI has a straightforward and effective protocol for research evaluation, most other organizations in Nunavut conduct reviews of research proposals on a more ad hoc basis. Gaining permission or co-operation may involve meeting inconsistent or unusual requirements, and much time can be taken up simply trying to determine what conditions should be met in order to proceed.

For example, the Department of Education required that I submit an application to the Nunavut Research Institute for a licence simply to access the Elders' Advisory Committee transcripts, which are undoubtedly part of the public record. For me to use excerpts from the transcripts, the department required that I approach each Elder individually and ask his or her permission to include a particular excerpt in this book. The NRI disagreed with this requirement and declined to grant me a formal licence, perceiving it to be unnecessary, but recorded my activity nonetheless. I did approach the Elders to request their permission in accordance with the department's wishes and to ensure full transparency on my part. I was obligated to use a number of proxy individuals located in the respective communities where the Elders live to deliver formal letters (in Inuktitut), to be signed by each Elder as an indication of his or her permission. It would have been nearly impossible for me to approach each individual myself for this purpose due to the extremely high cost of travel in Nunavut. I am lucky to have been able to leverage personal and professional contacts in order to meet this requirement. With regard to this process and any research in the Arctic, communication is commonly delayed, and attempting to conduct research from afar certainly results in a lack of the personal connections that are so important in gaining the assistance and trust of anyone involved in research.

In addition to the Elders' Advisory Committee transcripts, I searched a wide range of sources in an effort to draw out commentary by Inuit on education at its various stages throughout history. I collected Inuit voices from sources such as books, newspaper and magazine articles, and short stories as well as other reflections written by Inuit. I consulted transcripts of Inuit oral history that contain testimonies or memories regarding childhood and education. I used excerpts from interviews or research projects with Inuit, particularly those from which verbatim quotations could be extracted. I also accessed a few speeches by Inuit leaders. Much of this evidence offers a retrospective view of education, and many of the comments were made for other purposes or in other contexts, that may have had little to do with studying formal education. In terms of more recent history, Inuit have taken on leadership roles in the administration of formal education, and therefore some conclusions can be drawn about their perspective on education by analyzing the changes they have made to the system. I hope that these Inuit voices – set in the context of the scholarly evidence, Qallunaat perspective, and analysis I have added – are a prominent feature of this investigation. Such sources are intended to support the middle-ground perspective strived for in this history and to inform respectful, careful, and useful conclusions.

Acknowledgments

I WOULD LIKE TO thank the following Elders as well as Joe Karetak for permitting me to include their thoughts and words in this work: Mark Kalluak, Mariano Aupilardjuk, the late Gideon Qitsualik, Alice Ayalik, and Moses Koihok. I would also like to thank the Department of Education in Nunavut for its assistance with a number of components of this research.

Throughout the development and editing of this manuscript, I received thoughtful, encouraging, and constructive feedback from a number of individuals. I would like to especially recognize Ruth Sandwell for her support during the research process and for her major contributions to this work in its earliest iterations, as well as for suggesting that I pursue publication. Heidi Bohaker also provided important insight and feedback in the early editing stages. I would like to thank the two anonymous peer reviewers for UBC Press who validated the importance of this story and helped me to improve its presentation. I owe a particular debt of gratitude to Darcy Cullen at UBC Press, who has been an invaluable resource and support to me.

My husband, Phil McComiskey, deserves many thanks for his unconditional patience and support throughout this chapter of our life together.

My mother and father, Catherine and Cameron McGregor, are my greatest teachers, and I benefit from their experience, wisdom, and support every day. It is certain that I could not have brought this manuscript to life without them. The resources located, the questions answered, and the logistical challenges solved by them are too numerous to count! This book is a testament to the intention with which they have encouraged me to engage with, and reflect on, the world I experience around me. It is dedicated to them and to the passion with which they have lived and worked in the Arctic. Anaana, Ataata: Akuluk!

Inuit Education and Schools in the Eastern Arctic

Introduction

NUNAVUT TERRITORY IS by all accounts a unique part of Canada and of the world. It is the first and only large geographic and political jurisdiction where the majority of voters in a public government are of Inuit or – using a term more broadly familiar – Aboriginal descent. The people of Nunavut have emerged from the experience of colonization to re-establish control over their own lands and to form and exercise their own political and bureaucratic machinery in an effort to capture the tools of self-government. In contrast to this accomplishment, only a minority (albeit a growing minority) of students graduate from high school in Nunavut – the number varies between 25 and 30 percent. Substantially fewer students continue their education at the post-secondary level. Indeed, Justice Thomas R. Berger characterized the state of Inuit education as a "crisis" in a 2006 report to the Government of Canada.[1] The label "crisis" and the apparent contradiction between Nunavut's political achievements and its educational shortcomings beg the question: What does history tell us about the foundations on which education in the Eastern Arctic was built, the direction it has taken over time, and the meaning and importance of education to Inuit? What do we find by taking a close look at the role of curriculum, the role of teachers, the role of administration, and the involvement of parents in Eastern Arctic education?

This investigation is couched in a complex cross-cultural context that raises further questions: Can the colonial roots of this system, perhaps still perpetuated, be blamed for discouraging Inuit from pursuing academic accomplishment in the typical Western sense? Should we point to the cultural gap between Inuit students and parents, on the one hand, and Qallunaat, English-speaking teachers, on the other? What impact has come from the employment of Inuit as classroom teachers or from the increasing opportunity for Inuit parents to participate in educational decision making? How important is the recognition and integration, or lack thereof, of educational content, practices, and outcomes envisioned by Inuit to achieving a functional and relevant formal school system? What does this predicament of the modern school system say about the importance of education to Inuit as an ingredient of self-government, especially in the context of their preparation for the coming of Nunavut Territory?

Conversely, what important educational successes deserve distinct recognition, despite a low graduation rate? This book offers educators, administrators, and researchers a historical overview of educational change in the Eastern Arctic, focusing on the themes of cultural negotiation, decision-making power, and the role of tradition in education.

The modern context must first be put aside in order to examine historical questions about the profound changes in education that accompanied sustained contact between Inuit and Qallunaat in the twentieth century. Change was complex, varied, and non-linear, but for the sake of clarity in this brief history, it is examined with reference to four designated periods. The earliest, the traditional period, includes the history of the Inuit prior to colonization by Qallunaat, which began around 1945. Although studying the traditional period presents methodological challenges, the identification of educational practices in existence before contact allows for the development of a definition of "Inuit education" in Chapter 2. This definition includes an exploration of both educational content and methodology, as well as an understanding of the ways education was socially and culturally situated. Using research that draws on as many Inuit sources as are available, this book endeavours to identify the most important aspects of Inuit education and to explain why they were effective. It addresses what were believed to be the necessary ingredients of an education that was intended to produce a happy, self-confident, and self-sufficient person in accordance with Inuit values and worldview. It examines why Inuit education was well suited to the structure of this hunter-gatherer society, which was largely defined by its relationship to the environment, and why it remained in practice up until the time of the abandonment of subsistence hunting and nomadic or semi-nomadic rounds after 1945. This history then proceeds to examine the trajectory of educational change during the three subsequent periods of formal education, termed "colonial," "territorial," and "local," respectively.

Three strands of investigation into each period tie this history together: (1) identification of aspects of Inuit education employed in the schools, what purpose those aspects were thought to serve, and to what extent that purpose was realized in practice; (2) characterization of the relationship between Inuit education and the Qallunaat, or formal, system of education; and (3) recognition of who initiated and controlled educational change. During the colonial period of 1945 to 1970, those with political power in the Eastern Arctic – the bureaucrats and administrators within the federal government – chose to introduce a formal school system characterized by an assimilationist policy agenda. However, just when the Qallunaat system of schools was being solidified, administration of education was transferred to the territorial government in

1970. The territorial period ushered in a new set of educational priorities that were better tailored for the Northwest Territories (NWT) but still primarily controlled by Qallunaat, an arrangement that characterized the schools across the territory until 1982. During the local period, which lasted from 1982 to 1999, most educational decision making occurred at the level of district education authorities and regional school boards, and it focused on the re-establishment of Inuit education through the school system. Local control of education through these mechanisms brought about a form of education widely contributed to, and supported by, Inuit. This had the best capacity to reflect Inuit culture, their relationship with the environment, and their vision of the future.

Chapter 3 explains how and why the Qallunaat formal school system was introduced in the Arctic during the colonial period and evaluates the impact of this change on the experience of young Inuit. The collapse of the subsistence hunter-gatherer economy occurred in response to a number of changes, resulting in the colonization of Inuit in the Eastern Arctic and their disempowerment. During the colonial period, education played a pivotal role in bringing Inuit into the settlements and keeping them there. What did formal schooling, in its various forms (i.e., religiously affiliated residential and day schools, practical programs for older students, or regional high schools) offer Inuit in terms of advantages in their transition to a new way of life? How did it facilitate or disrupt the acquisition of traditional Inuit education? I examine not only the goals of colonial educators but also how Inuit children and their parents responded to expectations that they learn and become like Qallunaat rather than according to their own heritage.

The subject of Chapter 4 is the educational change that occurred when responsibility for education was transferred from the federal government to the Government of the Northwest Territories in 1970. Using documentary evidence produced by the territorial government, such as educational reviews, curriculum guides, teaching materials, and official letters, this chapter explores the change that occurred when assimilation was no longer considered a reasonable goal for schooling in the Arctic. This exploration includes identification of the aspects of Inuit education that began to be employed in the Qallunaat system, the reasons behind this change, and the resulting effect on Inuit communities. Why and to what extent did Qallunaat support the recognition of Inuit culture during the territorial period? What role did Inuit themselves have in changing the education system?

Chapter 5 covers the local period, which lasted from 1982 to 1999 and describes the rise and fall of the regional boards of education in the Eastern Arctic. My case study of the Baffin Divisional Board of Education examines Inuit control of education through local and regional authorities. It serves to highlight the vision of education established through these mechanisms and the extent to which this vision lines up with traditional Inuit education. Which aspects of education were prioritized by Inuit? How were they manifested within the confines of formal schools? There is more evidence during this period of efforts to incorporate aspects of Inuit education into the formal system; such aspects must have been viewed as effective, but was this really the case in practice? The chapter then investigates how these changes had an impact on the capacity of Inuit to be economically self-sufficient and to prepare for the coming of Nunavut. This period coincided with the pursuit of Inuit political self-determination in the Eastern Arctic through negotiation with the federal government for a land claim and a separate territory. Through the Nunavut Land Claims Agreement, the Inuit voiced their desire not only to retain responsibility for their land, wildlife, and resources but also to be involved in social issues such as language use and adherence to Inuit values as the foundation for their children's economic and social future. What role was education seen to have both in the preparation for, and in the maintenance of, Inuit self-determination in the Eastern Arctic? Ultimately, this book works toward determining the point when responsibility for education was effectively returned to Inuit, and when the education system became one by which they could fulfill their vision of the past and the future, and support their children in becoming successful adults in Inuit terms.

Terms and Definitions

Terms like "colonial" and "local" and using them to designate time periods in this history imply greater absolutes than are intended. The four phases of educational history are labelled according to my understanding of the dominant experience of most people in the Eastern Arctic during each timeframe. In referring to the earliest phase as "traditional," I am not arguing that traditional pursuits and values disappeared entirely from daily life during the subsequent periods. Rather, traditional pursuits were the dominant experience of most people and broadly characterized the education they practised. Likewise, I am not arguing that the limits I have imposed on the colonial period can (or should) encapsulate the entire process of colonization or assimilation of Inuit in the Eastern Arctic. Instead, it is labelled thus to draw out a characterization of schooling and of the relations between Inuit and Qallunaat. The territorial period is essentially straightforward, referring to the diminishing role of the federal government in direct administration of services. However, some may question my contention that it led to the local period of the late 1980s. I use the term "local" partly to draw attention to the local education authorities and regional school boards, which took a very active role in education. In addition, the local period reveals that in the interim between the negotiations for an Inuit land claim in the late 1980s and the realization of Nunavut Territory in 1999, many Inuit turned their focus away from a territorial perspective and toward their communities, where they experienced greater self-determination. Although this book does not cover the post-1999 period, it is clear that by then education had shifted back to a territorial (i.e., Nunavut) emphasis. I use these terms to emphasize and organize the experiences and practices that dominated daily life. Further discussion and explanation of the periodization follows throughout the chapters, but it should be noted that each period exists in a fluid and overlapping relationship to the others and that the terms applied to them are primarily thematic.

Inuit, meaning "the people," is the term used by the Aboriginal population of Canada who live in the Eastern Arctic to identify themselves. The language of most Inuit is Inuktitut, which includes various regional dialects and is written in both syllabics and Roman orthography.[2] The Aboriginal people of Nunavik or Northern Quebec, Labrador (Innu), and the Mackenzie Delta (Inuvialuit) are also sometimes referred to as Inuit, but for the most part this book refers specifically to those who reside in what is now Nunavut Territory. Nunavut consists of an 85 percent Inuit population and very few other Aboriginal peoples; culture and language are relatively homogenous across the territory. The term "Aboriginal" is also used where I refer to other northern Aboriginal groups, such as in the context of the former Northwest Territories. The terms "Indigenous" and "Eskimo," which Inuit do not typically use, are included only if they appear in original sources being quoted.

Language can offer important insights into a culture and worldview, and throughout this book I use a number of Inuktitut terms for tools, ideas, or feelings, which will appear *italicized* and with translations provided within the text or footnotes. Indeed, many Inuktitut words are commonly part of English speech in Nunavut, perhaps the most significant of which is Qallunaat. *Qallunaaq* (singular) or *Qallunaat* (plural) (also spelled Qablunaat, Kablunait, and Kabloona) means "white man" or "European."[3] It bears the Inuktitut root word for eyebrow, which has brought speculation that the Inuit who first encountered Europeans were impressed by their bushy eyebrows. However, the word is generally used to refer to any outsiders to Nunavut or any non-Inuit; it is not necessarily ethnically specific to Euro-Canadians. Minnie Aodla Freeman offers a definition that speaks to another possible origin of the word: "Possibly an abbreviation of *qallunaaraaluit:* powerful, avaricious, of materialistic habit, people who tamper with nature."[4] I have not italicized the term throughout this book due to the frequency with which it is used.

Histories and discourses focused on Aboriginal people, tradition, and culture tend to use dichotomous language and, consciously or unconsciously, to reinforce binaries such as white/Indian, authentic/inauthentic, formal/informal. In some cases, these dichotomies are very real, but nonetheless, they can be detrimental by solidifying differences, diminishing commonalities, and thus closing the dialogue between ways of knowing, being, and doing. In trying to represent the experience of education in the Eastern Arctic, I cannot avoid identifying differences between Inuit and Qallunaat practices and ways of living and thereby potentially reinforcing such damaging dichotomies. For example, I refer to Inuit education as "traditional" and "informal," which will be viewed in opposition to Qallunaat education as "modern" and "formal." By using these descriptions, I do not intend to suggest that Inuit education is not vital or does not have the potential to be relevant in today's world. By calling it informal, I do not intend to convey that throughout history Inuit education has not been intentional or conducted with care. Indeed, the evidence presented here demonstrates quite the opposite. By the end of this book, the meanings of words like *tradition, culture,* and *education* will have taken on a new life through examination in this context. However, one cannot add depth and detail to our common understandings of concepts without starting from those common understandings. In Canadian society the word "education" implies formality because it happens according to agreed-on locations, schedules, standard grade levels, and rules of behaviour. These formalities do not necessarily apply to Inuit education, thereby rendering it (for these purposes), informal. Although I am aware of the problems created by language and the application of rigid concepts, I hope these problems will not unduly constrain the narrative of this history.

View of the Field

The history of education in the Eastern Arctic has been the subject of relatively little research or publication. A number of articles that appeared in the 1970s outlined the development of the northern education system, primarily summarizing official reports and statistics.[5] Northern scholars such as R. Quinn Duffy, David Damas, and Frank Tester and Peter Kulchyski have included chapters on, or references to, education in their general treatments of Arctic history.[6] All have treated education as part and parcel of the experience of colonization, permanent settlement, or mistreatment by the federal government during the drastic changes to Inuit life in the twentieth century. Frank Darnell is perhaps the pre-eminent circumpolar educational historian. He has referred to the Eastern Arctic within the context of his circumpolar view, drawing comparisons between regions in which many of the issues are similar but manifest themselves differently according to national particularities.[7] With Anton Hoem, Darnell has spoken to the social and cultural dynamics of educating "minority" groups and their relationship to dominant governments in contexts of "ethnic pluralism."[8] Darnell's discussion of creating education systems that both reinforce particular cultures and support multiculturalism is convincing and has done much to support this book. However, because his conclusions are drawn in a comparative format across a number of regions, they also warrant greater, more detailed examination in the context of the Eastern Arctic. Mary A. Van Meenan's 1994 doctoral dissertation also uses circumpolar comparison to evaluate the relationship between government and the Inuit in the sector of education.[9] Her study draws broad strokes in covering the history of educational administration from 1900 to 1990 in the Northwest Territories and Siberia, eventually arguing in favour of local control of education by Inuit. In particular, she details the shortcomings of, and levels a great deal of criticism against, the Canadian government for its approach to creating a system of education for Inuit. Education in the Eastern Arctic appears in these works as a subject subsumed by other comparisons and larger narratives, suggesting that a detailed examination of the influences on, and results of, educational change is not only still pending but may also have the potential to offer insight into a number of other historical themes.

Ann Vick-Westgate's monograph *Nunavik: Inuit-Controlled Education in Arctic Quebec* represents a recent and comprehensive effort at recording the history of Inuit leadership in education in the nearby region of Northern Quebec.[10] Vick-Westgate draws attention to the process of reclaiming the formal school system in a cross-cultural and postcolonial context through local control of education. She suggests that leadership in educational change largely came from outside of the Nunavik schools – from parents, community members, and leaders who were not formally affiliated with the formal school system. Vick-Westgate also relies on the testimony of Inuit, allowing her history to flow directly from their voices. She draws parallels and demonstrates shared themes between the history of education in Nunavik and the history of education in other First Nations and rural Canadian communities. More importantly, she effectively illuminates educational change in one previously under-researched rural region of Canada and offers the voices and experiences of Inuit to the historical dialogue on education. I hope this book can begin to accomplish the same for the Inuit of Nunavut.

This book draws on themes and issues in the history of rural Canada and rural education to explore and situate changes in Inuit education. Although circumstances, local particularities, and even time periods differ greatly, many comparable themes and experiences are shared by southern rural Canada and other parts of the North. J.D. Wilson's examination of teaching in rural British

Columbia in the early twentieth century suggests that in comparison to urban schools, rural schools operated according to a different set of standards, including the highly demanding jack-of-all-trades role expected of teachers in rural communities.[11] Neil Sutherland has documented the demands on children of rural farming families in contributing to the economic viability of the family in addition to attending school.[12] These experiences in rural contexts clearly mirror those of the Eastern Arctic's early educators and of Inuit children who were commonly pulled out of school on a seasonal basis to participate in hunting trips. Mike Corbett provides an argument in support of rurality as a motivator and explanatory factor for resistance to education in Canadian communities.[13] His suggestion that schooling was largely perceived as "disconnected from life" in rural areas based on their economic activities applies to this northern context as well, although there is an added element of cultural and ethnic relevance here that he does not examine closely. The field of rural history is particularly pertinent to this book because it demonstrates that relationships – between communities and educational institutions, for example – cannot necessarily be considered consistent within each province or territory; rather, they are significantly impacted by factors such as proximity to urban centres, population density, economic pursuits, and local culture.

Research significant to this book has also occurred in the fields of anthropology and education. Historians must distance themselves, to a certain extent, from the frameworks by which anthropologists approach their subjects.[14] As well, the historic relationship between anthropologists and Aboriginal cultures has been subject to criticism, particularly when such studies result in essentialist or reductionist conclusions that operate to reinforce colonialism.[15] Anthropologists have a long history of involvement with Inuit in the Eastern Arctic, the most famous of whom are Knud Rasmussen, Franz Boas, and Diamond Jenness.[16] Indeed, whereas history is scant in supporting our understanding of Inuit culture and way of life through time, anthropology is substantial. More recent and useful anthropological studies operate less by way of contained and focused methodological application and more according to what we now call ethnography. John J. Honigmann and Irma Honigmann's 1965 report from Frobisher Bay (now Iqaluit) provides insights into the adjustments and challenges experienced by Inuit at the time of, or just after, the transition to permanent community settlement.[17] Jean Briggs's account of a year of study with the Utku Inuit, near Gjoa Haven, illuminates the "traditional" way of life (practised even as late as 1963), describes her observations of the inner, emotional patterning of Inuit in this context, and provides important conclusions about the nature of family and parenting in Inuit culture.[18] Hugh Brody's *The People's Land* and *The Other*

Side of Eden are highly significant and candid analyses of the experience of a hunter-gatherer society merging with a Western capitalist society through the process of colonialism in the late twentieth century.[19] Lastly, Arlene Stairs has done much to contribute to understanding Inuit identity and has drawn attention to linguistic nuances such as the different words used for traditional learning and formal learning.[20] These studies offer insight and reinforcement both to references made by Inuit informants and to my conclusions about the nature of Inuit culture and practices.

Fiona O'Donoghue,[21] Joanne Tompkins, and Lynn Aylward provide the foundation of current research on the Eastern Arctic in the field of education.[22] All three draw on themes of ethnicity or race, culture, and equality in schools, particularly in terms of educational leadership and professional development. Fiona O'Donoghue and her co-authors identify the paucity of sources that reflect Inuit perspectives on education, and indeed on the history of education in the Eastern Arctic in general, as a significant challenge to the work of developing best practices in education. They argue persuasively that the collection of this history could potentially bring great benefit to Inuit education in Nunavut:

> The history of Inuit education in the Qikiqtani (Baffin) Region needs to be written and published for sharing with new educators in orientations and professional learning experiences. Best practices identified by Inuit can provide examples of transformational practice to guide education as it evolves in Nunavut. This research started to explore aspects of this history through the personal recollections shared during the intense discussions. Participants expressed a need to share the many stories of successful Inuit leadership in a variety of contextualized educational initiatives. They believe these stories reveal a particular and powerful form of Inuit leadership.[23]

As this statement implies, the importance of the history of education is not only reflected in a record of graduation statistics but also lies in education's close relationship to cultural continuity and change. Darnell and Hoem offer insight into this relationship, first by defining culture and then by explaining how culture is sustained through education. Culture is shared knowledge and a common worldview that inform ways of living. Darnell and Hoem argue, "Simply stated, we see culture as the stored composite of knowledge a nation or a people has at its disposal. In keeping with this use, culture forms the basis for understanding and mastery, for a single individual, a society or a nation."[24] Education is linked to culture because it offers intergenerational knowledge transfer: "It follows, therefore, that if social groups are to survive, and this is one of the basic dilemmas of all indigenous peoples in the Far North, their cultures must be transmitted from generation to generation. Education and systems of education, regardless of form and locus of control, are inextricably a part of this process."[25] Education in the Eastern Arctic first served Inuit in their hunter-gatherer society as a means of cultural and economic continuity. It then came to represent the strongest agent of colonialism, language loss, and cultural change as they came in contact with Qallunaat. It is now expected to act as an agent of cultural reinforcement, preservation of Inuktitut, and Inuit self-determination. Inuit care deeply about their youth, and they have worked hard to develop and implement the Nunavut Land Claims Agreement as well as territorial legislation that better manifests the future they have envisioned for their children; but there is much work to be done. There must be alignment between the dominant form of education, which is formal schooling, and the cultural needs, desires, and future envisioned by Inuit.

Where does history fit into this equation? As argued by Linda Tuhiwai Smith, who provides one of the most insightful commentaries on the relationship between academic research and Aboriginal peoples in her book *Decolonizing Methodologies,* Aboriginal history has a sensitive relationship to the present and future. Smith argues that history has been detrimental to indigenous peoples because of its reflection of power:

> In fact history is mostly about power. It is the story of the powerful and how they became powerful, and then how they use their power to keep them in positions in which they can continue to dominate others. It is because of the relationship with power that we have been excluded, marginalized and "Othered." In this sense History is not important for indigenous peoples because a thousand accounts of the "truth" will not alter the "fact" that indigenous peoples are still marginal and do not possess the power to transform history into justice.[26]

Indeed, although the Inuit and the Arctic have never have been absent from the Canadian consciousness, they have been marginalized and rendered as stereotypes or, worse, associated with extremes such as the proverbial igloo-dweller and the primitiveness of early Inuit art or, more recently, an unparalleled suicide rate and the cruelty of the sealskin fashion industry. As is often the case, these hyperbolic perspectives reveal little about the historic and contemporary complexities.[27] Nonetheless, the discipline of history and the ways of thinking promoted by dominant societies cannot simply be ignored or dismissed by Aboriginal peoples; Smith concedes that the effort to decolonize research must be engaged by them:

> A dilemma posed by such a thorough critical approach to history, writing and theory is that whilst we may reject or dismiss them, this does not make them go away, nor does the critique necessarily offer the alternatives ... This means struggling to make sense of our own world while also attempting to transform what counts as important in the world of the powerful.[28]

Scholars like Smith have made clear to historians that particularly for minorities who are asserting themselves within their nation-state, often on the basis of historical claims, the past has the potential to advance the development of a positive identity and access to rights based on that identity.[29] Mary-Ellen Kelm argues that belief in the objectivity of history – such as has been demonstrated by the legal system in the past – is based on a false perception of the discipline, but it is not an uncommon assumption.[30] Therefore, historians must be aware of the purposes for which their history may be used, including the influence of present political circumstances. Even in prioritizing Aboriginal perspectives, Kelm states, historians cannot decontextualize Aboriginal experiences from the colonialist framework in which they existed (and perhaps still do); equally, history cannot be decontextualized from the modern reality of Aboriginal relations with the dominant society.

Power is and has been, as outlined above, a preoccupation in research, particularly in Aboriginal history. My research looks closely at the power relationships between Inuit and Qallunaat within the education system and, to a lesser extent, at how the education system may operate to affect power relationships in the Eastern Arctic more generally. Put very simply, this work could be seen as the story of loss of power held by Inuit and the path toward re-empowerment with respect to education. Issues of power are featured in my discussion of the purpose of education, Inuit experiences of the early colonial education system, the ways that Qallunaat norms trumped Inuit values in the classroom in the territorial system, the role of Inuit as educators and educational decision makers in the local period, and the relationship between education and self-determination in the post-1999 period.

Despite the extent to which power is examined here, both subtly and explicitly, I have chosen not to impose a theoretical framework on it. Due to its history, the word "power" brings with it a great deal of baggage, in the form of language, discourse, and theory, as well as imbedded assumptions. Yet it is not a word that is commonly used by Inuit to describe or explain their experience of colonialism, the quest for a land claim, or their involvement in the education system. Words like "control" and "self-determination" or phrases like "having a say" are more often employed. Partly because my sources do not easily or specifically support a theoretical analysis of power in this context, and partly because of

Figure 2 A modern Nunavut classroom: Inuit students learning from Meeka Kakudluk. Inuktitut syllabics are featured on classroom walls. Iqaluit, Nunavut, 2008. *Source:* Photograph reproduction authorized by Curtis Jones (for the Department of Education), Nakasuk School, Iqaluit, Government of Nunavut, 2008.

my own position of liminality herein, I have avoided developing a definition of "power" or using a theory of power as a lens or organizing principle by which to view this history. Formulating such a theory would constitute important future work, which the evidence and conclusions from this history can inform.

Setting the Scene: Schools in Nunavut Today

For readers who have not experienced education in this context, the following general description is intended to offer insight into, and establish a greater familiarity with, schools as they operate now. Most communities in Nunavut are only big enough to support one K to 12 school or one elementary and one secondary school. Only in the past twelve years have all senior grades been offered in each community. Schools are usually the biggest buildings in the community, and apart from a nursing station or a detachment of the Royal Canadian Mounted Police, schools are the most evident institutional or government presence. For the most part, schools run on the same daily and annual schedule as schools in southern Canada. Some let students out earlier in spring and start earlier in the fall to accommodate spring hunting or camping trips. School is inevitably interrupted by extreme weather, either storms or extreme cold, at various times throughout the year, and regular practice dictates that if the school shuts down for a storm, the entire community stays home. In the deep of winter, it is dark when students arrive at school and dark when they leave in the afternoon as well. However, everyone in the communities, including school children, gets a break to go home for lunch every day. Outdoor recess is still mandatory, and eagerly anticipated by students, except in temperatures of -50 degrees Celsius – in which case the school would probably close anyway! After school, hockey and indoor soccer are the most popular team sports offered, but volleyball, basketball, and speed skating are also common. Weekly games against other teams are impossible given the cost and time involved in getting to another community by airplane for competition. As a result, most athletes spend the entire winter practising and playing against their teammates, all in preparation for one big annual tournament in a central location.

The inside of these schools may give more clues to differences in the nature of education in the Arctic. The content of bulletin board displays, classroom walls, and school decorations certainly reflects the Arctic environment but also the use of Inuktitut. A majority of students in these classrooms are Inuit, with only one or two Qallunaat students per grade. Teachers, especially at the secondary level, are more likely to be Qallunaat, but Inuit teachers and staff have a strong presence in every school. Most communities offer Inuktitut-first-language education to students up to grade 4 and Inuktitut as a language arts period in grades 4 to 12. In Nunavut today, all curriculum materials under development are based on Inuit culture, but over the past twenty years opportunities to engage with Inuit culture in school were more varied. Some fairly consistent examples include a drum dancing component in music class, a traditional games component in gym class, a country foods component in health class, or a specifically labelled "cultural class." Relationships between students and Elders might be formed through traditional activities inside the school, or at an Elders' facility or community centre, or on the land. These are common examples of attempts to steep schooling in content and pedagogy that are culturally relevant and thereby to invoke Inuit education in the context of formal schooling. The frequency and success of such efforts differ according to local particularities but are part of an overall strategy that has been in development for decades.

My own experience of attending school in Iqaluit in the 1990s highlights the contradictions and negotiations still involved in the practice of Inuit education within the school context. I describe some of that experience here as an anecdote from which to draw out some of the questions that have led to this research.[31] I experienced the nuances of Elders in the classroom once a week in grade 5. Our class was separated by gender, with the girls being sent to learn sewing from local women Elders and the boys to learn carpentry from male Elders. For a time, this class took place in a *qarmaq*[32] that had been erected outside of the school as an appropriate setting for the purpose of cultural programs. More often, I recall going to the library or an empty classroom. Here, the differences between a class with Elders and a class with a Qallunaat teacher quickly became apparent. The women would be seated on the floor in a corner. They always sat on the floor, legs stretched straight out in front of them, not leaning on any wall or support, for the entire time we would see them. I don't know many Qallunaat who can sit for longer than a few minutes in that position. They would most often be dressed in a brightly floral top, with leggings that did not necessarily match, and *kamiks*.[33] They usually had CBC Radio, broadcasting in Inuktitut or playing the much-loved accordion music, buzzing in the background.

I was a shy kid, one of two Qallunaat girls in the class, and the Elders did not speak English. The first moments of each class, when they might greet us or explain something, were excruciatingly embarrassing for me. I didn't know whether it was appropriate for me to make eye contact or ask a question or whether I should just pretend to understand. I tried not to speak, fearing that my English might be insulting to them, so I just waited for a cue or mimicked my classmates. At the end of one class when an Elder was marking our names on our sewing projects, she picked mine up and evidently asked one of my classmates what my name was. This girl looked at me with hesitation for a moment, and then said "Ha-ta." I recoiled for a moment, thinking a trick was being played on me, but the Elder nodded, wrote my name in Inuktitut syllabics, and showed it to me. My classmate said that "Ha-ta" was my Inuktitut name. I was pleased that she had found a name for me that could be written in syllabics, and I quickly memorized the word.

We did not sew with caribou skins or sinew in cultural class. We used felt material and embroidery thread to make pink or purple pincushions (in the shape of teapots) and Christmas decorations (in the shape of mittens). There were a few instructions and a model available to us at the beginning of class, but most of our time was spent in near silence. Or perhaps that's the way I remember it because I didn't understand the conversation. When I made a mistake or got stuck at a difficult stage, my project was plucked from my hands and corrected by the Elder. She would show me the proper method in slow, exaggerated motions, the rest of the girls looking on. I was careful to copy her demonstration, knowing her eyes remained on me until I improved. I was proud of my sewing projects, and by the end of the year I was also proudly more comfortable with the Elders. I certainly thought that because I could sew and decorate a pink teapot pincushion while sitting on the floor and because my name could be written in syllabics, I had been initiated into Inuit culture.

The experience of sitting in a school sewing small decorative items, with materials and tools that were by no means traditional, offered us only an approximation of the experience of Inuit education. Yet, as my initial discomfort demonstrated, the experience of education with the Elders was foreign enough in relation to regular school activities and experiences that it left a significant impression on me. It must be noted that most of the rest of the school week was spent learning in a context more consistent with formal schooling in southern Canada. Our homeroom teacher was a male Qallunaaq who used a curriculum designed for schools in southern Canada in which "success" was measured mostly using Qallunaat marking schemes; I was more "successful" than my fellow students. The classes with the Elders were certainly more than our Qallunaat teachers could offer us but were still less than ideal.

My experience of cultural class very likely differed from that of my Inuit classmates. After all, efforts to create school experiences that reflect Inuit culture and education are clearly intended to meet the needs of the Inuit majority. Perhaps their conversations with the Elders, whom they knew or to whom they were related in some way, gave them comfort and a feeling of connection to their past, to their families, and to their culture. Perhaps more was communicated in those classes than I could begin to perceive. Perhaps it was a time during the week when they felt the school belonged to them, not the other way around. I also wonder whether the Elders felt rewarded as a result of their weekly classes with us.

Emerging from the scenario described above are questions such as: How did the school system in the Eastern Arctic, typically modelled on curriculum developed in southern Canada, determine that turning students over to Inuit Elders for cultural class on a weekly basis was an important component of the curriculum? What purpose is envisioned by teachers and administrators for classes such as this? What is deemed to be the importance of these experiences to Inuit, and how effectively do they engage Inuit students? How do these experiences relate to the process of completing an education intended to prepare people for employment and economic self-sufficiency? Do experiences like sewing with Elders capture the essence of Inuit culture and tradition? Do they serve a social function by "preserving" Inuit tradition and culture for the benefit of future generations? And finally, is the inclusion of Inuit educational experiences a result of more progressive views of education by Qallunaat, or a result of greater ownership of the formal system by Inuit teachers, parents, and community members? In summary, how has the traditional Inuit approach to education been incorporated into the formal education system in Nunavut?

These questions suggest that an investigation of tradition must be undertaken. I have intentionally chosen not to start by offering a definition of "tradition" derived from the work of theorists and historians. Although this is a departure from common academic practice, I feel that it more appropriately fits the spirit of avoiding the imposition of Qallunaat perspectives and of giving space to the Inuit voice. As Linda Tuhiwai Smith argues, theory has been oppressive to Aboriginal peoples, but it is also a tool that can be appropriated in "attempting to transform what counts as important in the world of the powerful."[34] Consistent with this point, I have worked toward using theories of tradition as tools in better representing this context, once it has been fully described. The history begins with an exploration of what constitutes the traditional Inuit approach to education in this specific historical context. Having identified the important aspects of the tradition, we can then trace how it operated through time, the endeavour that constitutes the greatest share of this book. Finally, having built a definition of Inuit education that is supported by Inuit sources and evidence, we can reflect on the relationship between this particular tradition and the broader concept of "tradition" as it operates in Western or scholarly discourse. However, in recognition of what may be a common understanding of tradition, it is important at this juncture to clarify that the terms "tradition" and "traditional" as they are used here do not connote a single, unchanging, and "primitive" past that exists in opposition to modernism as imposed by colonizers.[35] We should maintain openness to the possibility that tradition is a living and changing process, in which both the bearers of the tradition (Inuit) and the bearers of alternative paradigms (Qallunaat) participate.

1

History of the Eastern Arctic: Foundations and Themes

Inuit and Their Environment

THE FOLLOWING BRIEF outline of the history of the Eastern Arctic prior to 1945 assists in setting the stage for a discussion of education and the relationship between Inuit and Qallunaat. It is important to note the dominant role of the environment in bringing people to or keeping people away from the Arctic, in addition to strongly shaping the lives of those who live there. Only sixty years ago, one would have been hard-pressed to find a regular southern Canadian who recognized the word "inuksuk"; indeed, it would have been difficult to find a southerner who recognized the word "Inuit." Equally, one would have been unlikely to come across an Inuk who had used a telephone, heard of Adolf Hitler, or seen more than two hundred people in one place. Aboriginal peoples in southern Canada had been managed by the federal government for decades by the time the first generation of Inuit in the Eastern Arctic were subjected to full colonization after the Second World War. It is the environment that defined the time and the way that colonization occurred; the nature of the Arctic ecosystem protected Inuit from contact for a longer period of time than was the case for other Aboriginal groups in Canada. Indeed, in the early stages of northern exploration and resources exploitation, Inuit helped Qallunaat with travel and survival skills to a far greater extent than any knowledge or practical skill was transmitted in the other direction.[1] John Amagoalik, known as the "Father of Nunavut," writes about this differing nature of colonialism based on the challenges of surviving in, let alone conquering, the Arctic: "The would-be colonizers had to arrive by dog teams and soon discovered that their fingers were so numb from the cold that they couldn't even unzip their own pants. Many older Inuit smile and chuckle as they tell stories about having to unzip the pants of the 'big boss policeman' so he wouldn't pee in his pants."[2] The means of survival in this environment was so foreign to the Qallunaat that they were held at bay, and their first encounters with Inuit were often in search of help.

The Inuit were a hunter-gatherer society established in an environment with a relatively low level of resources in comparison to other areas of Canada. Although natural resources differ between the three major regions of the Eastern Arctic – Qikiqtani (Baffin Island), Kitikmeot (the western and High Arctic islands), and Kivalliq (the west side of Hudson Bay) – some generalities can be observed. For example, arable soil is scarce and produces little; some 75 percent of the landscape is covered by bare rock or by ice.[3] It is invariably cold in Nunavut; winter is a long season, with mean daily temperatures in Pond Inlet, for example, averaging -32.4°C in January, -34.1°C in February, -30.03°C in March, 1.8°C in June, 6°C in July, and 4.2°C in August.[4] Environment Canada reports the low diversity of both animals and plants in this zone; indeed, fewer than 10 percent of Canada's mammal species occur here, although three of these are sizable: the muskox, caribou, and polar bear.[5] Despite the very low number of plant species in the Arctic, there are several species of berries that were important to the Inuit diet. The plants that do exist in the Arctic ecozones are particularly adapted to the climate in their distribution, abundance, and size, and most were traditionally used for various purposes.[6] Despite the low mammalian speciation, hunting for land and sea animals as well as fishing and gathering characterized life in the Arctic. Wildlife provided the basis for nearly all of the resources available to Inuit; clothing and footwear were made entirely from animal furs or skins to stand up to Arctic conditions. The tools were specialized and carefully formed using bone, horn, antler, or ivory.[7] Richard Harrington, a photographer who travelled among Inuit in the late 1940s, offers a glimpse into their resourcefulness:

> Seal fat was rendered into oil for the kudlik. Animal bones were used to make tools or weapons. The skins were stretched out to dry and then used for a multitude of purposes. Polar bear skins were usually used on the sleeping platforms of the igloos, and so were seal skins. Seal skins made particularly watertight boots. Caribou skins were used to form the summer tupiks, and were also the usual materials for clothing. The women would spend untold hours chewing pieces of skin to soften them. The chewed skin, from which the hair had been removed, would often be soaked in urine, and then the women would continue chewing on it until it was as soft and velvety as chamois. Then, using sinew, they would sew the skins into the artiggis, kulitaks, parkas, pants and boots that are so perfectly suited to Arctic weather.[8]

This thin range of resources indicates that Inuit have been remarkably adaptive to an unaccommodating environment. Survival was tenuous enough that taking chances with any resource could be risky. Renée Fossett explains that every generation of Inuit would inevitably experience at least a dozen periods of short-term scarcity, which were for the most part manageable with the application of traditional knowledge, but longer-term scarcity that was unpredictable or unusual could be extremely dangerous.[9] As a result, the traditional semi-nomadic lifestyle included transience governed by seasonal hunting routes, migrations in times of scarcity, and dependence on small but strong family groups. George Wenzel characterizes these groups as "Reciprocal relationships that include shared social responsibility as much as they do kilograms of meat, in which all community members contribute their knowledge of animals and the environment, energy in hunting and processing food, and equipment and/or money as they are able."[10]

Like populations of other Aboriginal peoples, and other hunter-gatherer societies, Inuit populations were small, and their social structures and political organization appeared relatively simple. Decision making and leadership traditionally occurred on an informal basis involving the nuclear family or, at most, several families. Although the advice, opinions, and leadership of an individual such as a strong hunter or knowledgeable Elder may have stood out in small Inuit communities or families, deference to such a leader was often contingent on that individual taking into consideration the needs and wishes of everyone involved.[11] In addition to a lack of hierarchy in social organization, the economic system was limited to subsistence activities with little specialization. These characteristics, common to other hunter-gatherer societies, have left Inuit subject to prejudice in Western thought, including the disciplines of history and anthropology, because of the belief that societies that are less complex are also less productive and effective, thus creating the ultimate dichotomy between hunter-gatherer and industrial ways of living. However, as Marshall Sahlins argued in 1966,[12] and as Hugh Brody has echoed,[13] these characteristics of Inuit society – low population density, less accumulation of material possessions, and more hours of leisure – more appropriately offer evidence that they actually secured a high level of affluence. Inuit enjoyed a life of challenges that they could most often accommodate, as their persistence in the Arctic over millennia attests.

Inuit maintain that they struck a balance with the Arctic environment, a balance that could have lasted in perpetuity. Jose Kusugak, a political leader and respected spokesperson for Inuit, claims: "We have lived in the Arctic for many thousands of years. The Arctic has sustained and defined us. We are a part of the Arctic landscape and seascape and the Arctic landscape and seascape are a part of us."[14] However, Inuit also often describe the environment in terms of its capacity to destroy them through reference to the concept of *sila*. Although the term is complex, the following definition offered by Alex Spalding, a specialist in Inuktitut, gives us a sense of *sila:*

> *Sila* can be used in three principal ways: as an indicator of environment, an indicator of locality, and an indicator of intelligence or spirit ... In a world like *silajjuaq* [the all-encompassing sense of *sila*] ... we have synthesis, one might say, of all of

> these: that which supports life and physical being, that which defines horizons and limits, and that which regulates and clarifies mind and spirit. In this concept, one feels a unity of microcosm and macrocosm, near and far, inner and outer, that is, one living physical and spiritual unity of being. These are the outlooks and values of all peoples who are wise from their contact with the air, earth and water.[15]

Sila is also commonly thought of by Inuit as the weather spirit of the earth, and it is revered. In times of hardship, it is feared for its power and for the instability it creates and against which they must fight for their food.[16] The traditional knowledge necessary to interact with or respond to *sila* is characterized by an Inuit representative organization as: "An in-depth understanding of the distribution and behaviour of the northern environments we experience in different seasons of the year, and an understanding of the different living resources that need these environments for their own survival."[17] As a result of this worldview and collected knowledge, a culture and livelihood were established. In other words, many Inuit feel that the environment directly shaped their ways of being and doing. John Amagoalik explains, "The land shaped our mind and language, our culture, our legends, our philosophy and our view of life."[18] Scholars such as Peter Jull echo this Inuit self-image and the effects of that approach on their entire lifestyle:

> The full relationship of these northern peoples to their renewable resource base is not completely understood, but it underlies every aspect of their being, from songs and family customs to political organization and the settlement of disputes. The relationship of a people to a territory was primarily based on resource use, and the style of managing that territory and allocating and sharing its yield, no less so.[19]

There is little doubt that the relationship between Inuit and their environment has been a significant determinant in the history of the Eastern Arctic.

Encounters with Qallunaat

Inuit encountered Qallunaat in their homeland as early as the sixteenth century, when sporadic Northwest Passage exploration expeditions arrived, surveyed, and left, usually without a great deal of interaction. Any contact that did occur between Inuit and Qallunaat brought with it disease; Robert McGhee argues that European diseases such as smallpox were first recorded as spreading through Inuit populations as early as the 1770s.[20] Eruptions of smallpox, polio, and tuberculosis persisted well into the twentieth century.[21] Regular visits between

Inuit and Qallunaat began in the 1820s, particularly as a result of intensive commercial whaling by British and Dutch whalers, who were interested in highly valuable bowhead whale oil. The whaling period occurred between the 1850s and 1880s and exerted an enormous strain on numerous Arctic resources.[22] Inuit traded with the whalers, mostly for souvenir goods rather than staples, and some were employed as ice pilots and hunters for the Europeans.[23] However, although British whalers and American explorers rapidly charted the Arctic throughout the eighteenth and nineteenth centuries, their presence did not fundamentally alter the way of life of the majority of Inuit.

The establishment of Hudson's Bay Company (HBC) posts and missionary efforts had a greater effect on Inuit. As opposed to the spontaneous trade with whalers and explorers who visited Inuit camps, significant changes to the repertoire of tools available occurred with regular access to HBC traders. Inuit who lived on the west side of Hudson Bay (southern Kiralliq), could travel to Churchill to trade at the HBC post, and Fossett reports that by 1830 every hunter in that area would have possessed a gun.[24] Robert Paine characterizes this relationship as "transactional" because "each side was able to derive benefit from the other, even though their respective bargaining powers were unequal."[25] Trapping of white fox became a viable economic pursuit for Inuit after the establishment of an HBC post at Chesterfield Inlet around 1911, Eskimo Point (now Arviat) in 1921,[26] and twenty-one other locations before 1940.[27] The HBC stocked its posts on an annual basis, by ship, and Inuit gained access to staples such as tea, flour, and sugar as well as to tools such as fabrics, firearms, and ammunition.

Closely aligned with the spread of the HBC was the coming of missionaries and the introduction of Christianity. Missionaries established themselves in some northern locations prior to the twentieth century. The earliest and most important mission begun in the Eastern Arctic was that of Edmund James Peck at Cumberland Sound (near Pangnirtung) in 1894.[28] Reverend Peck is known best for developing the syllabic representation of Aboriginal languages, first with Ojibway and Cree in Ontario and later with Inuktitut. Peck spent eight years in Cumberland Sound translating gospels into Inuktitut and teaching syllabic literacy to Inuit. Conversion to Christianity happened quickly, as in most Aboriginal communities approached by missionaries. Christianity's presence in the Eastern Arctic was prevalent by the late 1920s and early 1930s. Catholic and Anglican missionaries competed for souls in the communities of the Eastern Arctic, leaving a spotty pattern of affiliation. As a result of Peck's translations, Inuktitut hymnals, prayer books, and Bibles were an important resource in that endeavour.

A small amount of instruction by Qallunaat missionaries, particularly under the auspices of religious observance, resulted in the enthusiastic and widespread appropriation of syllabic Inuktitut literacy. So completely did this system spread among Inuit that syllabics were in use on northern Baffin Island well before the first missionary arrived there.[29] Once settled, missionaries offered basic instruction in Inuktitut literacy, Western hygiene, and arithmetic. Donald Marsh, an Anglican minister who lived in Eskimo Point between 1926 and 1943, said the following about the "curriculum" at his mission school:

> We didn't expect nor hope to train Eskimo children to speak English; to whom would they speak? The trader? He spoke pidgin Eskimo and always used someone to interpret for him if he couldn't manage himself. It's generally useless to learn a language unless you can constantly use it. Simple hygiene, how to add, subtract and do small sums in arithmetic, all of which would help in trading, were the basics given to every child. To read and write in their own language helped them to read their Bibles and prayer books as well as to communicate with people far off, and some history and general knowledge of the world gave the children and adults a bit of background of a life apart from their own.[30]

Missionaries like Marsh would preach and teach from a central location, usually situated near a Hudson's Bay Company post. They would also teach on an itinerant basis, travelling by dogsled or boat with a guide to visit Inuit in their camps covering hundreds of miles of territory. In other words, these early educational efforts by missionaries catered, by necessity, to the way of life pursued by Inuit and therefore differed greatly from the approach of the later generation of residential schools.[31] The influence of the missionaries certainly did put an end to some cultural traditions, such as taboos associated with shamanism, but by introducing Inuktitut literacy, they offered Inuit a highly significant tool for communication.[32] Unfortunately, as will be discussed further, when responsibility for education was transferred to the federal government, this Inuktitut literacy was rejected by educators in favour of English.[33]

The increasing dependency of Inuit trappers and traders on the HBC affected their relationship to some wildlife resources, and the cultural impact of the introduction of Christianity should not be diminished. However, the viability of a nomadic subsistence lifestyle remained intact for most Inuit until the collapse of the fox fur trade in 1930.[34] The presence of the military and the Royal Canadian Mounted Police (RCMP), which started in 1903 with two posts,[35] grew steadily as sovereignty became a serious concern in the early twentieth century. However, Inuit were discouraged from camping or staying near the established RCMP posts. Prior to the Second World War and the subsequent interest taken by the federal government in Canada's Arctic, Inuit had no treaties with the nation of Canada, essentially no legal status under Canadian law, and access to very few government services or relief measures. Most important for the purposes of this book, few Inuit had access to formal education. The influence of the Canadian government was therefore limited. This brief introduction to the pre-1945 period is supplemented throughout the remainder of this chapter, and much greater detail with regard to Inuit culture and way of life prior to colonization is included in Chapter 2.

Aboriginal History and Education in Canada

Historians of the North rely on the broader body of Canadian Aboriginal history as a context in which to identify themes and from which to draw comparisons. The formal education of Aboriginal people in Canada has become a widely studied subject, particularly as it offers a measure of the inequality spawned by colonialism. Research into sexual and other forms of abuse of residential school pupils by clergy and religiously affiliated educators that came to light in the 1980s has received the most publicity.[36] The Report of the Royal Commission on Aboriginal Peoples (RCAP), published in 1996, devoted a significant portion of its hearings to the experience of Aboriginal people who attended residential schools. According to the RCAP, education was a cornerstone for the assimilationist policy employed by the Canadian government: "Of all the steps taken to achieve that goal, none was more obviously a creature of Canada's paternalism toward Aboriginal people, its civilizing strategy and its stern assimilative determination than education."[37] Although Aboriginal communities across Canada were subjected to education in this spirit at different times, for different durations, and under slightly different models, the results show a depressing similarity in broad outline. Marie Battiste effectively sums up the legacy of federal responsibility for Aboriginal education:

> Through ill-conceived government policies and plans, Aboriginal youths were subjected to a combination of powerful but profoundly distracting forces of cognitive imperialism and colonization. Various boarding schools, industrial schools, day schools, and Eurocentric educational practices ignored or rejected the world-views, languages, and values of Aboriginal parents in the education of their children. The outcome was the gradual loss of these world-views, languages and cultures and the creation of widespread social and psychological upheaval in Aboriginal communities.[38]

The late introduction of federal schooling and religiously affiliated residential schools to the Northwest Territories, and particularly the Eastern Arctic region, did not prevent Inuit from also experiencing this loss and social and psychological upheaval. As Lynn Aylward argues: "Cognitive and professional imperialism and cognitive manipulation have played a significant role in the educational policies of the northern territories of Canada. The history of the government's policy and action is replete with contradictions, racist assumptions, and superficial community consultation."[39]

Federal jurisdiction over Aboriginal education lasted until 1969, when the federal government's "White Paper," or *Statement of the Government of Canada on Indian Policy,* recommended the devolution of educational responsibilities to the provinces. This policy recommendation prompted a passionate response from the National Indian Brotherhood, titled the "Red Paper Policy," which was later distilled into *Indian Control of Indian Education.*[40] This document argued that the transfer of responsibility for Aboriginal education to the provinces was unacceptable and that it should instead be rendered to the Aboriginal peoples themselves: "We must, therefore, reclaim our right to direct the education of our children. Based on two education principles recognized in Canadian society: *Parental Responsibility* and *Local Control of Education,* Indian parents seek participation and partnership with the Federal Government, whose legal responsibility for Indian education is set by the treaties and the Indian Act."[41] At this time, Aboriginal education was viewed primarily in terms of its capacity to protect and preserve Aboriginal culture and language.[42] In resisting the mandate of the federal government's White Paper, Aboriginal communities secured the right to jurisdiction over their schools, and since 1972 band-operated schools have grown steadily. However, these schools continue to struggle to meet provincial standards and regulations while remaining true to Aboriginal visions of culture-based curriculum.[43]

This struggle points to the fact that Aboriginal education is required to make a difficult compromise between two purposes: (1) the preparation of Aboriginal students for economic success in a system primarily underpinned by Euro-North American culture and (2) the revitalization of Aboriginal traditions and cultures – not as a relic of the past but as a key to the future of Aboriginal peoples. Battiste explains:

> It was also important that the educational processes of Indian education should strengthen First Nations languages and cultures, build upon the strong foundations of ancestral heritage and culture, and enlist the invaluable advice and assistance of elders. The very tenets of Indian education had to change from accepting acculturation and cognitive assimilation as final ends to revitalizing and renewing language and cultural identity and dignity.[44]

In other words, Aboriginal educators discovered that the growing gap between Aboriginal youth, their heritage, and their prospects for the future could not be resolved simply through incorporating some Aboriginal content into the formal education system. Rather, it would take an ongoing negotiation to meet success in either purpose of education identified above.

The complete integration of Aboriginal people into the Canadian economic system has still not been fully realized despite Aboriginal oversight of schools. Marlene Brant Castellano and her colleagues reported in 2000 that an analysis of census data from 1981 to 1996 showed only a marginal increase in Aboriginal students pursuing post-secondary education: "The promise of an education that delivers the skills to survive in a post-industrial global economy while affirming the ethical and spiritual foundations of Aboriginal cultures is far from being fulfilled."[45] Therefore, Aboriginal education has had to grapple with the search for an entirely new system: "While the last three decades have been marked by the resilient struggle of Aboriginal peoples to regain control of education, the 1990s have produced concentrated efforts to rethink Aboriginal education and to articulate what is 'Aboriginal' about Aboriginal education."[46]

What is Aboriginal education in Canada now, and what significance does it have in comparison to non-Aboriginal education? The report of the RCAP suggests that preparation and support for Aboriginal self-government should be the highest priority of Aboriginal education: "Preparing Aboriginal people to assume the complete range of responsibilities associated with self-governance must be recognized as a top priority in postsecondary education. At this historical juncture, Aboriginal people, governments, educational institutions and professional organizations all have crucial roles in building the capacity of Aboriginal nations and their communities to exercise self-government."[47] The RCAP report is particularly poignant with reference to the creation of Nunavut Territory, where the establishment of self-government has literally been the most significant occupation of Inuit for several decades and arguably remains one of the most important functions of the education system.

Status of the Inuit

Although First Nations and Inuit peoples are often lumped together in federal departments and public consciousness in Canada, there is actually very little commonality between them in terms of their relationship to the federal government. Inuit surely count as a First Nation in a literal sense, in that they were resident in Canada long before the coming of Europeans and other immigrants to North America, but the Canadian Inuit as a people do not have any national treaties with the federal government comparable to First Nations treaties. Inuit groups have chosen to negotiate rights and privileges for themselves based not on a national racial or ethnic status but on the condition of their residency in areas defined by land claims.

Historically, there is very little Canadian legislation that refers directly to the Inuit. The Constitution Act of 1867 affords exclusive legislative jurisdiction to the Canadian Parliament over "Indians, and lands reserved for the Indians."[48] In 1929 starvation in Northern Quebec among Inuit raised controversy between Ottawa and Quebec about which level of government was responsible for relief provisions. *Reference re. Eskimos, 1939* of the Supreme Court of Canada finally decided that the term "Indians" in the Constitution Act of 1867 should include the Inuit, based on the historic usage of the term "Indian."[49] The Constitution Act is important because it defines the federal legislative jurisdiction over Aboriginal peoples and affirms their existing rights. It also provides the legal basis for the Indian Act of 1876, which affords Indians basic health, education, and tax-exemption benefits as well as band assets and reserved lands. However, the *Reference re Eskimos* decision does not apply to this legislation, so the Inuit remain exempt from it.[50] Despite reluctant recognition by the federal government that the Inuit are subject to federal jurisdiction, and despite the Citizenship Act of 1947, which made them Canadian citizens, the Inuit were not permitted to vote in federal elections until 1962,[51] and the first Inuk member of Parliament was not elected until 1979.[52]

More current legislation includes the Constitution Act of 1982, which defines the Aboriginal peoples of Canada to include the Indian, Inuit, and Métis; however, no further definition of who these people are exists in the document.[53] As Bradford W. Morse points out, this lack of definition raises sensitive and complicated questions about what degree of ancestry makes one an Indian or an Inuk. He asks, "50 percent? 1 percent? Or should the test be a cultural one? The government resolved the problem by allowing Native organizations to determine eligibility for themselves."[54] The updated Indian Act of 1985 dictates a complex web of status and non-status First Nations (referred to as "Indians" in the Act) with differing levels of rights and benefits.[55] However, Inuit groups remain legally excluded from the Act; they do not have their own legislation, and they did not have any other treaties with the federal government prior to modern land claims such as the Nunavut Land Claims Agreement. Natalia Loukacheva, who has compared the legal status of the Inuit in Canada to the Inuit in Greenland, argues that "the lack of treaties shows that colonizers did not recognize Inuit as sovereign people."[56] Therefore, the basic health, education, tax-exemption, and title benefits available to all Indians are not automatically available to the Inuit, whose status in law remains essentially undefined.[57]

Inuit Land Claims

The Inuit movement for self-determination was largely motivated by environmental consciousness and concern for the wildlife, land, and other natural resources that had sustained them and actively influenced their culture for thousands of years. As the Arctic increasingly became an area of military and economic interest in the Cold War period, Inuit felt threatened by their lack of involvement in decision making. Yet, by the 1970s, Inuit were seeking to assert their Aboriginal rights and land claims and to negotiate at the highest level of government in Canada. Jack Hicks and Graham White, analysts of political change in Nunavut, argue that what might be called "Inuit nationalism" was a "paradoxical result of Inuit contact with – and subsequent domination by – Euro-Canadian society," whereas all previous identification and loyalties would have occurred only at the local and family level.[58]

Particularly in response to the discovery of the oil fields in Alaska and to the ensuing Mackenzie Valley Pipeline proposal, the Inuit representative organization called Inuit Tapirisat of Canada (ITC) was created in 1971.[59] Its goals were stated as follows:

- to promote public awareness of Inuit rights in Canadian society
- to provide necessary information to Inuit on their own situation, government plans, aboriginal rights and legal matters
- to help preserve Inuit culture and language and promote dignity and pride in Inuit heritage
- to assist Inuit in their right to full participation in Canadian society, that they may determine those things of a social, economic, educational and political nature which will affect them and future generations; and
- to unite all Inuit of Northwest Territories, Arctic Quebec, Labrador and Manitoba and to speak for them with regard to political support and publicity.[60]

It is clear from the transcript of the inaugural meeting of ITC that Inuit were concerned about not fully understanding the federal laws and regulations that applied to them, their own rights in Canada, and how to exercise control over their lands.[61] ITC's core pursuit was the creation of a proposal for an independent territory belonging to the Inuit of the Eastern Arctic. This involved the development of in-depth land-use studies, which have identified all activities pursued by Inuit in the region, both historically and presently, so as to establish occupancy.[62] Inuit had no physical barriers, markers, or indicators such as fences and roads to delineate their territories, and indeed their culture makes little provision for the concept of land ownership.[63] But concerns regarding their economic future and the threat of large natural resource-development projects left them no choice but to adapt their culture to these foreign concepts and to skillfully employ them where necessary to achieve their goals. Asserting the right to self-government in one's own territory was the first step in this process. Loukacheva characterizes this change as follows: "There is no notion of self-government or rights in the Inuit tradition or language because the Creator endows the order of everyone and everything. However, because of the transition to modern society and strategic purposes of survival of a distinct Inuit culture, Inuit had to adapt unfamiliar concepts of human rights, Aboriginal rights, governance and autonomy."[64]

By 1976 Inuit representatives had drafted and submitted a proposal for the creation of their own territory to the federal government under Prime Minister Pierre Elliott Trudeau.[65] The document focused on Nunavut, as well as on a social and economic support system for Inuit involvement in all government activities. According to R. Quinn Duffy, the document reflected the unwillingness on the part of Inuit to be perceived as dependent on the federal government's "handouts," and it clearly indicated that no "special status" was being requested.[66] ITC was forced to withdraw its proposal in 1977 because of evidence that the proposal was unworkable, largely due to the low number of educated and experienced Inuit at the time but also due to the undefined issues of land claims and individual compensation.[67] Negotiations thereafter with the federal government were extremely slow-moving, and Inuit representatives were up against a number of seemingly impassable roadblocks.[68] ITC's multiple priorities involving the various other Inuit groups also further complicated talks. In 1980 ITC prepared a new proposal, of a vastly different tone and nature, entitled *Parnagujuk: "A Plan for Progress."* The negotiators had clearly learned from their first attempts and were recasting priorities in ways that would be more palatable to the federal government; according to Duffy, they "showed a commendable degree of political realism."[69] However, it appears that they also chose the path of least resistance by committing themselves to pursuing greater control over environmental, economic, and administrative decision making in their territory rather than claiming self-government based on their Aboriginal rights and status as a First Nations people.[70]

Following the *Parnagujuk* proposal, the Legislative Assembly in Yellowknife began an investigation into public opinion about the division of the NWT, initiating a 1982 plebiscite that produced a record voter turnout in the Eastern Arctic and showed 56.65 percent to be in favour.[71] In 1982 the NWT requested that the federal government divide the territory, but the government remained reluctant to take action until land claims had been settled for the region. Also in 1982 the Tunngavik Federation of Nunavut (TFN), which later became Nunavut Tunngavik Incorporated (NTI), took over leading negotiating responsibilities from ITC.[72] On behalf of the Inuit of Nunavut, TFN signed the 1990 Agreement-in-Principle with the Government of Canada and presented the

Inuit of Nunavut with the land claim, ratified by 69 percent of the eligible voters in 1992.[73] In 1993 the Nunavut Land Claims Agreement (NLCA) was signed by the TFN and the Government of Canada in Iqaluit, and in Ottawa that same year Parliament passed the Nunavut Land Claims Agreement Act and the Nunavut Act.

Inuit secured various rights and privileges through the NLCA, including title to 350,000 square kilometres of land; priority rights to harvest wildlife; three national parks; a public territorial government with new institutions to co-manage land, water, wildlife, and so forth; capital transfer payments; a 5 percent share of royalties from oil and gas revenues of Crown lands; Inuit employment support programs; and a $13 million training trust fund.[74] The NLCA was conceived to apply to "beneficiaries," who must hold Inuit status with Nunavut Tunngavik Incorporated, which maintains representative powers for the Inuit of Nunavut. This organization describes its mission and activities as follows: "NTI is responsible for the management of all Inuit-Owned Lands in Nunavut and acts as the advocate of Inuit interests in Nunavut. The organization also provides a number of programs to Inuit, including support to Inuit development corporations and community economic development organizations, an Elders pension plan, a harvester support program, and a bereavement travel program."[75] Essentially, NTI was given responsibility for developing the enrolment list for NLCA beneficiaries, a process wherein the definition of an Inuk was left to their own discretion and was based on individuals identifying themselves.

Peter Jull has argued that the 1993 agreement was the start of a new era for the Inuit of Canada, one in which they redefined the relations of Aboriginal peoples with the national government and captured the attention of their fellow citizens:

> Indeed, the Nunavut self-government and claims teams maintained high moral and intellectual ground in constitutional, cross-cultural, and environmental matters, e.g., parading the quest for a Nunavut territory as Canada's first "made in Canada" constitutional reform process since white settlement. Inuit were no longer the forgotten people ... This amounted to a subtle psychological winning of the South, a match for the earlier Southern physical possession of the post-war North.[76]

The rights and benefits, and the recognition, awarded to the 35,000 Inuit of Nunavut are undoubtedly of considerable significance. However, Hicks and White question the extent to which the terms of the agreement really represent a significant departure for the Canadian government: "The Nunavut 'package'

– the provisions of the Nunavut Land Claims Agreement, and the resulting division of the NWT and the creation of the Nunavut territory and the Government of Nunavut – was designed to both accommodate Inuit self-government aspirations yet fit comfortably within established traditions of mainstream Canadian governance. It is not a radical departure."[77]

Hicks and White raise an aspect of the history of Nunavut that has received little attention: What did the federal government receive from this agreement? In settling the land claim with the federal government and establishing a public government, the Inuit were required to legally rescind the opportunity to pursue further claims based on their Aboriginal status. The section of the NLCA that pertains to this trade appears in the *Certainty* section but is also referred to as the extinguishment clause. This clause has been criticized by historians and legal specialists alike for its limitation on Aboriginal rights and status in Canada. Frank Tester argues that "the extinguishment clause is the most political clause in the agreement, and it has the most serious implications for any, not just for Inuit, but for any First Nation anywhere in the country; the extinguishment clauses are I think the most offensive, controversial and the most important aspect of any modern treaty."[78] Loukacheva echoes Tester's criticism of the clause: "Arguably, this clause brings some colonial legacy features to the Agreement."[79] Inuit also felt insulted by this demand on the part of the federal government, but according to Paul Quassa, a lead negotiator, they chose not to risk losing Nunavut by disputing it: "It was very hard for us [Inuit] to do that. It is colonial legacy when you have to give up a certain thing in order to get something. This is not the Inuit way ... We had to accept it, but in turn we said: 'give us Nunavut government,' 'give us Nunavut territory.'"[80] Here is evidence that the negotiation for a land claim and new territorial government in Nunavut involved more compromise than Inuit expected, and perhaps the federal government was less flexible than it has claimed. The determination on the part of Inuit to achieve their goal regardless of the terms is admirable, but it is also appears that the full implications of their pursuit have not been realized. Further discussion of the implementation of the NLCA, specifically its impact on education, follows in the Conclusion of this book.

Historically, Inuit lived and thrived in a region of geographic, economic, and cultural isolation from the rest of Canada, and the population of "newcomers," or Qallunaat, still remains low. They have tried to chart their own course in negotiations with the federal government despite the complexity involved. They have expressed the desire to avoid some of the constraints of other First Nations policies, especially economic dependence and cultural assimilation. In an interview regarding the decision of Inuit to pursue rights based on residency rather than ethnicity, Jose Kusugak reinforces the point that Inuit have chosen to be

"Canadians" first: "What makes us real Canadians? We must have a good understanding of what it is to be Canadian. Not just to be on welfare. I think it's better choosing to pay taxes so that we can have a voice within Canada. And stand up by ourselves like any other Canadian."[81] Others, like Frank Tester, connect the history of mistreatment of many Inuit to the modern treaty, suggesting that the government is perpetuating an unjust relationship: "They [the federal government] claim that Inuit are just regular Canadians, no special status, but there is a whole history of treating them differently from other Canadians."[82] With patience and determination, Inuit were able to find common ground with the federal government. The creation of Nunavut Territory has thus far been seen as a monumental achievement in fulfillment of Inuit self-determination, environmental protection, and cultural persistence.

Traditional Ecological Knowledge and Inuit Qaujimajatuqangit

The nature of the Arctic environment, the traditional Inuit lifestyle, and the social norms by which they educated their children are further discussed in Chapter 2. At this juncture it is important to note that the ways Inuit live with, and know about, the environment (the main "subject" of Inuit education) differ greatly from the approach taken by Qallunaat. This difference is commonly remarked on by contrasting the Inuit basis for understanding, termed "traditional ecological knowledge" (TEK), with the Qallunaat basis for understanding, called "science." Traditional knowledge, traditional ecological/environmental knowledge, indigenous knowledge, or local knowledge, as it is variably called, has almost become a cliché in our society. In the past twenty years, it has gone from being a form of knowing looked at with great skepticism, and given only cursory legitimacy, to one that is nearly unquestioned based on romantic notions of Aboriginal authority.[83] The definition of TEK is a thorny issue. In 1993 the World Conservation Union created a Working Group on Traditional Ecological Knowledge that defined TEK and its relevance in the following way:

> Traditional ecological knowledge thus involves a people's understanding of environmental structures and processes. It is a knowledge which has an immediate relevance and application for specific societies in particular environments. On one hand, it is a unique and distinctive example of how human populations understand and relate to local ecosystems; on the other, it can represent the employment of functionally parallel solutions to similar problems in biologically diverse and geographically distant environments.[84]

This definition is useful because it highlights that the most critical components of TEK exist in contrast to standard scientific approaches: it is a resource that cannot be considered universal, standardized, or tested with controlled variables.

In Canada we have tended to place TEK alongside "science," or Western ways of knowledge production, call them equal, and then proceed to highlight all the areas where they complement one another and ignore those where they do not. The goal has remained to fit what Aboriginal TEK tells us into Western frameworks of knowledge in order to determine what we "know." For example, in her study of local knowledge, Julie Cruikshank points out, "In much of the resource management literature, there seems to be a growing consensus that indigenous knowledge exists as a kind of distinct epistemology that can be systematized and incorporated into Western management regimes."[85] Shepard Krech III also problematizes the stereotypes of TEK and in doing so raises many of the limitations of using traditional knowledge to bolster scientific or ecological structures of knowing.[86] He says that he does not contest the validity and the extent of TEK but argues that it cannot be considered without conditions since it is not static or universal and is influenced by characteristics of the person who is sharing the knowledge (i.e., age, gender, family history, and so on). Moreover, it can be problematic to determine whether the knowledge is rooted in the past. He states: "Although it is assumed to be anchored in the past, 'tradition,' a vexed concept, is mutable, open to external influence, and at times invented anew in succeeding generations."[87] Krech appears to come close to invalidating traditional knowledge, which is a sensitive and controversial pursuit. However, his points remind us of the true nature and function of traditional knowledge, which has recently been bent beyond recognition often for social, economic, and political reasons.

Historians and anthropologists know that TEK is not static; like oral history, it is constantly under production and flux according to the teller and the meanings that information takes on as circumstances change. Cruikshank argues that local knowledge, like oral history, is fundamentally changed the moment it is "defined and bounded as 'systems' of knowledge." She says, "this sets in motion processes that fracture and fragment human experience."[88] However, our Western knowledge frameworks privilege information that is always right or that is right for the longest time until proven wrong. Therefore, our understanding is that TEK is consistent, "old" content known by people who are aware that their ancestors have been here longer than ours. This is a simplification, but not by much. What we are missing is an understanding of and appreciation for the ways of knowing and the ways of knowledge production in Aboriginal cultures, which often present more significant differences than comparisons of the data or "known" content between TEK and Western knowledge. Krech points out that TEK is culturally situated: "Because it is cultural, it is premised on, for example, theories of animal behaviour (ethology), ideas about habitat locations or the presence of other-than-human beings, and definitions and metaphors specific to particular cultural systems. Indigenous ecological thought, the culturally based comprehension of ecological systems, varies according to culture, and therefore ecology is at base ethnoecology."[89] This reminder is equally applicable to the knowledge produced under scientific and Western knowledge frameworks. Derek Rasmussen analyzes the ideologies, assumptions, and foundations of Qallunaat knowledge, pointing out, for example, that "the ideology of print means that everything is seen in terms of the written word and the apotheosis of achievement; literacy is the benchmark for intelligence, illiteracy equals incompetence."[90] More often than not, the ways that knowledge is produced and the lens through which it is viewed are forgotten in favour of simply evaluating and comparing data and content. As George W. Wenzel has argued, the appropriate employment of TEK continues to present researchers with challenges: "Immediate concern must centre on 1) the problem of possible misinterpretation of traditional ecological knowledge through its cultural decontextualization and 2) the conundrum presented to researchers by our adherence to a perceived reductionist methodology. Not surprisingly, the fact that these two matters are not easily separated makes each essential to the discussion of traditional ecological knowledge."[91]

Given that local and traditional ecological knowledge is culturally situated, how does the general term "TEK" function specifically with reference to Inuit culture in the Eastern Arctic? This book actually avoids the term "TEK" in favour of *Inuit Qaujimajatuqangit* (*IQ*). *IQ* is preferable in this context because it is the term currently used by Inuit in Nunavut to represent what is traditional: "*Inuit Qaujimajatuqangit* means knowledge that has been passed on to us by our ancestors, things that we have always known, things crucial to our survival – patience and resourcefulness."[92] Hugh Brody suggested in his 1975 *The People's Land* that the idea of tradition in general is closely linked in Inuit culture and Inuktitut to what is "real." Brody explains the importance of the term *Inummariit,* or "the real Eskimos":

> *Inummarik,* "a genuine Eskimo" or "a real person": *Inuk* (an Eskimo) + *marik* (genuine). The plural is *Inummariit,* "the real Eskimos." The combination of these two examples shows the structure of a third term, *inummarittitut: Inuk* (an Eskimo) + *marik* (real) + *titut* (in the manner of), hence "in the manner of a real Eskimo." Some people are said to eat, work, talk, or even to walk *inummartittut.*[93]

Brody goes on to connect the concept of being a "real" Inuk to what is privileged as tradition: "*Inuit* conceptions of tradition lie, therefore, within the compass of the meaning of *Inummariit* or *Inummaritut.* The common use of these terms displays a strong consciousness of tradition."[94] In other words, it remains a great compliment to be referred to as an *Inummarik,* so being educated in *IQ* is of high importance. Furthermore, *IQ* is preferable because it reminds us that Inuit TEK is culturally situated, being steeped in the beliefs, values, and worldview of Inuit: "*Inuit Qaujimajatuqangit* embraces all aspects of traditional Inuit culture, including values, world-view, language, social organization, knowledge, life skills, perceptions and expectations."[95] What are recognized today as being the main principles of *IQ* are described in the Appendix.[96] As the principles demonstrate, *IQ* is not limited to data or content but encompasses Inuit ways of knowing, being, and doing. *IQ* also privileges experiential knowledge; there is a component of it that is alive only when the teller and the audience are able to experience the knowledge in ways of living.[97] If one is not there to listen, to observe, to try, a great component of knowledge is missed. We hear this from adults who regret not spending more time on the land with their parents learning the techniques of hunting, weather prediction, igloo building, and so on. They may hear many, many stories in their lifetime about such things, which we might classify as the passing on of oral history, but without having been there, many Inuit feel inadequate and unknowing.

Education and Culture

Thus far I have referred to education in a broad sense, but the historical meaning and practice of education for Inuit differed greatly from the concept of formal education pursued by the Qallunaat. This difference grows out of the same differences between Western knowledge and *IQ*. Jeanette Armstrong argues that education in Aboriginal communities is about the practice of everyday living, focused on training future generations for a healthy existence within their social order (and within a productive environment), and that education is thus culturally defined. Education is a "natural process that was integrated into the daily lifestyle of the culture" based within the family.[98] The impact of education being delivered by the family is of great significance in distinguishing Aboriginal education from formal schooling: "It is through family-based learning that quality is ensured as the young are taught with the utmost care through natural parental instinct for continuation and survival."[99] Armstrong further explains that the education of children thus tends to reflect closely the needs and stage of learning demonstrated by each child; it is child-centred. Lastly, she points out that Aboriginal education can be referred to as a natural process because of the way that it reflects both the natural rhythms of the day's activities and the experiential basis of educational methodology: "Experiential learning during work activities was the medium for learning."[100] Armstrong argues that much of the traditional teaching and learning among Aboriginal peoples thus occurred according to terms that cannot be achieved within the confines of the classroom. Chapter 2 discusses the extent to which each of these general characteristics of Aboriginal education matches Inuit education specifically; here, they are intended to offer a basic summary of the Aboriginal approach.

Anthropologists and scholars have commented on the experience of learning in the Inuit way. According to both George Wenzel and Arlene Stairs, in the North Baffin dialect of Inuktitut there are words that differentiate between formal education and Inuit education.[101] Stairs explains:

> Inuit clearly recognize the radical difference between formal education and traditional learning, labelling them, respectively, *ilisayuq* and *isumaqsayuq*. *Isumaqsayuq* is the way of passing along knowledge through observation and imitation embedded in daily family and community activities, with integration into the immediate, shared social structure and ecology as the principal goal. The focus is on values developed through the learner's relationship to other persons and to the environment. In terms of the present speculations, *isumaqsayuq* may be understood as education leading to ecocentric identity. In contrast, *ilisayuq* is teaching that involves a high level of abstract verbal mediation in a setting removed from daily life, with the skill base for a future specialized occupation as the principle goal. *Ilisayuq* may be understood as education leading to egocentric development, to success in an egocentric contractual culture.[102]

Hugh Brody also describes, in more personal terms, his experience of learning Inuktitut from an Elder in Pond Inlet as offering him much more than lessons in language:

> Again and again a lesson that I had expected to be about language had also been, or become, a lesson about other things – how to hunt, how to behave when talking, how to use the telephone, how to play checkers. When I had asked Anaviapik to teach me Inuktitut, and when he had said he was eager to do so, I had thought we were talking about words and grammar, about speaking, while he had supposed we were talking about a way of being. He had embarked upon the task of teaching me how to do and be *Inuk-titut*, "in the manner of an Inuk."[103]

Therefore, in addressing the integration of aspects of Inuit education into the formal school system, the challenge lies not only with the content and with developing materials that are culturally appropriate but also with the pedagogical approach, the values that shape that approach, the understanding of relationships, and the local contingencies that surround the teacher and learner. Education is fundamentally linked to the purposes, worldviews, and cultural foundations of the people who are being educated, and these largely differ between traditional Inuit education and formal Qallunaat education.

Even with decades of shared encounters, massive technological change, and recently the common concern for climate change, Inuit and Qallunaat continue to experience life in the Arctic differently. Through the mechanisms of government and public policy provided first by Inuit representative organizations and now also by the Government of Nunavut, Inuit have expressed the importance of maintaining many aspects of their traditional culture and relationship with the environment. The pursuit of self-determination was based largely on the Nunavut Land Claims Agreement, which stipulated rights and responsibilities with regard to the land, sea, wildlife, and subsurface resources. It also included a political aspect that allowed Inuit, who comprise the majority of the population in Nunavut, to make decisions about their homeland in terms of language use and cultural sustainability. It would not be unreasonable to argue that Nunavut was largely conceived of in the interest of ensuring that the relationship between humans and the environment in the Arctic is shaped by Inuit culture, not that of the Qallunaat.

2

Living and Learning on the Land: Inuit Education in the Traditional Period

No credence can be given to the view that education began in the Arctic District in 1949 with the construction of the first schools. An effective education system enabled the Eskimo people to exist and thrive long before the Kabloona [Qallunaat] were aware of the Eskimo's existence.

– Ivan W. Mouat, educational administrator, "Education in the Arctic District"

The Inuit language and culture is designed to help the society to survive in a harsh environment, by putting a lot of emphasis on practical lessons. When teaching a child to think and develop their skill and knowledge base, we should do so with a lot of love, kindness, understanding and patience being continuously present. Recognizing a child's character will help determine the types and methods of teaching that will work best for the child, as each person has a different way of processing how they generate thought or process ideas.

– Joe Karetak, *The Inuit Version of Where Our Thoughts Are Believed to Be Generated*, a reflection paper resulting from a meeting of the Elders' Advisory Committee

Education was crucial to the well-being and survival of families and persons in the Arctic. It was also fully integrated into childrearing and life-long experience, which can make it difficult to extract from the study of other aspects of Inuit life. Children were educated for the purpose of being successful in a hunter-gatherer society that was nomadic, sparse in population, and family-centred. The purpose of education was to learn to know, be, and do in the age-old manner of an Inuk. That is to say, although environmental knowledge was a crucial component of Inuit education, there was more involved than simply learning technicalities, such as the types of snow from which one could build an igloo. It was also essential that learners be prepared to practise, demonstrate, and experience what would become their means of survival: a sustaining relationship with the land, sea, sky, and other beings. A foundational quality of Inuit education is the caring that existed between learner and teacher. Education meant providing resources to young family members so that they might prosper and live through hardship. Education also meant a number of older family members acting as teachers to a child or youth at different times and in different capacities. Therefore, in addition to the generic survival skills necessary to life in the Arctic, education was often conducted with the goal in mind of discovering the special interests and skills of the learner and determining where the learner would fit into the family and the small community around the family. These are the characteristics of an education that proved successful in the context of traditional Inuit life.

In defining Inuit education, this chapter offers a number of Inuit voices. As mentioned, due to the holistic nature of Inuit knowledge and the lack of distinction between childrearing and education in traditional culture, I draw generalizations regarding education based on accounts of various subjects. On each point regarding the traditions of Inuit culture, I try to include evidence from Inuit perspectives, as well as reinforcement from other scholarship. Transcripts of meetings of the Elders' Advisory Committee, a body within the Nunavut Department of Education, provided important evidence of the traditional experience of education.

The historical period in question is difficult to define in absolute terms, but what I refer to as the "traditional" period occurred prior to sustained contact with or permanent settlement by Qallunaat. This period reaches as far back in history as the memories of Elders and their oral history allow. Our knowledge of this period is also informed by the glimpses of Inuit life captured by whalers, explorers, anthropologists, and other visitors to the Arctic who kept journals and made reports of their journeys among the "Eskimos." Although there was undoubtedly a degree of change in Inuit society during this period, the characteristics listed here serve to justify the term "traditional" as the dominant experience of most people in the Eastern Arctic at this time.

The Purpose of Inuit Education

Any examination of Arctic history conveys the important and active role that the environment played, in terms of both its affordances and its constraints, in determining the shape of human experience. The history of education is no exception. Adaptation to the environment has demanded, and arguably still does demand, a life-long learning process, dedication to which is critical to successful survival in the Canadian Arctic.[1] Inuit have historically engaged in integrated life-long learning about the land, sea, wildlife, and the relationships that constitute the Arctic environment. This learning has produced traditional knowledge, one component of a greater framework of Inuit tradition now called *Inuit Qaujimajatuqangit* (*IQ*).[2] Inuit education is not only distinguishable by its content but also encompasses ways of learning, ways of doing, and ways of being that are deeply rooted in cultural practice and social relationships. For example, the teaching and learning methods historically pursued are fundamentally experiential. It appears that this approach to education has served Inuit well, given their long-sustained dwelling in the Eastern and High Arctic despite the harsh conditions. The following analysis further elucidates the purpose of Inuit education, followed by a closer look at several specific aspects of that education. To determine the purpose of Inuit education, it is necessary to take a closer look at the worldview and livelihood traditionally practised. The preparation of young Inuit to be successful adults involved the development of skills and knowledge necessary to perpetuate a productive relationship with *sila;*[3] this was the most significant purpose of Inuit education.

History offers us insight into what can transpire if Inuit youth are not properly educated by their Elders. There is evidence that technologies can be lost between generations, particularly if a population is situated in a location with significant communication and trade barriers. Lyle Dick offers the extreme example of a family grouping of Greenlandic Inughuit losing the knowledge of boat or kayak building following an epidemic in which the Elders of the camp died. The younger generation had not yet learned the necessary skills, so for several generations these people existed without kayaks, and their standard of living suffered significantly. Without kayaks, it was exceedingly challenging to hunt seals, whales, and other marine life that would have formerly constituted a major portion of their diet. Until they were retaught the technology by their Inuit cousins who migrated from Baffin Island many years later, these Inughuit suffered the consequences of having lost the opportunity to learn the skills necessary for survival from their Elders.[4]

This history illustrates the crucial importance of conveying knowledge, skills, and techniques to each new generation. Therefore, education occurred on an informal but necessarily rigorous basis, as competency in survival skills was crucial to the integrity of the family.[5] Inuit were raised to learn by observation and thus to benefit directly from the knowledge and practices of their Elders. This is clearly part of the reason Elders are highly respected in Aboriginal and subsistence-based cultures. Renée Fossett aptly refers to Elders as "uncertainty specialists": "As was the case with linguists, travelers, navigators, and shamans, elderly 'uncertainty specialists' were appreciated as repositories of knowledge that contributed to the security and survival of the community."[6] Learning and practising skills such as skin preparation, butchering, igloo making, and weather prediction, regardless of one's gender or age, could mean the difference between life and death. Alootook Ipellie, a prolific Inuit writer and illustrator, succinctly summarizes the importance of receiving an education in survival: "Living within an oral tradition meant that each generation had to hand down the language and culture by word of mouth. This also meant that most Inuit needed the ability to retain detail, even the most minute descriptions, about certain things that were important to their continued survival. Failure to do so might mean serious injury or fatality."[7]

The Practice of Inuit Education

As the purpose and importance of Inuit education have now been established, a description of the social practices of Inuit culture will help to situate the "when" and "how" of education.[8] Inuit society was based around the family. Parents were responsible for choosing partners for their children, and betrothals were often arranged at birth or when children were very young. At a time when a young man was deemed a capable hunter and a young woman was of child-bearing age, they would be allowed to live together, or the man would take his wife back to his family's camp if he lived away. The process of learning to be a mother and wife begins from birth, but particularly once married; a young woman would be expected to observe her mother-in-law closely and learn from her. Several generations often shared tents or igloos, and women were expected to maintain healthy relations with their husband, family, and community.[9] As noted above, respectful treatment of Elders and a willingness to continue learning from them well into adulthood were values that could be essential to a happy life in a small community or family grouping. As Bernard Iquugaqtuq states, "If the sons and daughters didn't listen to their parents in those days, they would die young or have a hard time in later years. The ones who would listen to their parents would live longer and have a happier life and be respected by other people."[10]

The division of labour in Inuit society was largely gender-based. Although women and men were often equally competent or knowledgeable, the conventional distribution of responsibility left the household management and food gathering to women and the hunting to men.[11] One Inuit woman remembers the distribution of labour according to gender: "It was the woman who looked after the woman's side. She would teach us how to sew; how to make things; how to cook; how to survive; and how to scrape the hides and dry them the proper way. All sorts of things that men couldn't do. They could, but in those days they didn't!"[12] Women, often with a baby in their *amauti*[13] and several young children to feed, had to stay close to the camp, whereas men could depart for long days of hunting and take greater risks with their physical safety: "The women used to stay in the camp and look after everything while the men were hunting. They were the planners. They looked after the future for their children and grandchildren."[14] Marriages were for the most part considered companionate partnerships rather than romantic pairings, and they would last a lifetime.

Divorce was very rare and virtually unheard of once children were born to a couple. One of the most dominant experiences for Inuit women was reproduction. Children, particularly males, were seen as gifts to the family and very valuable. Women were nearly constantly pregnant or nursing; many women had a child in their womb or were breastfeeding until menopause. Apphia Awa, an Elder featured in one of the few books written about Inuit women, had twelve natural children, six boys and six girls.[15] Marriages that did not produce children were thought of as unfortunate.[16] If a woman was unable to have children or, under various other circumstances such as the particular need for a male or female child, adoption was a common solution. Adoption was, and still is, a widespread and highly regarded practice in Inuit culture, further illustrating their flexibility in social relations and under changing circumstances. This system of socialization, education, and subsistence necessitated prolonged close relationships between parents and their children.

For parents, not only bearing children but also teaching them and seeing them grow into successful hunters and mothers were the most meaningful experiences of their lives. Rachel Qitsualik explains why the special place of children in Inuit society has developed:

> A great deal has been written about how Inuit love their children. In an exceptionally harsh world, any culture becomes especially preoccupied with its youngest generation, which only makes sense if you think about it. After all, the more unkind the times, the more the survival of the culture itself comes into question. And there were times, among pre-colonial Inuit, when raising a child to healthy adulthood was quite an accomplishment. The consequent appreciation of their children is probably the reason why Inuit have traditionally fussed over them, indulging the very young to a degree that disgusted the first visiting Europeans.[17]

The important place of children in Inuit society was also manifested through the tradition of naming a new child after a respected Elder who had recently died. Although Inuit did not necessarily ascribe to true physical reincarnation, they did believe that the soul of an Elder, and therefore the *isuma*[18] of an Elder, could be present in a new child. Jean Briggs offers further insight into the concept of *isuma* and how it operates to determine a measure of maturity in Inuit culture:

> Underlying both the conscious training and the other experiences that Inuit children have are certain ideas concerning the nature of human cognition or *isuma. Isuma* refers to consciousness, thought, reason, memory, will – to cerebral processes in general – and the possession of *isuma* is a major criterion of maturity.

> Saying that a person has *isuma* is equivalent to saying that she or he exercises good judgment, reason, and emotional control at all times, in addition to the skills appropriate to his or her age, gender and role.[19]

Treating a child with disrespect or imposing one's will on a child was equal to acting in that manner toward the child's Elder namesake and was therefore unacceptable. This belief significantly shaped the relationship between parents and children, and it explains why the Inuit parenting style was, and still sometimes is, interpreted by Qallunaat as highly permissive. Hugh Brody refers to Inuit society as both individualistic and communal, identifying parenting as a clear example of the extent to which Inuit tolerate individualism: "The Inuit way is without authoritarianism; parents are inclined to trust children to know what they need. Individuals have to be left to make decisions for themselves; and children are individuals just as adults are, since they carry the names – for which we may say souls – of their late and much admired relatives."[20] This view of children, as mini-adults who simply need to be reminded of or re-familiarized with the knowledge that lies within them, exists in direct contrast to the Western *tabula rasa* concept applied to children. This Inuit perspective is crucial to the following discussion of traditional education.

Some of the qualities expected of an adult include the *Inuit Qaujimajatuqangit* principles, as I have referred to them. For more evidence of the qualities children were expected to develop, a study of the understanding of intelligence in Inuit culture, carried out by two anthropologists in the community of Holman, is useful. Between 1978 and 1995 Richard G. Condon and Pamela Stern conducted anthropological studies on various topics that were indirectly related to the concept of intelligence. They identified every reference to someone being "smart" or acting in a "smart way" in their data from this period to figure out what intelligence means to Inuit. They concluded that childrearing practices, even across the Arctic in communities from Alaska to Greenland, consistently placed a high value on industry, innovation, patience, and emotional evenness.[21]

Before Inuit methods of education are described, one final point should be made regarding the social dynamic of their society. Perhaps the most commonly highlighted attribute of Inuit is their capacity for adaptation and flexibility. Inuit highly value problem-solving skills, and *Qanuqtuurungnarniq*, or the concept of being resourceful in solving problems,[22] forms one of the central traditional principles of *IQ* and Inuit culture. The late Gideon Qitsualik explains why resourceful problem solving is important for young Inuit to develop:

> It is not always possible to pass on all the knowledge you have accumulated, even though you know a lot about it, you can't explain about everything, all the time,

> it just does not work like that. It is better a person is able to devise and develop solutions as they come up, only because it is impossible to predict and tell someone every little pitfall they may run into, no matter how much information we can provide in prevention, the method to dealing with problems, is to be able to create solutions, look at your options, if you have any, and do it as efficiently as possible.[23]

Brody provides insight as to how this flexibility has emerged from the Inuit relationship with the environment: "Hunters are always ready to move. This is a matter of economics. It is also a cultural habit, an approach to life, a way of dealing with the psychological and spiritual as well as the material demands of existence. Flexibility and mobility are at the heart of living in the north."[24] Fossett describes in greater detail what is meant by flexibility in practical terms:

> The first five of the six strategies for reducing uncertainty [practised by Inuit] – mobility, storage, diversification, exchange, and technological innovation – imply human adaptation to the environment. Individuals and societies learn the rules of the natural world and live within them. A precondition of successful use of any one of the strategies is, then, an investment of intellectual effort in order to understand the natural law, and to shape social and technological behaviour so that human beings might take the resources necessary for survival without disturbing the rights of non-human persons who share the land, and without endangering their own collective survival by depleting limited resources.[25]

This adeptness at flexibility and Inuit willingness to change in response to circumstances are remarkable, but these traits are especially evident when contrasted with the approach of European adventurer-explorers who frequented the Arctic in the late nineteenth and early twentieth centuries. According to Lyle Dick, "During the first half century of Euro-North American exploration in the High Arctic, most Western visitors failed to approach this region on its own terms. Typically, they regarded the environment as a hostile wilderness to be overcome, rather than accommodated, and early attempts to impose European techniques of travel, provisioning, and shelter often enough yielded disastrous results."[26] Philip Lange has added to this dialogue on Inuit flexibility by characterizing it as the basis for social interaction among Inuit:

> What I want to show is, first how flexibility as a principle of social action subsumes, at least in the Inuit case, two other crucial notions: creative action and consensual relations. I also want to draw attention to both the deeply imbedded place that

> the notion of flexibility has in traditional Inuit culture, and its enduring place as an adaptive and integrative mechanism in contemporary Inuit society.[27]

These points about the flexibility of social relationships in Inuit culture are revisited throughout this book as the nature of traditional educational practices is further illustrated.

Eber Hampton describes Aboriginal education in Canada according to the following characteristics: "All traditional Native methods occurred within cultural settings that were characterized by subsistence economies, in-context learning, personal and kinship relations between teachers and students, and ample opportunities for students to observe adult role models who exemplified the knowledge, skills, and values being taught."[28] This summary is largely applicable to Inuit education. In order to establish a framework by which to compare Inuit education to formal Qallunaat schooling more specifically, emphasis will be placed on three aspects: (1) in correlation with the Inuit worldview, education is focused mostly on knowledge and skills relating to the environment; (2) a distinguishing feature of Inuit education is that its methods are fundamentally experiential; and (3) education occurs on an informal and learner-centred basis, grounded in both the flexibility and the close relationships that characterize Inuit society. Although it may be obvious at this juncture, the latter point also indicates that Inuit education is, at its core, locally driven.

Knowing, Doing, Being

The first important aspect of Inuit education is its content, the pursuit of "knowing." As a result of the constraints placed on Inuit by the Arctic ecosystem, their daily pursuits demanded a high level of environmental knowledge. The *IQ* principle of *Pilimmaksarniq* refers to skill and knowledge acquisition that may be considered a comparable concept to what the Qallunaat would call "environmental education." The principle has been defined by Elders working with the Nunavut Department of Education, who further note that "capacity building is central to the success of Inuit in a harsh environment. Building personal capacity in Inuit ways of knowing and doing are key expectations for students. Demonstrating empowerment to lead a successful and productive life, that is respectful of all, is a powerful end goal of our educational system."[29] This definition was written in 2000 for the purposes of shaping the modern education system and can thus shed only limited light on the historical experience of education. Nonetheless, on the basis of this statement, several interesting points can be made that help to reveal the nature of Inuit education.

First, the most important skills and knowledge to be learned are linked directly to the environment, which is described as "harsh." In other words, the basis of leading a "successful and productive" life begins with the capacity to protect oneself from an environment that can be threatening and that is therefore due respectful study. Second, it is made clear that Inuit have particular ways of "knowing and doing," which in the modern context of this definition likely refers to the desire to distinguish between Inuit ways and the ways of Qallunaat. It also suggests that Elders believe that knowing and doing in the traditional ways are not lost to history but remain vital. Children were expected not only to absorb traditional environmental knowledge but also to demonstrate environmental stewardship – in Inuktitut, *Avatimik Kamattiarniq*. *Avatimik Kamattiarniq* is one of the *IQ* principles, loosely defined as responsible behaviours that act to protect the relationship between Inuit and the environment. In a Nunavut Department of Education meeting to discuss the definition of this component of *IQ*, one Elder, Mark Kalluak, offered his understanding, including how it may be applied in a modern context:

> We are the keepers of the environment, of the animals, of the water and the Sila (environment), and we occupy this land. We should take care of it, the same way we take care of our personal items, the way we take care of our ski-doos or any other things we try and make sure they don't get broken and keep them in good working order, [so] we can keep using them. The water and land we harvest from must be taken care of and used properly, like it always was, in the old days.[30]

As another Elder, Moses Koihok, described, these responsible behaviours were carefully taught to young Inuit:

> This principle seems to be the most consistently supported and practiced belief by all of the Inuit people, no matter where they come from. We hear the same things about how as young Inuit people growing up, how important it was to the Elders this concept be practiced consistently, we heard of people being scolded when someone did not listen to the laws that govern *Avatimik Kamattiarniq*, and I really appreciate hearing about it, the way we were made to understand to all of the children early, because it always talks about keeping the environment we live on clean, no matter where you live, [you are] on the environment.[31]

An example of demonstrating environmental stewardship is the expectation that nearly every part of a hunted animal should be utilized. John Amagoalik explains: "We regard other living things as integral parts of the whole and therefore must sustain their integrity. We understand that waste now means want later. We know that there must be a balance between take and return. Our environment has dictated these laws to us."[32]

The second aspect of Inuit education deals with methodology and learning to "do." Observation, practise, and experience were the most common and favoured methods of facilitating skills and knowledge acquisition. Jacopie Kokseak remembers with fondness the experience of receiving an education from his father: "When I was young my father and I used to have good times. I did not know that I was being given an education. Without my knowing it he was teaching me ways of doing things. I can remember thinking to myself that I would be very glad when I would be able to do all these things myself."[33] As described here and in the discussion of learner-centred education, children encountered learning opportunities as they helped or mimicked their older relatives during the course of contributing to their family's responsibilities. Education was conducted in the context of the demands and challenges of everyday life, and the reward of education lay in adult recognition of a child's capability and autonomy.

Inuit children were not expected to ask many questions, as asking questions was considered a sign of unknowing, that *isuma* was lacking, to which vague or evasive answers might be offered by the teacher.[34] Indeed, "Why?" was thought to be a considerably rude question.[35] Rather, learners should first closely observe their parents or relatives, who would demonstrate and might offer a description of how a task should be done. Then the learner would be expected to practise the traditional method or technique until he or she mastered it fully. However, according to Barnabus Pirjuaq's memory, Inuit also believed learners would best discover explanations or techniques independently: "Before the Qallunaat came, children were also taught by being made to do things on their own."[36] Learners embarking on a task for the first time might not be offered any advice so that they would experience it for themselves and make mistakes if necessary. The anthropologist Renée Fossett says that her experience as a learner, although an adult and a Qallunaaq, included being intentionally left to learn for herself:

> During the 1960s, the decade in which I lived in Inuit communities, some of my acquaintances were willing to attempt my education by the methods to which I was accustomed. They simply answered my questions and corrected me when I got things wrong. Many, however, preferred to teach by putting me in situations where, they thought, I could see for myself. The assumption that "observers were always capable of understanding," made by many Inuit teachers and informants over the centuries, was charitable and flattering, but perhaps not always realistic or wise.[37]

Fossett conveys how this method could pose a frustrating prospect, but despite her opinion, it was intended precisely to instill in the learner a keen sense of self-reliance. It was believed that this system would support the development of an individual who could feel independent, self-directed, and unique among his or her peers. This belief is evident in Pudlo Pudlat's description of how he learned to hunt:

> The way I learned about being a hunter was by going along with the men for the day. No one said to me, "This is the way you do this and this is the way you do that." In those days, we just learned by example, by watching and trying. For us, when we were learning about life, about life skills, it was from experience, from watching and by example. The teacher was there, but he was not there to tell us, "Hey, that's a mistake."[38]

After learners discovered the basics of a task, such as seal hunting, they might receive advice or direction to consider for their next hunt. Adults would continue to observe their Elders and receive additional instructions so long as there were new and different techniques to learn. Referring to the way his father taught him to hunt, Peter Paniloo remembers, "He would watch me while I was hunting, sometimes with binoculars from a distance. Afterwards he would tell me where I had made mistakes. And when I became more independent in my hunting, he advised me further for my advancement."[39]

Another important part of Inuit education is the legends, stories, and histories that comprise their oral culture. Most Inuit became literate in the early twentieth century as a result of missionary work in bringing Christianity to them through the syllabic system of writing Inuktitut. Before that time, they relied solely on oral transmission of knowledge and history. Many hours in the deepest part of the cold and dark winter were passed with varied types of entertainment. Much time was spent retelling the history and legends of their ancestors. This is an important component of the experience of young Inuit in learning where they have come from and how or why the practices they see used around them developed. Mark Kalluak explains:

> Before the writing system was introduced in the Canadian Arctic, story telling was one way in which a small portion of our history was preserved. The elder women were especially noted for their ability to recite Inuit legends in a way that made a person feel as though he were part of that story. Inuit legends, like any other stories, carry with them a lesson or principle to remember, and I believe that this is why they were quite important to our people.[40]

This was also the context in which the teachings of shamans, who maintained the deeply spiritual connection between Inuit and their environment, were shared. Gathering in a large igloo for these events, not only would youth listen to the stories of their Elders, but they would also hear songs and throat singing and would watch drum dances or re-enactments of legends with masks. Shamans might call out to the spirit world and become embodied by those spirits, conveying messages, predictions, or taboos. These evenings of cultural transmission were intensely experiential.[41] Although I cannot do justice to the significance and many purposes of these practices in the confines of this book, the rich oral methods of social and spiritual education provide another example of how culture, history, and their relationship to the environment were reinforced through experiential means.

The third aspect delivers the "being" of an Inuit education and relates to the integrated practices of childrearing and education, which were nearly indistinguishable in Inuit culture. Education occurred on a casual, but constant and integrative, basis most commonly between a young person (learner) and older family member (teacher). As was the case for most Aboriginal cultures in Canada, the relationship between teachers and learners was imbued with love and caring due to the kinship between them: "In traditional Aboriginal communities, learning is an intimate process. Traditionally, teachers loved their students dearly. Teachers were moms, dads, grandparents, and other loved ones."[42] Inuit education, therefore, was often an individual experience, insofar as it catered to the unique traits of each child. Learners were treated according to their ability and curiosity, and they were not pushed to mature beyond their own capability. The editors of an oral history of Nunavut generalize on this point based on their collection of Inuit testimony: "Inuit considered each child unique; as an individual who developed, learned and matured at his own speed."[43] If learners showed interest, they would be challenged by their teachers.

A certain degree of convention was inherent in the knowledge taught and methods used, but this was due more to their effectiveness than to a desire for standardization. The learner could certainly suffer both material and social consequences for failing to master the practices of his or her ancestors, but as previously discussed, innovation and problem solving were also highly valued. Although traditional education may not qualify as a formal "system," there is clear evidence that at least some teachers had a vision of the range of experiences that would be necessary for their students' success as adults. Here is one example of this systematic approach, as described by Emil Imaruittuq:

> When boys were being brought up it was better to treat them roughly – but not at all times, as there are times that a boy should be treated tenderly. In addition to that, there should be some times when the boy is awakened even if he has not rested completely. One should not allow him to sleep all he wants to; there should

> be some times when he is made to stay awake even when he is not fully rested, and there should also be times when he is permitted to sleep all he wants. This also applies to work. He should be allowed to work as far as his ability allows, and there should also be times when ease is maintained in his work. It is best that he be given responsibility that he can carry mentally. In this way his mind is being developed in line with his physical capabilities ... He should also be allowed to do what he wants periodically.[44]

He describes that a balance was required between permissiveness and pressure. Also, this account reinforces the belief that children would not mature at a certain age of majority, but only when their individual physical and mental development matched the expectations of adulthood – at whatever age that occurred for each individual. Although learners would not be forced to follow a schedule, laziness was looked down on, and as the day's tasks unfolded, the learner was expected to follow along, participating to the best of his or her ability. Speaking to the experience of young girls, Apphia Awa remembers: "We were always helping our mothers, cleaning the skins, sewing, taking the bucket out, getting ice, making oil for the lamps, and chewing sealskins. Working like this, it was like going to school, because we would be woken up early in the morning to start our daily work."[45] Discipline by parents was neither strict nor physical, but proper behaviour was enforced through social means until children became self-regulating and demonstrated that they understood how crucial self-discipline was to survival in the Arctic.[46] Alice Ayalik lists the principles of a work ethic she learned from her grandmother:

> The other thing my grandmother taught me was to finish what I am sewing. I tried to run out and play before I had a pair of mitts finished, and there were 2 parts to the lesson. The first part of the lesson was to finish what one starts, play later, and the second part was, to protect yourself and others from the cold elements, it is important to finish sewing first, and you will be protected better, with new warm mitts.[47]

In accordance with the conventional division of labour by gender, generally women were responsible for the education of their female children, whereas men taught their boys, a tradition described by John Bennett and Susan Rowley:

> Although children often acquired other skills, their gender determined the nature of their education. Boys, wanting to imitate their older male relatives, learned the skills of the outdoors: hunting, traveling, making tools and other equipment.

Figure 3 Pennyloo returns with his grandfather from fishing for salmon trout in Eclipse Sound (near Pond Inlet), October, 1951. *Source:* National Film Board of Canada, Library and Archives Canada.

> Girls, following in the footsteps of their mothers, grandmothers, and aunts, learned the complementary skills of the home: preparing skins, making clothing, tents and qajaq coverings, and the like.[48]

One individual was not necessarily designated as a child's teacher. Like other social practices, childrearing and teaching responsibilities were fluid among the social group or community, as Rachel Qitsualik explains: "In old Inuit tradition, it was every community member's right to coddle and interact with the young. It was almost as though a child were communal property, raised by all. But, then, members of any particular camp were almost all related."[49] A teacher could be any family member who chose to take a learner on a trip or who asked a learner to help with a task. Mariano Aupilardjuk confirms that uncles were often important teachers for young hunters:

> You see I had uncles, and all had different things or ways they would ask like to do this, as each had different skills or ways of doing things. One uncle was really tiring to go out with him and was always really strict, so I did not really like going out with him. But it turns out, as I look back, [he] was the one who was teaching me the most important things, that I would use the rest of my life. My other uncles never would pressure me, so I would just enjoy myself whenever I went with them. But I did not pick up any skills or learn very much from them, and the one I thought was the worst, left me with knowledge that has been very useful to my life. So serving others well, [is] truly the best method in teaching us to learn skills, acquiring knowledge and gain wisdom. I am truly touched, remembering back how useful serving is to learning how to live. I felt very strongly and wanted to say this.[50]

It is clear from this description that Aupilardjuk had a special relationship with one of his uncles, which resulted in a particularly effective teacher-learner experience. He had interactions with various older relatives who could have taken on the role of teacher, and some did so more effectively than others.

Tradition and Change

It is difficult to determine how or to what extent Inuit education changed over the generations, particularly as Qallunaat made early encroachments on the Arctic, but increased contact with Euro-Canadians and their culture has allowed us to better observe the characteristics of Inuit education through comparison. The importance of both a learner-centred approach and direct experience to

Inuit education methodology became much more obvious in contrast to the Qallunaat method of education, which was focused on standards, consistency, and the binary opposites of true and untrue. For example, when Qallunaat explorers or anthropologists asked for directions to an important location, Inuit could be put off by their aggressiveness and invasiveness. Nonetheless, Inuit would usually share their knowledge, but they would carefully qualify it as provisional because it represented only their own experience. Knud Rasmussen articulates this characteristic:

> The difficulties of understanding and teaching were neatly summed up in the early 1920s by Ikinilik, a man from the Great Fish River. Having done his best to explain his views on how the physical and metaphysical realms worked, he concluded by recognizing that self-knowledge, like other kinds of knowledge, is clouded by subjectivity, and that all transmitted knowledge is inherently imperfect. "Of course it may be that all I have been telling you is wrong. For you cannot be certain about a thing you cannot see. And people say so much."[51]

Contrary to the tendency of westerners to perceive Aboriginal traditional knowledge as something broad and static, which each informant relates with a measure of consistency, Inuit often express modesty about their own knowledge and remind those who receive it that it is based "only" on what they have seen and heard. This social practice reinforces the emphasis placed on individual experiential knowledge.

As is often the case, people may not recognize the most important aspects of their culture until they come upon another. Indeed, for this reason there are relatively few references to education in oral history collections, and those that occur are often included under the categories of childrearing or social relations. Traditional Inuit education was not a separate pursuit for the benefit of children but was integrated into the daily experience of all Inuit to such an extent that it hardly demanded reflection. This is the mark of an education system that best suits the society that it serves. It was focused on skills and knowledge acquisition that would support young men in becoming successful and safe hunters and young women in raising children and sewing protective clothing. Broadly speaking, this education reflected the central concern of life in the Arctic: meeting the needs of human life faced with the demands of a harsh ecosystem. Therefore, although an individual Inuk's education could vary considerably from that of his or her peers, respect for the land, and by extension respect for one's Elders due to their greater experience on the land, was compulsory. The accommodation of *sila*, which could be highly unpredictable despite the best application of traditional knowledge, also required flexibility, excellent problem-solving skills, and a high degree of independence and self-reliance. These necessities, manifested through the oral culture of Inuit in the Eastern Arctic, established education as fundamentally life-long and experiential.

Inuit increasingly encountered Europeans in their homeland as the Hudson's Bay Company personnel, Anglican and Catholic missions, Royal Canadian Mounted Police, and American military established semi-permanent or permanent settlements across the Arctic.[52] These institutions had varying levels of influence on and engagement with Inuit; some offered services or supplemental economic, social, and technological assistance. Their impact on culture and lifestyle can be considered relatively limited in comparison to their impact on other First Nations in Canada during the nineteenth century.[53] John Matthiasson, an Arctic anthropologist, calls this period "Contact-Traditional" because, although communities were being established, many Inuit still chose to live on the land: "The camp people were traditionalists in many respects, still dependent on hunting for most of their food, speaking Inuktitut in their homes, maintaining a fairly conventional Inuit family structure, and, I am convinced, believing that they were living much as Inuit had lived for centuries. In psychological identity, they were in fact Inuit."[54] However, this long-maintained way of life in the Arctic was rapidly ending. The scale of change approaching them was unprecedented. As their economic system bent to accommodate the pursuit of trade with the Hudson's Bay Company, the social organization of many family groups changed too.

Vast societal changes alter the demands on a system of education, and if complementary or compensatory change does not occur in each realm, significant dislocation is nearly impossible to avoid. In the mid-1970s an informant named Taqtu reflected, "When I was a child, they taught me how to hunt, how to survive, and how to support people. It was the only game; we had to have meat so it was something that we had to know. It's not the same now. Today it's more important to be able to work, carve, make money – that's what there is now."[55] Unfortunately, we do not know whether Inuit could have continued to pursue education that melded their traditional culture with the changing basis of their economy. We do not know whether they could have diminished the dislocation felt by their children in the face of two very different worlds. Instead, the Qallunaat brought their system of education to the Arctic and gave Inuit little choice but to hand over their children.

3
Qallunaat Schooling: Assimilation in the Colonial Period

The government had made it mandatory for all school-age children to start attending school. It touched on absurdity. The parents ended up tagging along just so their children could enter the academic world. Their status as heads of families was diminished because the principals and the teachers had the sole authority to teach Inuit children whatever was on the curriculum. As a student participant, I got a glimpse of the Qallunaat world in my studies. But not a single subject was devoted to my culture and language.

– Alootook Ipellie, "People of the Good Land"

These schools are designed to teach the Eskimo how to live in the white man's society, yet not one of them teaches either the Eskimo language or Eskimo folklore. Moreover, they do not teach the Eskimo how to hunt and trap. If the Eskimo does not obtain employment within the white man's industry, he is entirely unsuited to live in the North. In this way, education can be a curse rather than a boon. This also serves to tie the Eskimo tighter to the "apron strings" of the kablunait [Qallunaat].

– Robert McAlpine, "Kablunait and Innuit: The Effect of the White Man upon the Eskimo Minority"

Between the mid-1940s and early 1970s, Inuit lost their autonomy in their Arctic homeland. These difficult years saw the closing stages of reliance on their subsistence-based economy, seasonal rounds, and cultural and political independence in the Arctic. A majority of Inuit settled in communities, received some form of welfare or relief from the government, and found that Qallunaat were increasingly interfering in their lives. Some Inuit felt that it would be best for them and their children to become more like the Qallunaat, who appeared materially wealthy and powerful. Others resisted the changes expected by members of the Royal Canadian Mounted Police (RCMP), nurses, and teachers. However, regardless of what any parent believed, by the late 1950s small schools had been erected across much of the Eastern Arctic, and Inuit children were exposed to the paternalistic, assimilative approach of Qallunaat educators. Inuit parents had no say as to how or what their children learned in school.

This change not only involved the introduction of a new education system but also proved detrimental to the Inuit one. Indeed, the purpose of early schools was to teach Inuit children to know, be, and do like Qallunaat in order to prepare them for employment on Qallunaat terms. It appeared that the system of experiential, learner-centred, environment-based education could not co-exist with that of the formal school system. Many Qallunaat and Inuit felt that the transition to a life more reflective of Qallunaat ways and the implementation of formal schooling marked the passing of the relevance of traditional Inuit knowledge, culture, and education.

The Qallunaat system of education differed vastly in content, methodology, and social underpinnings; these differences and the way they were experienced by Inuit students and Qallunaat teachers form the central focus of this chapter. The introduction of the formal education system was detrimental because it took control over the future of Inuit children away from parents and Elders. It was culturally assimilative and the most significantly disempowering colonial practice imposed on Inuit. Moreover, economic development did not coincide with educational development, and the jobs promised to Inuit who did finish their education or practical training did not materialize. Therefore, the education system did not facilitate self-determination, a positive self-identity, or economic self-sufficiency.

To support these arguments, I rely heavily on Norm Macpherson's *Dreams and Visions,* a collection of reflections by teachers, educational administrators, and some students who participated in the education system across the Northwest Territories from the time of the earliest schools until the late 1970s. *Dreams and Visions* also includes excerpts from official letters, government documents, and other articulations of the institutional perspective. Much of the value of *Dreams and Visions* lies in the candidness of the letters and memories that have been reproduced, as well as in the breadth of material. It covers a large time period and touches on most of the communities of the NWT at least once. It is important to note that this source does not offer much insight into the views of Inuit, a gap that is partly explained by the relatively low employment or involvement of Inuit adults in the school system for most of the period examined in *Dreams and Visions.* Another important source of evidence for this chapter is scholarly monographs, most of which are anthropological, that provide insight into the experience of colonization. I have tried to incorporate as many Inuit memories and views as possible of this difficult transitional period and of the role of education therein. There are, however, relatively few sources that provide insight into the daily experience of federal community schools from the perspective of students. Inuit are often reluctant to recount experiences of anger, embarrassment, or conflict. As has been the case throughout this book, I must sometimes draw wide conclusions based on the comments of only a few spokespersons. One of the spokespersons on whom I consistently rely is the late Alootook Ipellie, a prominent Inuit writer, artist, and historian from Iqaluit, who did not hesitate to commit to paper his views on the past.

Referring to this period as the colonial period, like any other generality, raises many questions. Is the term "colonial" really appropriate in representing the experience of Inuit? Did this period begin with the long-term establishment of federal government involvement in administration of the northern territories, or did it begin long before when southern economic systems began to change Inuit livelihoods and pursuits? Did the colonial period end with the advent of Inuit representation in the NWT Legislative Assembly in 1967, with the signing of the Nunavut Land Claims Agreement in 1993, or with the creation of Nunavut Territory in 1999? Is the colonial period really over?

The term "colonialism" is often used but not often defined. Giving shape to the term is a task that can be daunting to historians, due to the peculiarities of making the theory fit the circumstance or vice versa. It can also present a difficult prospect in terms of representing the agency of both colonizer and colonized with accuracy and sensitivity. Duane Champagne argues that most theories of colonialism overemphasize power and materialism and under-represent the colonized culture and community.[1] Instead, he offers a multidimensional theory of colonization in which political competition, economic incorporation, cultural exchange, and biological resistance are the major factors of analysis. Each factor may operate autonomously, but examining them together in one "model" can provide "a more holistic explanation for the outcomes of colonial relations."[2] Champagne prescribes that the analysis should then take into consideration the colonized (in this case Aboriginal) communities and their historical contingencies in order to identify change and continuity resulting from colonization:

> By focusing on the issues and strategies of the colonized nations and understanding the colonial context through the cultural, political, and economic requirements of self-preservation forced on the colonized by the colonizer's power and interests, the present theory avoids the deterministic and coercive explanations usually given to colonial contexts and the view that the colonized are helpless victims of the inevitable domination.[3]

Applying Champagne's model, the experiences of Inuit in the Canadian Arctic can be appropriately termed colonialism because, like other Aboriginal communities, they experienced the dislocation of sudden political competition (primarily with Euro-Canadians but also with Americans and other circumpolar nations), economic incorporation (first through trading and trapping and later through full incorporation into the welfare state), cultural exchange (e.g., Christianity and formal schooling), and a lack of biological resistance to European diseases (e.g., tuberculosis, polio, smallpox, and influenza).[4] Their colonization is distinct, however, for its timing in the mid-twentieth century and for occurring over only a few decades.

Colonization of the Eastern Arctic

For the purposes of this book, the colonial period is considered to have begun around 1945, the point at which sustained and increasingly interventionist involvement by the federal government drastically changed the lives of Inuit, particularly as permanent settlements were established and Inuit were encouraged, coerced, or forced to relinquish their nomadic seasonal rounds. During the colonial period, administration of Inuit was a federal responsibility in Ottawa. Great contradiction and competing visions of the Arctic's future and of the government's responsibilities characterized the federal administrative approach. The overriding principle behind these bureaucratic policies was that Inuit could not continue to fend for themselves, as they did not understand enough about the world they were entering to make their own decisions. Ipellie suggests that "Canada was concerned about which bureaucrats would speak for the Inuit, federal or provincial. The idea of letting the Inuit speak for themselves never occurred to many of those in authority."[5] By 1970 administrative responsibility had been transferred to the Government of the Northwest Territories, and this marked a step toward political representation for Inuit through the Legislative Assembly and various other mechanisms. Therefore, although Qallunaat social, economic, and cultural structures and priorities remain ubiquitous in the Eastern Arctic, 1970 can be considered the date by which Inuit began dismantling the colonial period and embarked on the long road toward self-determination.[6]

Three broad points must be made regarding the colonial period to provide context for the introduction of the formal education system. The first point is that the period was characterized by a collapse of the traditional economic system as Inuit abandoned their nomadic hunting rounds for settlement in permanent communities. The speed at which this fundamental alteration to their existence occurred is one unique feature of the experience of colonization, matched by the unusually late historical period in which such changes occurred. An Inuk negotiator for the land claim described this change as going from the "stone age to the space age,"[7] and Frank Tester and Peter Kulchyski, authors of one of the most noteworthy treatises on Inuit mistreatment by the Canadian government, also refer to this particularity:

> The central historical dynamic that came to link Inuit to non-Inuit society politically was put in place during the period of high modernism. Unlike Indian affairs, where a pre-welfare state employed largely coercive measures, in Inuit affairs it was a liberal form of welfare state, which gave the appearance of having a more benign face and which employed a greater reliance on ideology, that became the means for attempting assimilation.[8]

Through colonization, Inuit were taken from a world of subsistence economics and relative isolation from other societies and placed in a world that had seen global war, the atomic bomb, and the television. Tester and Kulchyski refer to experience during this period as "totalization" and detail the mistreatment of Inuit and the experimental nature of government policy in the Eastern Arctic.[9] They argue,

> as a totalizing force, the state operates in a very particular fashion. Its goal is the establishment of a material and social reality conducive to the accumulation of capital. The social reality effectively means the creation of a people who are prepared to sell their labour power in a marketplace of labour relations. This implies a process of dispossession: of separating people from their means of subsistence, which in most cases and for most cultures, is the land.[10]

I support Tester and Kulchyski's argument that the various ways the government gained control over Inuit all share a significant commonality: they undermined the essential relationship between Inuit and their land. Thus the intervention on the part of the Canadian federal government in their lives after the Second World War precipitated abrupt cultural decline and resulted in significant economic dependence.

As has been the case since trading in the Arctic began, Inuit increasingly adopted Qallunaat technologies or resources such as rifles and staple foods from the Hudson's Bay Company. Zebedee Nungak remembers the significance of these new tools and how they shaped the Inuit view of the Qallunaat: "At this time the Qallunaat seemed almighty in so many ways! Their technology was wonderous. They could fly airplanes and talk to each other over vast distances on radio. They lived in warm wooden houses and seemed to lack for no material thing."[11] However, the cost of these goods exceeded any potential income from hunting, particularly after the end of the fox fur trade. Instead of trade, Inuit were offered credit or government assistance, and this led to reliance on subsidies for food, gasoline, and firearms.[12] For most, the logical solution was to live a semi-nomadic lifestyle; John Matthiasson's anthropological work suggests that during what he calls the "Contact-Traditional" period, Inuit were happy to commute into the community from their camps as required and then return to the land.[13] The missionaries and even the early government welfare teachers settled at the trading posts and interacted with the local population during their periodic visits to restock supplies. This itinerant contact, however, was not always sufficient in administering services to these new Canadian citizens.

Permanent settlement in centralized communities was not traditionally undertaken because it was not conducive to the Inuit subsistence lifestyle. Settlement meant that subsistence hunting was no longer environmentally or economically viable. George Wenzel provides a simple picture of the environmental problem of making the transition to settled life:

> Rather than small groups exploiting resources contiguous to their indigenous village, centralization meant an enormous increase in local hunter populations from communities that were not situated with hunting in mind. Because traditional transport, notably dog teams, limited the distance at which hunting could be conducted, this demographic change meant a greater density of hunters and, thus, the potential for overexploitation of the local resource base.[14]

Not only were hunting activities and the health of wildlife populations at stake, but settlement also did not reflect their unique relationship with the land. The structure of kinship and social relationships, the remnants of shamanism, which were already disappearing under the weight of Christianity, and many cultural practices, including traditional education, became irrelevant to the daily lives of Inuit in communities. Within a short time Inuit were seldom doing as their ancestors had.

Nonetheless, there were myriad reasons why Inuit were attracted to permanent settlement in communities in the 1950s. Apart from the instances of clear coercion by the government, most came off of the land in response to the structural shifts of life in the Arctic, such as the aforementioned access to resources. Several notable hunters, such as Joseph Idlout, resisted and delayed settlement until it was absolutely necessary – that is, until they could not support their families solely by hunting and trapping. Idlout later discovered community life to be unbearable.[15] Other than the economic needs met by visiting the Hudson's Bay Company or employment in the few unskilled labour jobs provided by the military or the RCMP, access to health care and education were the most significant factors in permanent settlement. Some Inuit were experiencing a crisis level of starvation and epidemic disease. Increasingly, contact with outsiders was ravaging families.[16] David Damas suggests that settlement in communities was largely a by-product of the government's attempts to provide services to Inuit rather than an intentional policy associated with the welfare state.[17] Whether the government was acting in a genuinely altruistic manner is debated by academics, but what is certain is that with the welfare state came cultural assumptions that were to be highly destructive.

Thus the second broad point about the experience of Inuit in the colonial period is that it involved an aspect of paternalism and cultural denigration by Qallunaat, specifically by the Canadian government, a history little known to Canadians outside the North. The cultural and political ideas associated with post-Second World War affluence and the Cold War were entirely foreign to Inuit and yet were wholly imposed on them by the government. One of the most significant textual remnants of this period is the *The Book of Wisdom for Eskimo.* Peter Irniq, former commissioner of Nunavut, remembers the condescending tone of the book:

> Even the Canadian government got in on the act, producing its own booklet, *The Book of Wisdom for Eskimo* first published in 1947. It also told us how to live, and addressed us like unknowledgeable children, telling Inuit women how to look after a baby, Inuit hunters how to hunt, and encouraging us to use plenty of soap and water.[18]

Paul McNicoll, Tester, and Kulchyski have shown how this book, a collection of basic hygiene and behavioural instructions in both English and Inuktitut with some illustrations, provides insight into the contradictory position the government found itself in during the colonial era:

> In its dealings with Inuit, the State's desire to avoid reproducing what it saw as the dependent relations existing with other aboriginal people in Canada has previously been noted. The dilemma clearly illustrated by *The Book of Wisdom for Eskimo* was how to assimilate without creating dependency. The unfortunate outcome was, for many, debilitating. The text attempts to undermine relations to wise individuals (isumatait), Inuit wisdom and the structure of Inuit families and camps. It is into an environment permeated by notions of cultural inferiority, previously unheard of relations to authority and rapid social change that many adults in contemporary Inuit culture were born.[19]

Apart from the implications of power – that Inuit were required to live under the authority of the Qallunaat king, the RCMP, and the Arctic administrators – this marked the beginning of the undermining of traditional knowledge and the associated Inuit ways of knowing and doing in the Arctic. McNicoll, Tester, and Kulchyski point out that as in religion, an important and tangible sense of power comes from the possession of book knowledge:

> That *The Book of Wisdom* is a text in book form should also not go unremarked. The concept of "wisdom" implies authority. There is a parallel here with the authority of the only other book most Inuit, at the time, had encountered; the Bible – the word of God – another "Book of Wisdom." Wisdom comes in book form. The book, a western modality of inscription, displaces the wisdom of an oral culture. *The Book of Wisdom* inaugurates a process where Inuit will come to see that knowledge must take this new form to be knowledge.[20]

This Western standard of the written word, against which Inuit knowledge was compared, was reinforced even more strongly in northern classrooms as the first schools were opened. The ignorant and experimental way that the government approached the provision of support and services to Inuit, once it did become involved, is made clear by the content of this book:

> *The Book of Wisdom for Eskimo* is therefore on the cusp of an era: it can be read as the last gasp of a deeply colonial era in which Inuit affairs were largely the purview of police officers and a backwater of government. It can also be read as a precursor to a new era, when significant resources and energies were devoted to Inuit affairs, though colonial relations, paternalism and the notion of Inuit as "primitives" continued to characterize Inuit-government relations.[21]

Inuit have referred to a feeling called *ilira, ilarasuk,* or *iliranaqtuq* in response to the influx of Qallunaat and their persistent instructions about living a proper Canadian life. One man, named Tunu Napartuk, offers a definition of the term:

> *Ilarasuk* is something my parents dealt with; it's how they regarded the Qallunaat doctors, the missionaries and the teachers who came north. It's a term that means when so much respect is given to someone that it borders on fear, it's more than being in awe of someone. It's when you take another person's word without ever questioning or arguing.[22]

Scholars have also recognized this tendency, which grew out of traditional Inuit relations and often resulted in miscommunication with Qallunaat:

> The word *ilira* goes to the heart of colonial relationships, and it helps to explain the many times that Inuit, and so many other peoples, say yes when they want to

> say no, or say yes and then reveal later, that they never meant it at all. *Ilira* is a word that speaks to the subtle but pervasive results of inequality.[23]

Testimony by Mariano Aupilardjuk, an Elder who was involved in this experience reveals the extent to which Inuit cultural identity was oppressed by Arctic administrators during the 1950s:

> Our laws, which existed and had some good in them, were struck down. As Inuit we are very agreeable, very easy-going and willing to get along with everyone. As we were introduced to western civilization, we looked up to them in awe. They seemed to be so advanced and powerful and seemed to have a lot of knowledge about everything. Because of this thinking we, and I include myself, stopped listening to our parents, we stopped following their way-of-life. I realized later that I was in an empty hole and it was all because I was now living in a lifestyle of my choice. When I look back, that is what I see, all the knowledge I would have picked up from my parents is not here with me, it is gone forever.[24]

In terms of practical consequences of *ilarasuk* for the economy, livelihood, and potential for Inuit to support and direct themselves, Alootook Ipellie likewise comments on the role of Arctic administrators: "When Inuit became helplessly trapped in the midst of their cultural upheaval, the administrators went out of their way to provide the goods and services to rescue them. Thereby this guaranteed the administrators the dubious honour of becoming 'saviours' of Inuit. Understandably, Inuit would flock around the administrators asking for assistance in the manner of orphaned children."[25] Alice French also describes the impact of the introduction of welfare:

> The biggest mistake the people outside ever made was sending men from the south, like welfare officers, to give away money for nothing. Family allowances were not heard of until these men came north. We helped one another when times were hard and lived without social welfare, and then we heard through the radio that one could go out and get something for nothing, instead of working for it. I do not condemn this system in itself for helping out the families that needed help, but it took away the incentive of the people to help one another.[26]

Moving Inuit off their land to provide them with a livelihood they had formerly achieved for themselves was the first step toward relinquishment of cultural identity. As a result, Inuit struggled to make sense of their new position in a culture they did not understand. Rendering their former means of survival impossible, settlement threatened the entire Inuit culture, and a majority of anthropologists at the time predicted that "it was only a matter of time before it disappeared."[27] This colonial process was carried out using methods that were alienating, repressive, and traumatic to Inuit, although the Qallunaat perpetrators were largely oblivious of these results. Ipellie describes this chapter of history as one in which Inuit were blinded by a "whiteout":

> As an Inuk living in the Arctic, you can expect to get trapped in a whiteout several times each winter. The cultural upheaval we experienced in our community in the late 1950s and early 1960s seemed in retrospect a lot like being caught in a whiteout – trapped and unable to go forward since you could not see clearly where you were heading. So, our society had to rely on another society to be the guide dog to our blind culture.[28]

Creating communities out of concern for Inuit welfare was not the only agenda of the federal Arctic administrators, which leads to the third characteristic of the colonial period. The Canadian government had an underdeveloped, if not entirely inconsistent, vision of what it was working toward in the Eastern Arctic. Administration could be characterized as initially reluctant and ignorant and then as assimilationist and experimental. There is little question that the Canadian government resisted involvement with Inuit, publicized by the anthropologist Diamond Jenness, who attributed this reluctance to government "myopia": "Without question it was [due to] the erroneous policy of the federal government, which accepted the responsibility for law and order in the Arctic, but refused to shoulder the other responsibilities that go with sovereignty."[29] This late arrival has been explained as the result of best intentions; the government did not wish to disrupt the lives of the simple nomadic "Eskimos" and see dependence on the scale of the Indian reserves result.[30] However, as the Cold War era progressed, the North became the comprehensive "welfare state" in North America; indeed, Inuit were referred to as "wards of the state."[31]

Many credit Farley Mowat's *The People of the Deer*, which was published in 1952 and documents starvation among the inland Inuit of the western Hudson Bay area, for bringing the harsh realities faced by some Inuit to public (southern) attention. Jenness attributes much of the change in government involvement in the postwar period to negative publicity stemming from military personnel and others who were witnessing the collapse of the traditional way of life:

> The war brought about another change. It rolled half-way back the long-closed doors of the Canadian Arctic and allowed the world to glimpse some of the things that had been happening (and not happening) behind them. Airmen and construction workers returned with first-hand descriptions of the Eskimo settlements

> they had visited, and foreign newspapers and magazines published accounts of Canada's north that reflected little credit on its administrators. High officials in Ottawa began to take notice.[32]

Regardless of the source of publicity, it is clear that decision making and policy were shaped more often by southern interests and priorities than by the needs or desires of Inuit. Shelagh Grant generalizes about the skewed priorities of the federal government throughout its involvement in the Arctic:

> For the most part, patterns of government response to northern issues have had a distinct exploitative character, justified as being in the "national interest" and consistent with various hinterland/metropolis theses. The origins of many policies are rooted in the events of the 1940s, with concerns for the environment and aboriginal rights only recently added to the list. Even here, southern priorities have continued to provide the primary motivation behind new policy directions and the speed with which they have been set down and implemented.[33]

Grant argues that since the 1940s the issue of sovereignty and national security has consistently been the greatest catalyst for government decision making in the North.[34] Other scholars would point to the early resource development in the form of the fur trade and add the later potential for mining and oil revenue as a close second priority.[35] Regardless of the reason, it was generally perceived to be in the national interest for federal bureaucrats, led by the Eskimo Affairs Committee from 1952 to 1962, to go about implementing an assimilation mandate in the Eastern Arctic.[36]

Federal Administration of Formal Schooling

This break with the precedent of financial restraint and neglect by the government was cemented by the appointment of Hugh Keenleyside as deputy minister of mines and resources (who also became commissioner of the Northwest Territories) in March 1947. Keenleyside went about reorganizing northern responsibility, and what was thought of as the "Eskimo problem" in Canada became the purview of the Department of Resources and Development in 1950. The Northern Administration and Lands branch directed policy, and the RCMP implemented policy and supervised Inuit in the Arctic.[37] Federal agencies and their representatives identified three administrative priorities: (1) improving access to education, (2) improving access to health care, and (3) increasing the ability of the Inuit to support themselves adequately in the emerging socio-economic sphere.[38] For Keenleyside, education was the greatest priority; he "declared that in the future the federal government would bear the full costs of new schools and payment of teachers' salaries."[39] Between 1947 and 1950, his last year as commissioner, Keeleyside opened eight new schools.[40] Mary Van Meenan, whose doctoral dissertation in philosophy compares policies for Aboriginal education in Siberia and the NWT, says the "first definitive statement on the government's intentions with regard to Inuit education" came in 1955, through the words of Jean Lesage, then minister of northern affairs and national resources: "The only realistic approach is to accept the fact that the Eskimo will be brought ever more under the influences of civilization to the south. The task, then, is to help him adjust his life and his thoughts to all that the encroachment of this new life must mean."[41]

The new life in the Arctic meant children must attend school. First, they were sent to the residential schools that were already in operation in centralized locations, some of which were expanded to receive children from around the region. The roots of residential schooling for Aboriginal students in Canada reach back to the 1880s, viewed then by the government as a fulfillment of an obligation to educate the "Indians" and to socialize them appropriately.[42] Although there are common themes between the context of Aboriginal education in the nineteenth century and the circumstances surrounding residential schooling in the Eastern Arctic, some characteristics cannot be applied across the board. For example, Jean Barman has offered evidence that the education of Aboriginal students, particularly girls, at early residential schools in British Columbia was conducted with the precise intention of keeping them marginalized and preventing them from progressing in white society.[43] I have not found any evidence that this was the case with regard to northern schools. Most teachers believed they were engaged in the important work of putting Inuit on an equal footing with Euro-Canadians by educating them, and equality was also stated to be the intention behind education by the federal government of the day.[44] Nevertheless, consistent with the experience of Aboriginal communities throughout Canada's history, residential schooling provided the most significant means by which Inuit were removed from their traditional subsistence lifestyle and inculcated with white, southern, Canadian cultural norms, which devalued their own. It is important to note that the early missionaries in the Eastern Arctic promoted the use of Inuktitut and encouraged the maintenance of the subsistence lifestyle.[45] However, the mid-twentieth century, some religious orders were running residential schools, such as the one in Chesterfield Inlet, with very different goals in mind. The Canadian government declined to articulate educational policy during this time or to directly manage schooling at all, preferring to leave such matters to the Catholic nuns and priests. According to Jenness: "This arrangement suited the government well, because it hardly dinted the federal treasury. Accordingly for the year 1922-23 the Department of the Interior contributed the sum of $3,000 to education in the Northwest Territories."[46]

For many students, the primary detriment of residential schooling was the physical separation from their families, cultural practices, and language. Residential schools were also intentionally designed to impose Western standards in every realm of their lives, manifested by the disallowance of Inuktitut and Inuit clothing and food and by the devaluing of Inuit social norms, beliefs, and practices. In residential schools, young Inuit were taught to forget Inuktitut and their culture and were taught that their former identities and traditions were worthless. According to John Milloy: "Children were to be divorced from parents and from their parents' lives on the land. Thus, through education, a people's connection with their culture, which was the land, their physical health, and spiritual balance was to be ruptured."[47] This embedded in many Inuit youth a sense of shame about their own culture and heritage.

The coercive way that children were enrolled in schools is remembered vividly by many. Maata Pudlat describes her experience of being forced by Arctic administrators to go to school in return for family allowance for her parents, which was a common practice across the Arctic: "We were still in the camp when the government came to our parents, and they told us, 'Your children have to go to school.' My parents had no choice. And if we didn't go to school, we wouldn't receive family allowance, Baby Bonus; that's what our parents were told."[48] Peter Irniq attests to cultural loss in his experience with residential school as a young boy. He has publicly described the impact of his generation being forced to attend residential schools in which they were taught the "proper" Canadian ways. When he was taken by a priest to attend school at the age of eleven in 1958, Irniq says:

> Little did my parents or I know that this was the beginning of leaving behind my culture, language, Inuit spirituality; and the practice of shamanism which we used for healing, special relationship among us Inuit, with animals, land, our past and the future. We were to be assimilated into the Qablunaaq [Qallunaat] world, to think like a European. The losses we experienced were to be permanent.[49]

The residential school that Irniq attended was the Joseph Bernier Federal Day School in Chesterfield Inlet, run by the Roman Catholic Church. Several other current leaders of Nunavut were educated at this particular school, and later many Inuit were sent to larger regional centres to live in hostels while attending high school. A few children, such as Peter Freuchen Ittinuar, who became the first Inuk member of Parliament, were even sent out of the North entirely to attend school.[50] In what Ittinuar calls "The Eskimo Experiment," these children were billeted with Qallunaat families in Alberta, Ontario, and Nova Scotia in the 1950s and 1960s and sent to school in order "to know if Inuit kids could compete in the southern education system."[51]

Arctic administrators knew of the challenges and inadequacies of the residential school system used for many decades with First Nations in southern Canada. However, with regard to the experiences of Inuit in the 1950s. Milloy argues, "No matter what the Departmental head office staff might say about the form, content, and intentions of their educational strategy, it would appear that in its delivery, once the children were taken inside the classroom and the door closed, it was just as intolerant of Aboriginal culture as old mission and Indian Affairs policy had intentionally been."[52] Rendering children even more helpless, some teachers at residential schools were sexually and physically abusive. Reports of this abuse were discussed publicly after Bishop Reynald Rouleau of the Hudson Bay Diocese was forced by testimony and evidence to apologize in 1996 to Inuit abused at the Joseph Bernier School. The bishop said, "Tragically, others among you were sexually abused as children. By taking advantage of the trust that you and your families had given to the personnel of the school, the abusers perpetrated a profound violation against you, physically, emotionally and spiritually, but sexually as well."[53]

Apart from the personal trauma, this means of control used by Arctic administrators had devastating consequences for family relationships, Inuit identity, and traditional culture because the youth of a whole generation were subjected to cultural oppression in their most formative years:

> Traditional Inuit customs and skills were forgotten as southern educators replaced the children's parents as role models and teachers of life skills. This meant culture shock and acute loneliness until the new language, structure and values were learned. However, many Inuit children could not adapt and became trapped between Inuit and settlers' ways. Parents became alienated from their children, and a phenomenal generation gap developed.[54]

In addition, Inuit children were not taught the survival skills and values associated with the environment because they were removed from the land, their homes, and their families. This resulted in a limited choice as to how they would make their living in the future. It increased their dependency on government provision of employment and services and necessitated their settlement in communities. For example, Alice French remembers being retrieved from residential school when she was fourteen, having lived there since the age of seven, to return to life on the land with her family. One male acquaintance remarked on the struggles she would face to become a successful female adult in the Inuit world:

> It's about time. Now that you are no longer a child, you should be at home helping around the house. What has school ever taught you except the English language, even to the point where you can not even talk in your own tongue? Can you scrape and sew hides for clothing? Do you know how to skin the furs that are brought home? What kind of wife will you be since you must learn all these things which go into homemaking before you get married?[55]

Indeed, those were challenges felt acutely by French: "I often thought I would never learn to do the simple things needed to live off the land. After the first month at home, my self-confidence suffered a lot."[56] These consequences followed French throughout her life because she had not become a woman in Inuit terms.

In addition to preventing Inuit girls and women from realizing the identities and roles formerly available to them in the family unit, the introduction of education was disruptive for their parents. In practical terms, without children at home, motherhood was no longer the central occupation of women. Women who had formerly been very close to their children, scarcely ever parting with them except in adulthood, were now separated from them at a young age. Apphia Awa remembers,

> Arvaluk and Simon were far away in Churchill, Martha was in Igloolik, Rhoda and Jakopie were in Pond Inlet. Joanna and Salomie were young, and Phillip was just a baby in my amautik, he wasn't even a year old. We asked them if we could keep one of our sons with us. We asked the teachers if we let them take Rhoda and Jako away, would they leave Solomon to stay with us?[57]

Separation was compounded by the knowledge that the future lives their children were being prepared for in schools did not require the expertise these women could offer. The Qallunaat language, skills, and knowledge trumped those of the Inuit by necessity under the heavy hand of colonialism. French describes this disconnection from her grandmother:

> My grandmother's biggest concern for me was that I had not been brought up in the traditional way of life, and she did not know how to deal with this. In the same way, I could not understand why someone should arrange my life for me. It did not help that I was seventeen, had been to school and learned a different

> way of life, and knew that most of the town people courted and found their own mates without the help of anyone arranging their lives.[58]

Young Inuit who were learning to be women in this new world, and also their mothers left at home, experienced significant trauma as they lost sight of the traditional roles and the relationships that defined them.

In the context of this book, residential schooling is particularly important because it fully interrupted any opportunity for students to receive an Inuit education. Precisely as a result of living away from home, students were prevented from participating in the tasks and experiences of everyday life, which would have provided them with the education necessary for sustaining their families. One of the earliest teachers in the Eastern Arctic, Margery Hinds, has remarked on the disservice of residential schooling to Inuit who were separated from their families and way of life in their most "impressionable years" because they were unable to practise the ways of daily life on the land:

> In the case of Eskimoes in residential schools or hostels, they are weaned from their way of life during their impressionable years, and then, when school days are finished, they are returned to their Eskimo homes minus the skills they would have acquired had they remained in their own environment; more-over skills that are essential to them in their lives as Eskimoes; skills that can only be acquired from Eskimoes living as Eskimoes.[59]

The attitude of educators toward Inuit culture and language also lodged in students' minds the perception that Inuit ways are inferior to Qallunaat ways. Students were taught that important knowledge must be found in books, not in one's mind; that remembering important facts makes you a good student, not demonstrating important skills; that listening, reading, and writing are what will make you successful, not innovation and practical experience; and that English is the language of the future, whereas Inuktitut is the language of the past. This is the greatest consequence of residential schooling identified by Irniq:

> Even more importantly, the problem lies with the ideas that lay behind what the Qablunaaq [Qallunaat] did: that we were primitive, ignorant, child-like pagans in need of civilization. What we need is a clear acknowledgement that these ways of thinking were wrong; that there are other ways of "making sense" that have merit, deserve recognition and are – for all of us – you as well as me, important to what I would like to call the re-enchantment of the world – the return to ways of being that respect mystery, tradition and cultures other than your own.[60]

Many teachers and administrators truly believed that the Inuit way of life was endangered and that the best future for youth was facilitated by a Western education that would make them employable. Indeed, although it was painful to see their children leave home, many parents also believed that sending them to school would secure their futures in the "white man's world":

> Later on the children had to go to school, which was all right too: they had to learn if they were not going to be staying out in camp. They had to take jobs, which was also all right. There was really no choice, and I accepted it gladly because our children had to learn. I wanted them to learn English so that they can have good jobs when they grow up.[61]

Unfortunately, the belief that jobs awaited all Inuit graduates was not supported by structural economic change. Paul Welsman points out that the lack of an economic strategy meant that these educational initiatives resulted in few opportunities for Inuit self-sufficiency. Welsman notes that a significant disconnection remained between the efforts to educate Inuit and the economic opportunities that were available to them:

> There was no assessment of the effect of the mission system on the native peoples' social, political and economic welfare. Nor was there any assessment of where future educational policies would lead the native peoples, or how the educational system fitted into the overall structure of development in the North. Instead, the Federal Government, which was responsible for native education through the Department of Northern Affairs and Natural Resources, developed an incremental approach ... Reports of the Department of Northern Affairs and Natural Resources and its successor, the Department of Indian Affairs and Northern Development, all stressed the quantitative gains made in the field of education.[62]

Regardless of the best intentions of the Qallunaat involved, the early formal education system represented a loss of power on the part of Inuit, a loss of participation in one of the most critical roles played by adults, and a loss of parenthood and control over the future of their families and their society.

Residential schools in the Arctic were not able to reach the entire Inuit population and were primarily used as a partial solution, or to fill gaps, while other plans were being implemented. In 1944 the federal government commissioned a report on the state of education in the NWT from Dr. Andrew Moore. His report offered some forward-thinking recommendations, such as that a middle-of-the-way curriculum should be developed, that education should be given to

Figure 4 Early school room, Chesterfield Inlet, 5 September 1958. *Source:* © Library and Archives Canada. Reproduced with the permission of Library and Archives Canada. Credit: Charles Gimpel, Charles Gimpel fonds, e004923401.

Aboriginal children in their own environment (i.e., in day schools), that schools could double as community centres, and that short courses for adult learners should be offered.[63] On other subjects, Moore was more conservative, suggesting that control of education should be more centralized and that a director with "wide powers" should be hired.[64] In 1946 the federal government appointed an inspector for schools, but it was not until 1949 that he established an office with one staff member in Yellowknife. Soon after, numerous day schools were opened. Those in what is now Nunavut included schools in Cape Dorset, Coppermine (now Kugluktuk), Coral Harbour in 1950, and Chesterfield Inlet in 1951.[65] By 1955 a new and expanded school system was announced, involving the building of schools in various regional centres, to be accompanied by hostels for student residences, one of which was in Frobisher Bay (now Iqaluit).[66] This was also the year in which the Department of Northern Affairs and Natural Resources officially took over responsibility for Aboriginal education from the Department of Indian Affairs. Norm Macpherson suggests that the creation of one jurisdiction of schools in the Northern Administration Branch of the Department of Northern Affairs and National Resources on 1 April 1955 might be considered the official start of the school system in the NWT. 2,067 students were enrolled and there were ninety-two teachers.[67] By 1968 nearly every settlement in the NWT had a school.

Arctic Day Schools

Several generalities can be made regarding the approach to education taken in the early day schools that increasingly dotted the Eastern Arctic throughout the 1950s. First, this approach offered a curriculum and methods of education that were foreign to the experience of Arctic life and Inuit culture. Second, it demanded demonstration by students of a number of social behaviours or characteristics that were contrary to those practised by Inuit. Particularly with regard to the day schools, teachers ran up against the culture and lifestyle of Inuit parents, which persistently disrupted their assimilationist efforts and demanded flexibility from them. Third, the education policies and expectations of the government and other Qallunaat outside of the communities seldom had relevance or offered responsiveness to local realities.

The curriculum used throughout the early years of federal schooling was theoretically consistent with what was offered to school children in southern Canada. Some communities in the NWT borrowed the Alberta curriculum, while most teachers in the Eastern Arctic employed that of Ontario. Regardless of the irrelevance of many aspects of a southern education to northern life, for some teachers this standardization was a source of pride and comfort:

> Aside from the language barrier, this classroom assumed the same atmosphere as any other classroom in the south. First of all, a testing program was introduced to determine where the pupils should begin. Then followed the issuing of books, and the general review of the previous year's work. The subjects taught are mainly the same except for the necessary Basic English program. Arithmetic, Spelling, Nature Study, Reading, and Writing are the main subjects, while Music and Art complete the program of studies.[68]

Not only were the subjects studied consistent with southern classrooms, but the content and materials were also pulled directly from shelves in Edmonton or Ottawa. "Dick and Jane" readers and other culturally foreign materials provided the basis for this northern education. R. Quinn Duffy points out that farm animals, traffic lights, and fresh fruit made regular appearances in northern classrooms despite their irrelevance to people still living a partially subsistence lifestyle in a vastly different environment:

> The curriculum in these and other Arctic schools was resolutely patterned on that of the urban and rural society of southern Canada. It started in Grade 1 with Dick and Jane on the farm, a subject utterly meaningless to Inuit youngsters. And so it continued. Texts and workbooks depicted a world of which Inuit children had no concept. Stories and lessons might deal with a zoo, a milkman, traffic lights or horses, all as strange to Inuit as the far side of the moon.[69]

Some classroom materials were employed as a means to teach English as a second language, but equally, they referred to the southern, urban landscape and generally lacked context in the Arctic.

The great distance between southern government administrators and the realities of life in the Arctic apparently contributed to the long dearth of relevant classroom materials. Norm Macpherson, hired as a high school principal in Yellowknife in 1962, remembers the reluctance of curriculum specialists to take on the challenge of northern education in the early 1960s:

> The Curriculum Section was a thing apart. To prepare or even assist in preparing a course of studies for little-understood ethnic groups, speaking in different languages, 2000 miles away from headquarters, was an almost impossible task. This fact seemed evident to a number of prominent educators who accepted the position as Head of Curriculum, did a tour of the Northwest Territories, and promptly resigned. At least this was the perception from a Field Superintendent's point of view because a succession of four Curriculum Directors came and went within four years.[70]

It was not until the late 1960s that materials began to be altered or developed from scratch by those in Ottawa responsible for curriculum, and even then, most action stemmed from the initiatives of teachers who had become frustrated with the irrelevance of their resources. Brian Lewis, a teacher who had spent several years in Cape Dorset, developed the idea of a primary-level Arctic Reading Series, which featured Inuit characters and their lives in an Arctic settlement. Printed in 1968, this was the "first organized attempt to introduce more relevant materials into Northern classrooms."[71] However, Lewis' recollections of working in the curriculum section in Ottawa only highlight its disorganization, "both in producing relevant materials for northern students and in delivering them to the classrooms."[72]

Moroever, as was the case with residential schools, English was the only language employed by teachers in the classroom, and it remained the main purpose and emphasis of schooling altogether. The language issue in particular became a source of great criticism of the early school system as Aboriginal people and others concerned with cultural preservation realized the risk of loss of languages like Inuktitut.

There was certainly no shortage of problems faced by educators in this era; as noted, the environmental and logistical challenges and constraints of delivering education were such that consideration of what occurred in the classrooms was secondary to providing those classrooms and teachers in the first place. Gordon Robertson, commissioner of the Northwest Territories from 1953 to 1963, has explained the lack of cultural relevance, particularly the decision to teach in English, from the perspective of Arctic administrators. It was due not only to their desire to see Inuit become successful Canadians by southern standards but also to the growing pains suffered by a new institution in a new land:

> If my recollection is right, there was only one teacher in the Northwest Territories who had any knowledge of the Inuit language. Apart from the missionaries there were none with knowledge of the Indian languages. The teachers were entirely from southern Canada and teaching simply had to be in English if it was to be given at all. A few years after the program was implemented a plan was worked out for training "teaching aids" – Indian or Inuit girls who had some knowledge of English and who could be trained to aid the teachers in the native languages of the children. It was only after the educational program had been in effect for some time and there were Indians and Inuit who had some basic education that it was possible to produce teachers who could teach in the native tongues ... I do not think it would have been wise to have left children uneducated for 5 or 10 years in order to train teachers who could teach in the native tongues.[73]

Although the language barrier remained a source of difficulty for both teachers and students in the Eastern Arctic, only a few years of adjustment were required for most children to adapt to this change. The social and cultural variances between the expectations of Inuit parents and southern teachers could involve a much longer adjustment period. These variances resulted in a greater potential for miscommunication and, indeed, alienation on the part of young Inuit. Many aspects of daily life taken for granted by teachers from southern Canada, such as the timely arrival of students at school in the morning, were major responsibilities for them in the Arctic. Inuit parents seldom imposed a routine on their children, allowing children to sleep, wake, and eat when it suited them. Particularly in the spring, when it stays light well into the night in the Arctic, teachers took it on themselves to send children to bed: "It soon got to the point where I had to patrol the settlement at eleven o'clock and chase all the pupils home. This was hard for the pupils to accept at first, but I think they finally realized that my suggestion of 'early to bed, early to rise' was the best solution."[74]

Issues such as daily routine, regular meals, and seasonal absences were obvious points of difference between Inuit and Qallunaat lifestyles that entered the classroom, but other expectations introduced by teachers were more fundamental to the process of education. John J. Honigmann and Irma Honigmann observed the disjunction between traditional and formal education when they visited the community of Frobisher Bay in 1959:

> Eskimo parents instruct their children with a minimum of accompanying explanation; they seldom try to explain why some task should be done or a skill mastered. An explanation, presumably, will be found in the situation by the child itself as he learns to understand it through becoming practically, rather than theoretically, involved in it. Of necessity, the school's curriculum forces teachers to ignore this educational technique – learning by doing – which many American-Indian people follow. Instruction in school is highly rationalized, with children constantly being given reasons for certain rules and expectations.[75]

The classroom environment presented young Inuit with content and methods of education that were entirely foreign to the traditional experiential learning of their parents and Elders. The means by which students were expected to learn and to think and the standards by which they were evaluated were all vastly different from Inuit tradition. Indeed, the fundamental premise of education was that it should help Inuit to function in a very different world, that of the English-speaking, employable Qallunaat man or woman participating in a Western democratic capitalist society.

Like the standardization of education through the imposition of a southern curriculum, the socialization of Inuit students according to southern Canadian standards and values was a great source of pride for some teachers. One teacher boasted, "Samuel, age 10, grade 2, is my brightest pupil. With much hard work and perseverance he should continue to climb the ladder of success in the white man's way of life."[76] This comment reflects one of the most problematic characteristics of education in the colonial period: not only did many people take this privileging of Qallunaat social behaviour for granted, but they also considered it to be beneficial for the students. As suggested above, these Inuit youth and their parents were not in a position to dispute or negotiate the system of education into which they were integrated. Even as beliefs held by administrators about the purpose and nature of education may have become more responsive to Inuit culture in the late 1960s, such change is not often reflected as swiftly in the actions of individual teachers and their relationships to individual students – especially if the teachers themselves are unconscious of the culturally biased lens through which they see the world. One teacher from Churchill Vocational Centre, which operated as a secondary and vocational school for Inuit from across the Eastern Arctic from 1964 to 1973, cites the point when he realized that this cross-cultural dynamic was occurring in schools:

> One of my interesting experiences or experiments in which I learned something was when I did a survey among the teachers and the students. It was a sort of typical sociogram – asking the students to pick out their favourite person and at the same time asking the teachers to do this as well.
>
> It was very enlightening to me inasmuch as the teachers (myself included) tended to select the students with attributes based on their own North American values and attitudes. It's incredible how important we find aggressiveness. Being first – meeting problems head on. We're taught to think like this, and so it wasn't unnatural that the teachers selected who were athletic, who were always speaking out in class, who were always first to answer questions and the people who were typically North American leaders in our eyes.
>
> When I looked at the students' results, they were always selecting those with characteristics that were based on the Inuit culture – very quiet and unassuming – people who would not tread too closely on another person's autonomy. So from that point of view, that little incident over the couple of months that I did the survey to me was very revealing.[77]

In hindsight, the inappropriateness of these practices becomes clearer, particularly in light of Inuit reflections on the experience of education. Duffy sums up this history effectively: "For too long and in too many classes Inuit were made to study materials and respond to motivations based on the alien culture of white, middle-class North America. The school system attempted to introduce them to a value system that stressed individual achievement, advancement and self-discipline in return for future rewards. This orientation often contradicted native values."[78]

It is arguable that most teachers were provided with too little preparation, training, and support for the cross-cultural context in which they found themselves. In 1970 Ivan Mouat argued,

> There are three major problems in northern education today. The first of these comes about because teachers should not enter classrooms where there are Indian or Eskimo (or Negro or Mexican) children unless they come prepared to face the problems and challenges of cross-cultural education. Problem one, then, is one

> of orientation of the teacher. Teacher preparation for northern classrooms is a requirement that has not been adequately met.[79]

Even though it was consistent practice to ensure prospective teachers were personally interviewed and briefed on the challenges of teaching in the Arctic, there was little other orientation offered them, and despite the variable assistance of a principal or teacher-at-large (i.e., teachers' consultant), many arrived in their communities alone. Indeed, the first pursuit of many early teachers could include finding or even building the school, locating school supplies, or even building their own accommodations. As in other rural areas of Canada, the turnover rate for teachers was very high, and students often encountered a new teacher each year or two:

> The severity of the environment combined with the cultural shock resulted in abnormally high turnover rates among teachers, especially in the Arctic District. In the mid 1960s, for example, in the eastern Arctic the official estimate of average teacher turnover rate per year was 28 percent. In most instances, teachers rarely remained in the north for more than one year and it was exceptional for the stay to be longer than two years.[80]

In 1970-71 the average retention rate, or number of years of teaching experience in the Arctic, for both male and female teachers was 2.95 years.[81] This reality did little to mitigate the challenges of familiarizing teachers with Inuktitut language and Inuit culture.

A significant reason for low teacher retention, and my third point about the school system in the colonial period, was the demand involved in trying to meet expectations set by the administration, while respecting the particularities of locality. For some teachers, it was easiest to bend the expectations of the administrators in Ottawa, or adapt to Inuit ways, rather than change the habits of the students and their families. In 1948 Dorothy L. Robinson was a teacher at the first Anglican day school in Tuktoyuktuk, which later became a government school:

> One irregular aspect was the time we started classes in the morning. When I arrived I realized that the whole community started the day late, especially the children. As it was easier to change my habits than those of the whole group, we started school at eleven in the morning, and then carried on longer in the afternoon. It worked, with far more regular attendance and fewer late arrivals than if we'd attempted to comply with government regulations (though annual protests came from Ottawa).[82]

For others, great frustration was experienced in finding that the instructions and demands arriving from the "centre" were not only unrealistic but also contradictory.[83] For example, many teachers were also designated as the welfare representative or medical specialist, but these duties were not supposed to interfere with the operation of the school. In addition, the rate of settlement was different in each community. If the community's Inuit housing program was developing quickly and successfully, then the measures taken to get students into school differed vastly from those required in places where people were less inclined to move into town. As late as 1965, in at least one location, the government was still picking children up in a plane from their family camping sites in the fall.[84]

Although official federal policy during the early years of government schooling was poorly defined and inadequate for the northern context, the direction assumed was consistently toward assimilation of Inuit in the interest of their future as Canadians. English was considered mandatory, Western concepts of proper hygiene and nutritional practices encouraged, Inuit culture looked down on as a relic of another time, and white welfare teachers reinforced as tutors to all Inuit, even the adults they encountered in the community.[85] The goal of education – despite a great deal of evidence from the history of First Nations education that suggested it was futile – was to give Inuit more economic opportunities by teaching them to be like Qallunaat.

Signs of Change

Paul Welsman was an outspoken commentator on the education system, and these comments on how and why the colonial approach had been highly dislocating for Inuit youth were published in the mid-1970s:

> The failure rate among Inuit has been especially high. Although the largest single group in grade one, Inuit comprised the smallest group by grade nine. The school system attempted to introduce native children to a value system which stressed strong individual achievement, advancement and self-discipline in return for future rewards. This orientation often contradicted native values. The Inuit people deplored the white man's excessive concern for self-discipline. His world was too rigid and insensitive to human relations, and this was reflected in his education processes. Native peoples also suffered from being more present- than future-oriented: the concept of long-term education was difficult to grasp.[86]

Welsman's depiction of the schools, as having a contradictory orientation to Inuit culture and values, was made when the context of education was changing substantially. While such insight may not have been common during the colonial period, there is evidence that some educators in the field were coming to realize that the expectations and decisions determined by bureaucrats many thousands of miles away were actually having a detrimental impact on Inuit youth.

Some of the earliest teachers in Arctic communities recognized their students' preference for experiential learning and for culturally appropriate reading material as well as the importance of the school meeting local needs. Long before it was politically astute to do so, a few educators realized that what they were attempting to do simply was not workable. That understanding led to impromptu departures from the norm, which in most cases proved successful. These exceptions contributed to the growing belief that the Arctic required its own unique system of education.

For some teachers and principals, the greatest cultural affordance they could offer was leniency toward absence from school, despite direction to the contrary, when children accompanied their families on hunting trips.[87] Arguably, these situations were hardly under the control of the educators, but their understanding of the importance of hunting and camping trips should nevertheless be noted. Honigmann and Honigmann explain:

> The school's greatest flexibility and boldest attempt at cultural integration occurs with respect to absenteeism for hunting and fishing. In spring, the principal permits children, whose families are going to coastal camps, to leave school before the end of the academic term in order to accompany their parents. At other times, too, the principal allows boys to enjoy the educational experience of accompanying a father or other relative on a hunting trip.[88]

For other educators, seeking alternative teaching methods was important to their success in the classroom. Margery Hinds, who taught in Arctic Bay and Cape Dorset as well as Northern Quebec in the late 1950s, observed the Inuit preference for active learning:

> Especially with Eskimoes it is necessary for lessons to include as many practical exercises as possible, otherwise talking and book-work are almost meaningless to them. The inventing of practical exercises, which I call number games, or reading games has severely tested my ingenuity. It has, however, been a worthwhile effort for such exercises serve to revise and test lessons that have been taught, and also provide activity.[89]

Hinds not only recognized the means by which these students were inclined to learn, but she also accepted them and adapted her teaching methods accordingly.

By the late 1960s teachers were paying more attention not only to their methods but also to the content of classroom learning. Some began the practice of inviting culture and community into the classroom:

> A lot of teachers tried to incorporate Eskimo culture in the curriculum to the extent they understood it themselves, which in most cases wasn't very much. Cultural inclusion programs, if they existed at all, were more or less periods in which some old-timer in the community would come in. Everyone would sit squarely on his butt and this old person would tell stories.[90]

Turning the classroom over to Inuit, beyond the incidental cultural interlude, was still unknown in the colonial period, although it was increasingly raised as an important goal. As noted in the previous section, Gordon Robertson has explained that although the language barrier was a significant hindrance for southern teachers, the dearth of educated Inuit to replace them in the classrooms was the greatest challenge. Some educators in the Eastern Arctic increasingly called on the government to take action to ensure either that Inuit were made teachers or that teachers were provided with much-improved training in Inuktitut and Inuit culture:

> If this is the Arctic, that teacher should be an Eskimo who not only knows the children and their language but who is trained thoroughly in the arts of formal teaching at this crucial first stage. Or, alternatively, the teacher should be someone thoroughly familiar with the Eskimo language and the people who speak it. In such case considerable training is essential. Whichever it is, the teaching should begin with the familiar and move at the appropriate pace to the new and challenging.[91]

R.A.J. Phillips was particularly forward-thinking, as this advice, published in 1960, was not heeded until the first teacher education program was conceived in 1967.[92] These examples still represent exceptions to the rule; for many Qallunaat teachers, coming to the Arctic remained a disorienting experience, and they were unable to dissociate themselves from their southern perspective and values.

As the years went by, educators and community members alike became increasingly adamant in their calls for education in Inuktitut, taught by Inuit teachers, using a curriculum and textbooks made in the NWT, and even based on an Inuit cultural approach. The roots of this change were set down by enterprising and forward-thinking teachers in the 1960s, and the next chapter will outline the massive increase in the momentum of educational change as it became a territorial responsibility.

There are numerous long-term consequences of the changes that occurred during the mid-twentieth century as a result of the separation of Inuit from their land and from the traditional political economy and culture associated with it. The nature of the Inuit family was drastically altered.[93] The contemporary social issues that can be linked to this loss of identity are widespread and include spousal abuse, alcoholism, and suicide. Again, Alootook Ipellie provides insight on this experience:

> For years, all three living generations had different goals and values, and all suffered. The educational system failed Inuit youth. They dropped out in swarms year after year, creating a society of half-educated young men and women who could not adjust fully to either of the cultures they were being brought up in. They became sons and daughters without destiny, without pride in their past and without much of a future – dropouts, social sores, listless vegetables. Many of them chose the easy way out by committing suicide.[94]

Hunting became merely a supplement to income, and sometimes more of a recreational activity. Generally, Inuit who have jobs do not have the time to go hunting or no longer possess the skills, and Inuit who do not work cannot afford it.[95] As the baby boomer generation in southern Canada was growing up in circumstances of unprecedented prosperity and stability, cushioned by the welfare state and federal policy, the same generation of Inuit was being rendered powerless in cultural, political, and environmental terms.

Success at integrating firearms, tobacco, cotton fabric, food staples, and eventually snowmobiles and other capital-intensive tools tied Inuit to the Western capitalist economy. This left many dependent on trapping and trading rather than on subsistence hunting, and soon trapping at the rates necessary to procure goods was environmentally unsustainable. With the collapse of subsistence hunting and fishing due to the growing reliance on staples bought in stores, and with the subsequent collapse of the commercial hunting and trapping economy due to the limited elasticity of the environment, came a population requiring significant government support. To hand out such support, permanent settlements, often built around Hudson's Bay Company trading posts, RCMP detachments, or military sites, were established. Frank Vallee effectively sums up the economic prospects of the late colonial period:

> Within a generation the whole economic base has shifted. A minority still make a living from the more or less exclusive combination of hunting and trapping. The majority get a little from these pursuits and what they do get is supplemented by income from sources which did not exist a generation ago: wages, sales of handicrafts, family allowances and various pensions, and relief. For most Eskimos the economic sphere is unstable, unpredictable. Less than 25 percent can be regarded as fully employed in some occupation. The single largest employer of full-time and casual labour is the federal government. Like the Indians of the Northwest Territories, the Eskimos have been able to take only minimal advantage of mining and other developments taking place on their own doorstep. There are several reasons for this, the chief one being lack of training and experience in industrial occupations.[96]

This fundamental alteration to human existence in the Arctic is without precedent. No longer were Inuit expected, or in some cases allowed, to stay on the land, maintain their ancient relationship with the environment, and support themselves as hunter-gatherers. No longer were they expected to maintain their language and culture; these were considered relics of a past quickly becoming obsolete.

With permanent settlements came two government services: health care and education. Inuit were thought to need preparation for the new environment – the coming of Qallunaat civilization to the Arctic and, with it, the wage economy. This new environment suggested that Christianity, English, literacy, mathematics, and behaving astutely in the social and cultural world of the Qallunaat were essential to Inuit success. The introduction of formal schooling, both through the removal of children to residential schools and through the regular attendance expected at community schools, was arguably the most powerful tool of the colonists. Inuit education and Qallunaat education did not easily exist in parallel because each was delivered by conflicting methods, demanded different social and cultural skills, and was conducted with vastly different ends in mind. Education, as traditionally practised, had been fully integrated into the daily experience of children, youth, and even adults. With those children absent at residential school or expected to attend community school for six hours each day, parents were no longer able to integrate education into the daily tasks of life. Traditional Inuit education continued to occur on a casual, seasonal, and much reduced basis within families, but the lack of time and opportunity were barriers impossible to avoid.

In addition, during the colonial period parents had no control over the education of their children as it was occurring in schools. The issue of local and Inuit control of education was becoming a public concern for both Qallunaat and Inuit by 1970. Mouat's criticism of the education system in the Arctic refers to this exclusion: "Problem three is perhaps the most serious and challenging problem of all – the lack of involvement by Eskimo parents in education planning for their own children. It has always been the Kabloona [Qallunaat] who knew best."[97] Although the first part of his statement is accurate, the second is meant to be tongue-in-cheek, but it reinforces that the Qallunaat believed they knew what was best. For many centuries before the coming of the Qallunaat, Inuit were entirely successful in raising and educating their children to function within a hunter-gatherer society. However, societal conditions changed drastically during the colonial period, and for a few decades the Qallunaat expected that Inuit would simply fit the mould of English-speaking, Western, industrial-capitalist society. Inuit had little choice but to respond by trying to accommodate this new life. Parents had little choice in sending their children to school, but they did so hoping that the result would be employment for their children in jobs like those done by the Qallunaat and thus provide a more secure means of support for the family. As has been the case in colonial cross-cultural encounters throughout the world for many centuries, the formal education system made it clear to Inuit that their ways had been trumped by Western civilization. As Qallunaat tried to shape the Arctic by their own standards, Inuit were further dislocated from the social, economic, and cultural experience that formed the basis of their identities. Schooling was the most overt assimilationist practice employed by the government in the Eastern Arctic; students were expected to leave behind Inuktitut and Inuit culture and ways of living in order to become successful Canadians in the Qallunaat image.

Because widespread residential schooling and assimilative educational content lasted for only one generation, many aspects of Inuit culture have endured. One interesting result of the early formal school system is that the education Inuit received served them in resisting federal paternalism and seeking self-determination in their own land.[98] Peter Irniq points out, "That is the terrible tragedy of all of this. Those of us who became the best educated and the most capable of leading the drive toward the creation of Nunavut – of talking back to the Qablunaaq [Qallunaat] – were also the ones to be most negatively affected by the same education that made all of this possible."[99] The formal education system did not succeed in entirely divesting Inuit of their past and their identity. It offered some Inuit the skills to operate in the Qallunaat world and to articulate that the Qallunaat did not always know best. Inuit took steps to reclaim their children by becoming involved in the education system, first as teaching assistants, then as teachers, and more importantly, eventually as members of local education authorities or regional school boards. In cooperation with territorial administrators, Inuit first brought their language into the classroom and then began developing local and culturally appropriate content for classroom materials. The greatest challenge in adapting the formal Qallunaat system of education to the Eastern Arctic has been changing the methods by which education is delivered. Chapters 4 and 5 outline these efforts to integrate the traditional education system with the formal education system.

4

Educational Change: New Possibilities in the Territorial Period

If participatory democracy is going to mean anything for the indigenous people of our north land, then there must be provision for the natural progression from interest to involvement, from partial control to full authority. This is one of the many challenges facing the Government of the Northwest Territories as it assumes responsibility for administration of the Arctic District on April 1, 1970.

– Ivan W. Mouat, educational administrator, "Education in the Arctic District"

It seems to me that the schools our children are attending teach nothing of the values to be found in the Inuit way of life. The school system appears to focus its attention on what is "good" in the white culture and not what is "good" in both. This has created a feeling among our children that the Inuit way of life is primitive and worthless. When our children come home [from school] they view their parents as being backward and worthless.

– Markusie Inualaak, letter, 1976

On 1 April 1970 the transfer of responsibility for education to the Government of the Northwest Territories,[1] based in Yellowknife, brought about a significant attempt to break with the past. In the 1970s the Department of Education came to focus on incorporating Aboriginal culture and language into classrooms. Administrative leadership in Yellowknife developed a vision for a made-in-the-NWT curriculum, and they expected teachers to fall in step. This vision was largely steeped in the belief that school should no longer separate students from their culture and traditions but should reinforce them in a variety of ways, notably by providing schooling in Aboriginal languages during the early elementary years, by developing programs and classroom materials that reflect northern content, by increasing the involvement of community members and parents in the education process, and by ensuring that teachers are able to support students in moving toward any future they might choose.

One important factor in the success of these goals was the training of Aboriginal teachers first as assistants and language or cultural specialists in an effort to bridge the language barrier between Inuit students and Qallunaat teachers and later, after the NWT Teacher Education Program was developed, as certified teachers managing their own classrooms. Initiatives such as the employment of Inuit teachers and the move toward culturally relevant curriculum content represent preliminary steps in reshaping the formal school system into one that incorporates some aspects of Inuit education. However, there is little evidence that these aspects were implemented *because* they approximated Inuit education or in response to the wishes of Inuit. Moreover, until the opportunity for greater local control through the Education Ordinance of 1977, this educational change did not reflect the needs and desires of Inuit students, parents, and community members. Integration of traditional Inuit values, knowledge, and educational methods into the formal system would remain limited, and the experience of formal education was still alienating and dislocating for many Inuit.

This chapter primarily examines Department of Education publications from the period, including philosophy statements, curriculum documents, classroom materials, and various reports. These documents are examined for references to content or methodology that correspond to Inuit culture, as well as for references to local control or Inuit involvement in education. In addition, northern magazines and periodicals, as well as Norm Macpherson's *Dreams and Visions*, are compared for references to education or schools that either support or contradict what the Department of Education describes. As is often the case for historians, it remains challenging to determine the extent to which official policy actually reflects the reality of life in the classroom. While researching, I kept the following questions in mind: What has changed? Who is responsible for this change? Who benefits from this change? How important was this change in contributing to a system that supports the development of an Inuit child confident in his or her identity? In spite of the new emphasis on Inuit culture, the evidence presented here demonstrates that much of the change seen during this "territorial period" – that is, prior to the creation of the divisional boards of education in the mid-1980s – was Qallunaat-driven. The formal system of education, despite its departure from assimilative goals, continued to manifest the Qallunaat belief that they knew what was best for Inuit. This can be explained by the fact that Inuit were not involved in any educational decision making.

Until 1969 the education system in the NWT was led by a federally appointed commissioner, who was by tradition the deputy minister of the federal department responsible for the NWT. The commissioner held wide powers; responsibilities included those typically held by a provincial minister of education, in addition to many related to other facets of northern life.[2] Transfer of responsibility for education to the government in Yellowknife began in April 1969 and was complete by 1970. This was part of the devolution of typically provincial responsibilities to the NWT that occurred in most sectors from 1967 to 1970. However, the commissioner continued to act as top bureaucrat until 1986.[3] Mary Van Meenan argues that continuity of federal involvement through the role of the commissioner perpetuated the federal system and that 1970 did not represent a significant departure in the approach to education:

> The territorial government's assumption of administrative control over education in 1969-70 did little to alter the course set by the federal government. New ideas and approaches were proposed but the same officials who had worked within the old system resisted substantive changes that would have made the system responsive to Inuit needs. At best, what developed was an educational system in which most Inuit had some exposure to education but few obtained high level results. The core of the problem was that neither the federal nor territorial governments understood the peoples they were trying to educate.[4]

Van Meenan successfully argues that departmental officials were still ignorant of many of the facets of Inuit culture and tradition, but in terms of "substantive changes" she overlooks some significant initiatives undertaken in Yellowknife, and her argument that bureaucrats were "resistive" is not, in the end, convincing. For example, a bold effort at reforming curriculum to make it more appropriate to northern circumstances was undertaken, starting with publication of *Elementary Education in the Northwest Territories K-6* in 1972. Although the structure of administration and accountability and the degree of local control did not change significantly until after 1977, greater emphasis on language, culture, and Inuit teaching staff started immediately after the federal handover. The following section outlines the changes that, despite being driven by Qallunaat perceptions of what would benefit Inuit, did represent a significant departure from the federal system in terms of the approach to education.

Criticisms of the school system became more frequent beginning in the early 1960s. Changes to formal schools were not only instigated by internal or logistical frustrations but also influenced by philosophical beliefs about education that were forming across the country. Two important educational trends developing across Canada during the late 1960s and early 1970s are of note: (1) the promotion of Aboriginal languages and the link between language and identity; and (2) the policy of multiculturalism espoused across the public domain. R.A.J. Phillips, director of the Northern Administration branch of the federal Department of Northern Affairs and Natural Resources, offers us evidence of northern educators looking beyond the practicalities of schooling to the overall impact of assimilative practices on Aboriginal peoples. Although writing well before this issue was popular in the mainstream, he articulates a concern for the preservation of Inuktitut:

> The teacher must not take away more than he gives. The preservation of the Eskimo language may have little economic importance in many settings but almost everywhere in the Arctic it will continue to have a psychological and cultural value. We must not have on our conscience the consequences of an indifference to the preservation of the Eskimo language. We would not wish to cause a future generation to revive from scraps that which could have been preserved from whole pieces.[5]

Phillips' comment, particularly the reference to "our conscience," suggests a colonialist attitude common at the time. However, his call for the preservation of language appears to be an early identification of the link between language and identity that the entire nation grappled with at the time of the Royal Commission on Bilingualism and Biculturalism, which led to the issuing of a Multiculturalism Policy on 8 October 1971 by Prime Minister Pierre Elliott Trudeau.

Some scholars argue that the recognition of multiculturalism as policy had a substantial impact on changes seen in the approach to Aboriginal education across Canada: "The impact of multiculturalism on the development of the discourse on Aboriginal education is rarely explicitly recognized in the public record. Nonetheless, one should bear in mind that there are important parallels between ideas and events that occurred in the respective spheres of multiculturalism and Aboriginal education."[6] The trend toward recognition of the pluralist Canadian identity, and the role of language therein, was occurring largely in response to the demands of francophones and Québécois, but it came to encompass Canada's other minorities, such as immigrant populations and First Nations.[7] Public schooling had been seen as an important instrument for assimilation and conformity across Canada,[8] but as Harold Troper and Morton Weinfeld argue, after 1971 cultural diversity was no longer viewed as a "problem to be solved."[9] The multiculturalism policy was undoubtedly beneficial in terms of establishing the principles of inclusion and equality on a national scale, but it has had other, more ambiguous impacts. For educators, the "pluralist dilemma" has emerged, presenting the challenge of accommodating educational needs of ethnic minorities while still meeting provincial standards or national expectations for social cohesion.[10] Multiculturalism has also overshadowed legitimate differences and inequalities, particularly in terms of the Aboriginal experience. Karen Mock argues that the emphasis on celebrating differences has actually prohibited the resolution of structural and social inequalities in Canada.[11] Canadians continue to engage in the act of balancing cultural sensitivity, the accommodation of diversity, and the practicalities of civil rights, the legal system, and nationalism. With regard to Inuit, multiculturalism did serve to recognize and protect their culture in schools, but its ongoing relevance to the social and political milieu of the Eastern Arctic is questionable.

During the colonial period, learning English was widely seen by both Inuit and Qallunaat as the most important outcome of education, but by the 1970s it seems many Qallunaat had come to believe that protecting and maintaining the use of Inuktitut would not threaten students' ability to learn English. Indeed, the NWT Department of Education promoted classroom instruction in Aboriginal languages, at least in the first three years of elementary school. Although this book is focused on investigating the incorporation of several aspects of Inuit educational practice into the formal system, the use of Inuktitut in schools can be viewed as providing a critical foundation for any other aspect. Indeed, much of the impetus for including cultural programs in the NWT education system originated with a preoccupation with language protection by Qallunaat educators. Language was the first component of culturally relevant education to be afforded significant legitimacy by the Department of Education, evidenced by the establishment of the Linguistics Division within the department in 1976 for the sole purpose of developing materials in Aboriginal languages.[12]

Territorial Administration of Education

The year 1970 presented the new territorial educational administration with the opportunity to make changes partly because it no longer had to allocate a high level of attention to physical expansion and infrastructure. The government was satisfied that the system had grown enough to ensure that all children in the NWT had access to formal education, with about 10,000 pupils in the school system.[13] With the basic physical system in place, administrators turned their attention to answering tough questions about the purpose of education. The challenge of taking stock of the successes and failures of education and determining its future direction was taken on by two review processes between 1970 and 1972.

The first of these reviews produced the publication *Survey of Education,* which was internally generated by the Department of Education and overseen by B.C. Gillie, director of education in Yellowknife.[14] The *Survey* claims to represent a consultation with teachers working "in the field" and living in the communities, as well as with administrative staff from within the Department of Education, on changes that they wanted to see made to the system. Gillie explains that open-ended requests for comments on any aspect of the system were sent to teaching and administrative staff, who returned written answers. These suggestions or concerns were collated by the department, and once a number of themes had been identified, it held several meetings with educational staff to further articulate desired goals and objectives for the education system. However, Gillie had final editorial control over the content of the *Survey*, and the format makes it impossible to tell which recommendations originated with teachers and which were instigated by the department itself. There are no direct quotations or specific references by which to determine its accuracy in representing teachers' views. If we assume that the views of teachers are well represented, as the *Survey* claims, then the changes inherent in these recommendations represent a shift from the view that the basis of education should be assimilation, to the view that it should be focused on recognition and preservation of culture. This document reveals that, given the opportunity, many teachers and administrators felt sweeping changes could and should make the system more relevant and therefore more beneficial to the students. Generally, the *Survey* also reflects concerns with multiculturalism and cultural pluralism that increasingly set the terms of discussions regarding First Nations and all "ethnic" groups in Canada in the 1970s.

In terms of its central philosophy of education, the *Survey* does much to indicate a desire to break with the record set by the federal education system. The introductory section, entitled "Purpose of the Study," acknowledges the previous lack of a coherent vision for the education system. It also self-consciously points out that the precedent of relying on southern models as a basis for northern education was misguided:

> When the goals of the northern system were subject to dispute and difficult to identify, there was a tendency to cling to the programme which was already tried and tested somewhere else on the Canadian scene. Hence the education program of the Northwest Territories has already borrowed heavily from the Provinces in one form or another. Many voices have pointed out that this was not advisable, since in the north were people whose educational needs were dictated by a social and cultural environment different from that found in most other parts of the country.[15]

Although the NWT has never been able to avoid borrowing from provincial models for some aspects of the curriculum,[16] this was an important recognition that led directly to curriculum and resource-development initiatives to make education more relevant to Inuit and other northern peoples.

The *Survey* further distances itself from the history of religion-based and residential schools by asserting that assimilation of Inuit and other Aboriginal peoples was no longer viewed as a desirable outcome of education. On the contrary, Gillie suggests that "conventional thinking" had come to prescribe the protection of Aboriginal language and culture, presumably an undertaking in which the school system would have a role:

> At one time it was conventionally accepted that some kind of assimilation or integration was the only possible approach for the problems of these people. However, within more recent years and in response to the protests of Indian and Eskimo people themselves, thinking has changed considerably and now supports the belief that some method must be found whereby the Aboriginal population in Canada may be able to retain much of its culture while learning to live in the general Canadian society.[17]

The source or evidence of protests from Inuit against assimilation or integration is unclear in the *Survey* and can be contradicted by a number of statements by parents who felt that it would be economically beneficial for their children to assimilate.[18] As a result of the territorial government's new position on northern education, the *Survey* indicates a broader understanding of who is being educated and why:

> The purpose of education is to provide for all people opportunity for maximum development of their aptitudes, skills and competencies along with an understanding and appreciation of the sum total of human experience. Such development should enable each individual to choose freely between different courses of action in such a manner that he can live a satisfying personal life while discharging his responsibilities as a participating member of a complex society.[19]

Despite being somewhat vague, this statement indicates the territorial government's desire to set a new foundation for the education system.

The *Survey* also offers a total of 223 recommendations on subjects large and small, demonstrating the extent to which those involved in education felt significant changes to the system were necessary. Of particular note, the *Survey* identifies the NWT as a multilingual society and argues that the promotion of Aboriginal languages is critical to supporting the identity of Aboriginal peoples: "Language is such a vital aspect of the culture of any people that its loss frequently constitutes a seriously traumatic experience for those involved and constitutes an automatic denigration of their whole culture."[20] As a result, according to the *Survey,* Aboriginal languages were to become the primary language of instruction for the first several years of elementary education, followed by the gradual introduction of English or French. In addition, the teaching assistant program, which brought Inuit or Aboriginal assistants into the classroom beginning in the late 1960s, is vehemently defended by the *Survey.* It suggests that the conditions of their employment should be improved and indeterminate positions created for them. In comparison to the previous federal system, the Department of Education espoused some ideas that were notably forward-thinking – for example, that compulsory attendance should be removed from school ordinances to accommodate hunting and camping trips. Indeed, recommendations such as this were so progressive that they sparked disputes and controversies. For the most part, however, the recommendations of the *Survey* were in some approximation adopted by the department within a matter of years.

Despite the scope of the *Survey,* there are a number of points that it neglects or on which it offers limited commentary. In various instances, the *Survey* recommends the inclusion of cultural content. For example, with reference to secondary-level education, it suggests: "That credit programmes in indigenous languages and cultures be made available in all schools."[21] At the elementary level, it suggests that cultural and survival programs be offered with the guidance of local people. However, these references do little to explain the importance of cultural content, to set expectations for the amount of integration of local and Aboriginal knowledge into the curriculum, or to reveal the methodological or structural differences between Aboriginal and formal education. Similarly, the *Survey* does little to recognize or address the confusion and alienation on the part of students and parents resulting from the cross-cultural school environment, conflicting social norms and values, and the replacement of parents and family members with Qallunaat as the primary educators. The only reference to this awareness on the part of educators is the stated goal: "To develop in each person, attitudes, morals, and social competencies that will enable him to function effectively within both the Canadian and global society."[22] There is no mention here of the difficulty and complexity of navigating between the social expectations, attitudes, and morals of the Qallunaat and those of the northern Aboriginal cultures. Indeed, this recommendation arguably takes for granted that these behaviours and codes are universal, subtly perpetuating an assimilationist approach. Later, the *Survey* does recognize that values may differ between cultures in the NWT, but this is primarily with reference to teachers helping their students to make choices about their economic future. Lastly, the *Survey* does not do enough to integrate the Department of Education's new view of education with the realities of preparing students for viable employment.

These shortcomings are primarily a result of two factors: (1) the lack of student, parental, and community contribution to the *Survey;* and (2) an approach that focused on making small accommodations to ease the introduction of students to the formal school system rather than on changing the foundations of the system to better approximate Inuit education. With regard to the first factor, the *Survey* points out the lack of involvement by parents and community members in the education of their children and recommends that more action be taken to establish school districts and to invite parents into the classrooms. Recommendation 214 states, "Virtually no progress has been made in the last decade in establishing local school districts."[23] This is an interesting point because it suggests that the Department of Education should accept some responsibility to engage parents in educational consultation and decision making, yet the *Survey* itself made no such effort. There is no evidence that the recommendations articulated by the department were made in response to the concerns of Inuit parents and students who were on the receiving end of education, so the validity of the *Survey* is limited. With regard to the second factor, the *Survey*'s lack of detail around dealing with the contradictions between Inuit and Qallunaat values indicates a limited recognition and understanding of the specificities of Inuit culture. Caught in the trap of multiculturalism, educators and administrators could not see beyond making northern schools more culturally inclusive in theory, to envision changes that would accomplish this objective in practice.

The second government review, which produced the 1973 publication *Report of the Special Committee of the Council of the Northwest Territories to the Study the "Survey of Education – Northwest Territories,"*[24] was conducted by a special committee sponsored by the Council of the Northwest Territories. It was, as its title suggests, issued in response to the Department of Education's *Survey.* The committee consisted of only four appointed members, namely Lena Pederson (chairperson), Bryan Pearson, James Rabesca, and Dr. Louis-Edmond Hamelin.[25] The committee held meetings in Yellowknife over a period of six days (without Dr. Hamelin in attendance due to an unforeseen illness), during which administrators from within the Department of Education were called on to discuss aspects of the *Survey* and to answer various questions. No references are made in the *Report* to incorporation of the views of teachers, students, parents, or community members.

The *Report* agreed with many of the *Survey*'s recommendations, and indeed generally pushed for even more progressive changes to the school system. For example, the basic aims of education identified in the *Report* include making education non-compulsory. The aims are listed as:

- to equip northern residents to live in the ever-changing and rapidly developing North

- to give everyone an opportunity to receive an education but in the area they are best suited for. However, the Committee does not believe education should be compulsory; and
- to have the opportunity to adapt to the white man's way but without losing their traditional way of life, their own language and their cultural heritage.[26]

This list is indicative of an effort to diminish the assimilative tendencies of the formal school system under the federal administration. A brief summary of the other most significant points made by the *Report* will serve to establish a comparison with the *Survey.* The *Report* strongly promotes Aboriginal-language education, even suggesting that the *Survey* placed too much emphasis on the teaching of English. Interestingly, part of the justification offered by the special committee is a desire not only to preserve language but also to remedy the communication barriers being experienced in families and to facilitate learning for adults as well as children: "Through giving the Natives the opportunity to retain their mother tongue, the children will be able to communicate well with their parents and keep their respect for their own heritage. The whole educational process should be slowed down so that the adults can be brought along in the learning process with their children."[27] Whereas the *Survey* makes a number of references to Inuit classroom assistants, the *Report* places more emphasis on the importance of training Aboriginal teachers: "The number of native northern teachers should be increased to as many as possible. They are of the greatest importance in achieving a healthy system."[28] It also places significant emphasis on establishing grade 9 in every community as quickly as possible and expresses disapproval of the hostel (i.e., residential) program.

Most of the suggestions of the *Report* indicate a stance strongly rooted in establishing a system that is more reflective of the needs of Aboriginal peoples, with one notable exception. The special committee expressed support for the northern-oriented curriculum introduced by the *Survey,* but it also pointed out the importance of maintaining educational standards so that graduates of the system would not receive an education of lower quality than was provided in other parts of the country: "In implementing a more northern-oriented system great care must be taken not to lower the quality of the educational process merely for the sake of change."[29] While quality is certainly an important consideration, this reluctance to initiate change that may have benefited students is uncharacteristic of the balance of the *Report.*

Lastly, the *Report* identified local involvement in educational decision making as a major priority for the northern school system in the future. Citing one NWT community that already had a school board in place, the *Report* argued strongly in favour of handing over significant administrative responsibility to the communities and parents:

> The responsibility for education must be given to the community. Every school should have its own local school board as has been established in Rae-Edzo. School boards should have full powers, including responsibility for the financial areas as without this their powers are meaningless. In addition to the schools being locally run they should be operated on a twelve-month basis and active parent participation should be encouraged.[30]

This concern for the role and views of parents and community members in education was further bolstered by Dr. Hamelin's comments. A summary of his response to a draft version of the *Report,* which he offered in lieu of participating in the committee's meetings, is available in Appendix B of the *Report.* His comments reveal unprecedented insight into the contradiction of movement in the school system toward cultural relevance without input from those who are on the receiving end of education. He points out the need for the participation of Aboriginal people on their own terms rather than in accordance with conditions offered to them by the Qallunaat:

> The opinions of the native peoples as to the kind of education system they want must be sought as they form the major part of the population in the North. This, however presents a problem as the questions seeking these opinions are formulated by the white people and also because the latter are not accustomed to actually listening to what the natives have to say, nor do they understand. This does not necessarily mean though that the white people do not want whatever is best for the native people.
>
> The Survey of Education is a great document but reflects the white views much more than an integrated white-native approach. It is more sympathetic to the natives than previous reports, however.[31]

The *Report* identifies a number of weaknesses inherent in the *Survey* and in the Department of Education's associated efforts to initiate educational change, but I would argue that Dr. Hamelin's articulation of the lack of local involvement is the *Report*'s most valuable contribution.

Inuit Teachers in the Classroom

One important outcome of the *Survey* and the *Report* was an agreement on the importance of increased opportunity for adult Inuit to participate in the education system as classroom assistants and, eventually, as certified teachers. A brief history of the classroom assistant program demonstrates the system's new willingness to make compromises to better reflect Inuit culture. The earliest Inuit classroom assistants were employed on an ad hoc, or local, basis in the late 1950s.[32] Norm Macpherson argues that the impetus behind the formalization of the teaching assistant program was to better communicate with young students who knew little or no English and to integrate them into the classroom more quickly. Aside from support in terms of language, the assistants provided a social and cultural bridge between children, their parents, and the formal education system: "In many cases, the classroom assistant is also instrumental in interpreting the school philosophy to the Eskimo community."[33] Classroom assistants were also encouraged to upgrade their own education and training through correspondence courses or, where available, through adult education programs, which made the teaching assistant program one of the best employment opportunities for Inuit at this time. By 1972 there were eighty classroom assistants employed across the NWT, and it was in this year that classroom assistants were recognized by the territorial government and no longer had to be employed on a casual basis.[34] The Department of Education could not have reasonably required Qallunaat teachers to learn and teach in Inuktitut. With the Aboriginal-language curriculum in development, another solution was devised; the classroom assistants program was expanded to become the NWT Teacher Education Program (TEP). There were other advantages besides language to increasing Inuit staff in the schools: improved communication with parents and the community; continuity in teaching staff, as Inuit were less likely to be transient; increased Inuit employment; and eventually, increased cultural content in the curriculum.

The NWT Teacher Education Program originally set up shop in Yellowknife in 1968 with fifteen pupils. After the first year, the program was put on hold pending a review of its success. The result was that the program was expanded to stretch over two years, moved to an adult training centre in Fort Smith, and became associated with the University of Alberta. However, throughout the 1970s there was ongoing tension between meeting the needs of Inuit in the Eastern Arctic and the needs of the rest of the NWT. John D. Lee, principal of TEP in 1980, vaguely described this problem as: "The whole question of resolving East/West differences with regard to objectives, program location and political aspirations."[35] My understanding of the differences referred to by Lee is that they were rooted in the contrast between the relative homogeneity of Inuit culture in the east and the multiplicity of Aboriginal cultures in the west. Courses were offered intermittently in Chesterfield Inlet and Frobisher Bay as a means of enticing Inuit into the program, but by 1979 these demands had resulted in a schism, and a separate TEP was established permanently in Frobisher Bay. According to Lee, in 1980 eighty-three Aboriginal teachers had graduated from the program since 1968, more than half of whom were still employed as teachers in the NWT.[36]

The classroom assistant and teacher education programs received a great deal of investment in the 1970s and represent a crucial step toward the development of an education system that could be responsive to Inuit ways of knowing, being, and doing. For Inuit to own the education system, they had to first become familiar with it and involved in its operation. It would still take a significant amount of work to change the system into something that was seen and felt by Inuit to reflect them. Nonetheless, putting classrooms in the hands of Inuit teachers, and providing a link between schools and parents and students, was extremely important in making education more responsive to their needs.

Curriculum Development in the Northwest Territories

Most educational adaptations seen in the early 1970s resulted from redefining curriculum and producing learning materials that were directed toward making educational content more familiar to northern students. Starting with the *Survey,* many theoretical suggestions and statements were made by the Department of Education to promote the development of northern curriculum and materials. Although it is difficult to establish how this theoretical shift was felt in the classrooms, there is evidence that new expectations were strongly enforced by the administration. So as not to lose the momentum of change initiated by the *Survey,* in 1972 the Department of Education introduced the first elementary curriculum guide made in the NWT. The so-called *Red Book,* entitled *Elementary Education in the Northwest Territories K-6,*[37] was written primarily by Paul Robinson, the department's chief of curriculum. It was closely followed in 1973 by the *Green Book,* entitled *Learning in the Middle Years,* which provided curriculum guidelines for the middle school level.[38]

Various generalizations can be made about both documents. They each include a lengthy introductory section that further elaborates the department's new philosophical basis for northern education, as well as sections devoted to each classroom subject, which include activity suggestions, lesson-plan resources, and other guidelines. Rather than offering a curriculum guide that sets out specific mandatory content and a list of learning objectives, these documents were to provide the framework by which Robinson expected teachers to design their own courses and lesson plans. In other words, the emphasis is placed on pedagogy and broad content rather than on specific curriculum outcomes.

This framework should have provided teachers with the opportunity to ensure that lesson plans were locally and culturally relevant. The idea that education should be responsive to each individual child's needs was taken quite seriously by Robinson. As Gillie stated in the *Red Book*'s letter of introduction to educators: "The learning situation must be developed around the strengths that the child brings with him to the classroom be they his own language, his cultural heritage, and his 'view' of the 'world.' In this respect the total learning program must integrate and facilitate the opportunity for children to engage in Northern learning experiences."[39] In addition, the *Green Book* states that teachers must invite local cultural specialists into the classrooms, further enhancing the opportunity for achieving local relevance:

> The involvement of Northern people in the classroom program is a vital necessity. The type of curriculum as outlined herein simply will not be effective without drawing upon the talents of settlement resource people. In a cross cultural setting, co-operative learning situations which involve the fully certificated teacher and the uncertified lay person in a team teaching arrangement can do much to realize the aims and objectives of Northern education.[40]

Recommendations in both the *Red* and *Green Book*s show evidence that the authors took the needs of the community into consideration along with those of the children and teachers. The department did not shy away from establishing priorities that were outside those traditionally associated with formal schooling, such as outdoor education, life skills, or survival courses on the land:

> Outdoor education is gaining in popularity in Canadian education generally. In the Northern context outdoor education affords the opportunity to bring school and community closer together. Not only are there a multitude of possibilities with regard to environmental studies, the ecology, conservation and similar interest areas, but perhaps more importantly, the child's educational program can be broadened to include traditional life skills programs: hunting, fishing, trapping, Arctic survival.[41]

Although this framework did encourage teachers to place emphasis on the individual learner and local needs, better approximating the format of traditional learner-centred Inuit education, there is little evidence to suggest that this change was driven by the intention to replicate traditional Inuit educational methodology. Rather, it was thought to be an approach more accommodating of the needs of Aboriginal learners, and it reflects newly validated shifts in educational practices among Qallunaat and in southern Canada during this period.

The books also both demonstrate that the department felt it was necessary to open a public dialogue on the cultural differences between educators and administrators, the education system, and Aboriginal peoples. From a historical perspective, these early curriculum guides provide some of the best evidence of the institutional view of Inuit-Qallunaat relations that informed educational policy in the 1970s. The *Red Book* offers one of the first departmental admissions of the colonialist overtones of the existing educational experience:

> The W.A.S.P. atmosphere of the average classroom can be very real. Such virtues as hard work and no play, competition, getting ahead, acquisition of material goods, applying oneself to a task in the hope of future rewards, can be ingrained in the Euro Canadian society ... In some ways many educators tend to see themselves as living justification for the validity of these values. In the Athabaskan-Eskimo societies middle class values can be hopelessly meaningless.[42]

This point is further fleshed out in the *Red Book* by a comparison table demonstrating the conflicts that can occur between deeply held Qallunaat values and those of Inuit. For example, the table shows that it is believed in Qallunaat society that "all men should strive to climb the ladder of success. In this sense success can be measured by a wide range of superlatives: first, the most, the best, etc.," whereas the Aboriginal perspective would more often approximate: "The influence of the elders is important. Young people lack maturity and experience. A man seeks perfection within himself – not in comparison with others."[43]

The *Green Book* perpetuates the style and voice of the *Red Book*. It starts with a section entitled "What It's All About – Young People," in which a number of significant challenges facing Aboriginal youth in the NWT are described. The language and commentary provide little comfort to middle school teachers but rather attempt to paint the social, cultural, and political situation in all its difficulties:

> By the time an individual has reached adolescence conflicts can develop as a growing awareness of the "facts of life" run counter to the indoctrinated stereotypes of the preceding years. For any young person, separating fact from fancy can be difficult. However, the Athapaskan, Inuit or Métis person confronts an even more trying situation as the harsher realities – poverty – prejudice – double standards – are not only seen, but experienced on a personal basis.[44]

Commentary such as this indicates that the department was conscious of the cultural negotiation occurring in their own schools and felt that its teaching staff should receive additional guidance on recognizing and dealing with such differences.

Indeed, Paul Robinson was infamous among educators for avoiding social niceties in favour of making departmental positions and expectations on sensitive subjects ruthlessly clear.[45] Unlike the *Survey*, which neglected to articulate specific expectations for cultural content in the classroom, Robinson made his expectations unmistakable:

> There is no hierarchy of cultures to suggest that the non-native cultures are more important, and therefore automatically deserving of greater emphasis. To put it another way, token approaches toward recognizing Aboriginal cultures whereby fifteen minutes per week are devoted to such things as instruction in syllabics, or Arctic survival skills are foreign to this curriculum. It is incumbent upon educators to ensure that parity reflects the time to be spent on cultural aspects of any program, course offering, or classroom activity.[46]

It is unlikely that classroom teachers had the support, in practice, to meet these expectations set by Robinson. The *Red Book* was sometimes referred to as a "compromise curriculum" due to its recognition of the limited capacity of Qallunaat teachers to implement Aboriginal-language programs and the need for ongoing materials development. However, this compromise did not apply to the department's expectation that teachers would do their utmost to realize the new vision of education as presented by the department and would acknowledge the many steps that still lay ahead of them:

> Allied with the foregoing is the necessity to consider that current practices of including some "first" language teaching, some trapping and other out-of-doors' experiences, some legends and story telling, etc., are but the tentative first steps in the direction of developing a truly multi-cultural education program. This is not to deny the importance that such activities have in our schools at this time. However, it would be misleading to suggest that this is all that is required. Until such time as people can see their attitudes and values reflected in the total learning experience, there is no room for complacency in this regard.[47]

The department's implied criticism of the old federal system and its identification of inequities that characterized northern life were not easy for all involved in education to receive. It is understandable that some teachers felt alienated or threatened by the language of these documents. If the curriculum guides themselves left any question as to the seriousness of the department, then the message of the "Dear Educator" letter of 1972 could not be avoided. As mentioned, the *Red Book* was distributed with an introductory letter from B.C. Gillie, drafted by Paul Robinson.[48] The letter read, "It may well be that a minority of personnel will not feel comfortable working within a system having these expectations. If this assumption proves to be correct for you, then the time is ripe to make your plan regarding the next school year."[49] Gillie remembers, "Quite naturally this message was not warmly received by all members of the N.W.T. teaching staff."[50] This letter of introduction shows that the Department of Education was committed to a new approach, no matter the expense to the old system, including the loss of experienced teachers.[51]

Increasing awareness of cultural differences and identifying systemic impediments to educational success were challenges taken on by these books with some success. Truly implementing pedagogical reform proved less feasible in practice. Gillie explained in retrospect that the practical provisions of the books were considered unsatisfactory to some northern teachers:

> Neither the Red Book nor the Green Book presented guidelines on how or what to teach, but rather outlined approaches, suggested strategies and offered a philosophy of teaching and learning. Indeed it was suggested by Paul Robinson, Chief of Curriculum, that teachers should be capable of preparing their own courses of study for their own pupils. Capable or not, the teachers of the Northwest Territories were, generally speaking, unable or unwilling to attempt to develop formal educational programs for their pupils. They pointed out that if provincial teachers were given course outlines in every subject, they expected no less from their administration.[52]

As Gillie points out, the *Red Book* and *Green Book* provide only a skeleton of directions for classroom proceedings, which, in practice, were not substantial enough to become the basis of all coursework. As is often the case, much of the change that actually reached students in classrooms was dependent on the individual teacher's motivation and will to meet these expectations.

Despite the many strong points made in favour of culturally appropriate education, in the mid-1970s teachers could not yet rely on the department to provide classroom materials that reflected northern life and culture. Although the Programme Development Division was growing, demands on it were very high in light of the new emphasis on Aboriginal language program development. It was not in a position to develop materials at every grade level and for every subject. Most of the northern content found in classrooms in this period had to be introduced on the teacher's own initiative. There is little evidence left of this hard work, except the memories of teachers who were struggling with an already heavy workload.[53] Therefore, it remains difficult to determine to what extent lesson plans and classroom materials actually fulfilled the vision offered by the *Red Book* and *Green Book* and the vision statements made by the department. It is likely that students, especially those in the upper grades, saw little change in practice. For the most part, they still received an education designed by curriculum specialists in Southern Canada.

There are some notable exceptions that demonstrate the type of classroom materials the department supplied to incorporate northern realities and northern voices into northern education. *Piksaaq* (Tools), published in 1974, is an example of multilayered learning material with culturally appropriate content, available fully translated into Inuktitut.[54] *Piksaaq* consists of 8.5 x 11 flash cards, in solid colours like red and yellow, each with a drawing of a different traditional Inuit tool on one side and an explanation of that tool on the other. Presumably, the teacher would hold up the flash card in front of the class and allow students to speculate on its use before reciting the explanation. In the English version, the description of each tool usually offers both its English and Inuktitut names (e.g., "Seal Float [Avatuq]"), the type of materials used to create the tool, and its purpose. The reason *Piksaaq* is described as "multilayered" is that many of the flash cards include quotations by Inuit that are about or include reference to the particular tool. Such excerpts by Elders or other Inuit suggest an approximation of including Inuit oral tradition in the lesson about Inuit tools. This methodology – learning about Inuit tools by looking at drawings of them on flash cards held up by the (likely Qallunaat) teacher – is not ideal. There is no concept of the size and scale of the tools, no opportunity to hold and feel the tools, no experience or practise of how the tools would be used, and likely not enough information for the teacher to answer questions about the tools. Nevertheless, a lesson with *Piksaaq* would offer recognition of the technology of Inuit culture, provide some insight into what is needed to sustain oneself on the land, and bring Inuit knowledge and an approximation of Inuit oral culture into the classroom.

Despite the comparatively drastic changes brought about by the territorial takeover of northern education and the abandonment of assimilationist objectives, the nature of classroom materials like *Piksaaq* and the expectations set by the curriculum guidelines reveal that the Department of Education had a great deal of work to do in order to catch up to its bold new vision of education. The Programme Development Division began the process by focusing on ways to bring what was familiar to Aboriginal students into the classroom – in other words, to increase the northern content of lessons that were already prescribed. The road to developing entire units, and eventually entire courses, of northern content that reflected Inuit knowledge and culture in terms of both subject matter and methodology, would be a long one.

Educational Philosophy and Legislation

It was recommended in the *Survey* in 1972 that the NWT needed a new education ordinance, but it took five years of drafting until this ordinance was approved by the Legislative Assembly in 1977.[55] The NWT had inherited its former educational legislation from the federal government, a 1956 ordinance based largely on southern models. To develop this new document, many northern organizations were consulted, including schools, local education advisory committees (where they existed), municipal councils, Inuit Tapirisat of Canada, and the NWT Teachers Association.[56] The resulting Education Ordinance of 1977 afforded a number of significant changes to the system and promoted education that was culturally relevant and responsive to local needs. In addition to making statements of support for cultural curriculum content[57] and for the employment of non-professional local staff to support the provision of cultural or lifestyle programs,[58] the ordinance offered local education authorities control over the language of instruction in kindergarten and the subsequent two years.[59] Although by 1977 several communities were already conducting the first years of schooling in local languages, this legislative solidification was important in building the capacity of such programs.

Arguably the most significant stipulation of the ordinance is the transfer of substantially greater duties and powers to local education authorities, particularly where resources were robust enough to warrant the creation of a "divisional" or regional board of education. Much of the ultimate authority for administration of schools was retained by the "executive member" of the Legislative Assembly, who, in 1977, was still the appointed commissioner of the Northwest Territories. However, the ordinance ensured northern communities the first opportunity to guide the administration of their schools if they desired. Local control could occur according to three different models, each with a progressively higher level of responsibility. First, a community education committee could be established consisting of five elected members operating in an advisory capacity to the local school principal and the regional superintendent. Second, an elected community education society could be created to replace any committee already in existence and would thereby receive a budget for the operation of school programs, maintain a more active role in school planning, and receive custody of education facilities. Lastly, a seven-member corporate board of education could be created anywhere an education society had been in existence for two years by petition of the executive member at least four months prior to a municipal election.[60] According to the ordinance, a board of education would be required to carry out duties that included receiving reports on the operation of each school at least once each month; reviewing education program plans; receiving annually moneys from the NWT Legislative Assembly and from the municipal council; providing, maintaining, and furnishing education facilities; executing plans for construction and alterations of education facilities; recruiting and appointing principals, teachers, and other staff; settling disputes between students, guardians, and teaching personnel; and employing a local superintendent of education.[61] By supporting local education authorities, this ordinance provided the grounds for change that would significantly alter the structure of educational decision making in the NWT during the 1980s and also facilitate a critical aspect of Inuit education. This is discussed in detail in Chapter 5.

Soon after the ordinance, in 1978, the Department of Education issued a document entitled *Philosophy of Education in the NWT*.[62] According to its introduction, this document was intended to update and reorganize the statements of philosophy made in the *Red Book* and *Green Book*. The *Handbook*, as it is referred to, contends that it clarifies the curriculum's core programs and a system of student evaluation. The introduction makes reference to the department's increasing preference for experiential teaching: "Although indicating a bias towards 'experience' and 'activity' approaches to implementation, the Handbook is non-prescriptive on this issue."[63] Despite being suggestive of methods used in traditional Inuit education, this reference is likely more a coincidence than an attempt to emulate Aboriginal pedagogy; however, it is indicative of changing practices. The *Handbook* reinforces the department's insistence on using a program that is "territorial," meaning created in the NWT, for some classroom subjects while also acknowledging the regional and local work that must be done to develop more robust programming.

The *Handbook*'s position on multiculturalism deserves consideration, both because of its emphasis within the *Handbook* and because of its limitations in applicability to the Inuit of the Eastern Arctic. The introduction states: "The Handbook reasserts the importance of multiculturalism and bilingualism in the NWT and the need to consider both cultural and linguistic factors in developing programs."[64] The absence of a definition of "multiculturalism" and the ambiguousness of the practical implications of a multiculturalism policy had long been a shortfall at the federal level, and this lack of clarity is perpetuated at the territorial level.

To elaborate on the departmental support for multiculturalism, the *Handbook* argues that an individual's success is related to the capability of the school to reinforce what they learn at home and from their culture:

> The concept of multiculturalism recognizes that each of our young people needs to develop confidence through a sense of self-identity and a feeling of self-worth. Good pedagogy tells us that as an individual, and as a member of a particular ethnic or cultural group, the student functions best if full use is made of the

> traditions and experiences which are integral to home and family, and therefore to student well-being.[65]

If promotion of multiculturalism results in heightened feelings of self-identity and self-worth among students, it is an admirable and highly positive pursuit, especially in light of the history of assimilation. However, a prescription for exercising multiculturalism in schools is lacking. For example, in suggesting how to implement a multicultural approach to education, the *Handbook* describes what can be gained through local or Aboriginal studies: "A vast range of undocumented experience, of individual and collective wisdom, of unused skills and of folklore exist. Learning about one's group can help to bridge the cultural and generational gap between young people and their elders, and can also contribute positively to the sense of self as a member of a family, a cultural group, and a community."[66] This statement borders on tokenism by implying that this undocumented experience, wisdom, and folklore are useful only as a means to make students feel more comfortable with their Elders. Much as oral history and traditional studies can and should create connections to the past, much greater meaning can be drawn from such studies by demonstrating their application and usefulness to the present and future. Despite implying an effort to foster a system of education that supports Inuit ways of being, the concept of multiculturalism is largely inapplicable to Inuit students since they form the majority culture and population in Eastern Arctic communities. Moreover, the department does not go so far as to acknowledge that many of the values, goals, and structures of formal schooling are equally culturally situated and are inherently in conflict with the social, cultural, and otherwise fundamental experiences at home. Although the *Handbook* certainly expands the dialogue on cultural negotiation and cultural inclusion in NWT schools, it remains a superficial treatment of complex cultural issues and offers too few specific directions to teachers on classroom implementation. On this topic, Lynn Aylward argues:

> Assimilation, through formal religious education of Inuit students, gave way to a more subtle approach in the 1970s of claims to affirm cultural diversity through integration, or the bicultural curricular approach of the "best of both worlds." However, a recurring theme of institutional yearning for "sameness," along with skewed theories of cultural deficiency, cultural deprivation, and cultural difference at work in northern schools, have meant that the philosophy of curriculum integration – mainstream or southern Canadian curriculum "infused" with indigenous knowledge – has become in fact a soft form of cultural and linguistic assimilation in Nunavut.[67]

There continued to be a gulf between the theory of improving student self-esteem and the practice of using multiculturalism to do so; this did not effectively translate into the incorporation of aspects of Inuit education in schools.

Defining and implementing the purpose of education both remained challenges. Paul Welsman reflected on the inconsistent relationship between education and employment: "A northern model of education must also answer: 'Education for what?' In the past the school system has been treated largely as an isolated institution despite the fact that northern students must not only be educated but must be absorbed into the economic system."[68] In the 1970s absorption into the economic system seemed to call for vocational education. It was believed by the federal and territorial governments that Inuit and other Aboriginal peoples would be needed for the practical occupations associated with employment in industries centred on infrastructure development and resource extraction. Therefore, where secondary-level programs were offered, highly academic pursuits were not prioritized by the Department of Education.

Vocational education began for students in the Eastern Arctic with the opening of Churchill Vocational Centre in 1964 and the start of an Apprentice Training and Occupational and Certification Program that offered students access to fifteen various trades.[69] In 1971 the Gordon Robertson Education Centre was opened in Frobisher Bay, with a residence to house students from the other communities.[70] Metal and wood shops and home economics facilities were used for training youth and adults. Other vocational programs were offered across the NWT and sometimes outside of the territory for men in construction and heavy-equipment operation to support the mining industry. Women were trained as practical nurses and, as mentioned, teaching assistants. However, much of this training came to naught because the employment opportunities did not arise as the government had expected. Mary Van Meenan argues:

> A basic weakness existed in the vocational education system. While the Inuit were being trained for basic vocational positions, the labour market in the NWT was shifting to an increasing requirement for skilled labour, and a decrease in unskilled labour. Thus the educational focus of the government, instead of preparing the Inuit to participate fully in the wage economy, was assigning them to a limited future with limited opportunities.[71]

Apart from this vocational focus, and more germane to this discussion, student access to secondary-level education was limited in a logistical sense. Students who were motivated to continue in school beyond the eighth or ninth grade were required to leave home and attend residential schools, which presented a significant deterrent for many students and their families. This was a major challenge to the education system until the late 1980s and 1990s when a majority of Eastern Arctic communities introduced grades 10 to 12. In terms of the path to employment, the department's activities were still not in alignment with the realities of northern life and the needs of Inuit.

The Impact of Schooling on Communities

One crucial insight into the territorial period of education remains to be discussed: the perspective of Inuit parents, community members, and students themselves on the role of schooling in their lives. Conducted on the cusp of the transition from the federal administration of education to the territorial period, one study published in 1970 comes closest to representing the views of Inuit children and parents, at least in one community, at this stage.[72] This research was funded by the federal government, but it was done at arms length through the National Museum of Man in Ottawa. David Omar Born, the researcher, investigated the "social psychological characteristics of the encounter between the Belcher Island Eskimo and the federal school program"[73] – or, more plainly, whether Inuit in this community perceived the school system to be meeting their needs. Born found that the education system was perceived to be the greatest Western, or Qallunaat, influence in their lives. He says, "As we have seen, there are a number of western influences, but the school program is the one which, to the Eskimo, is the most predominant and, in the words of one of the Islanders, the most 'pushing.'"[74] In 1960 a primary school was erected at "South Camp" to accommodate grades 1 to 3, and all older children were flown to Great Whale River (130 kilometres away) and housed in hostels under the supervision of Inuit "hostel parents."[75] Born argues that due to the introduction of formal schooling, "The Belcher Island Eskimo are faced with a complex of social and economic relationships which are largely alien to their traditional tools and modes of thinking."[76]

In contrast to the emerging Qallunaat concern for preservation of Inuktitut, Born found that Inuit felt the greatest benefit of attending school was the opportunity to learn English, which they believed was essential to getting Qallunaat jobs. Indeed, he reports that parents did not want their own language spoken at school in case it interfered with their children learning English. He includes the following example: "Q: Do you think the schools should teach about where the other Eskimo are and how they live? A: The children should learn English."[77] Subjects such as mathematics and biology were met with mixed enthusiasm, and studying government was thought to be beneficial if: "It would help the Eskimo 'get more' from DIAND [the Department of Indian Affairs and Northern Development]."[78]

Apart from language, Inuit identified practical education as a desirable outcome for schooling: instruction in health, childcare, manual skills, and home economics. Born describes the economic bind that Inuit were experiencing, created by their dependency on government welfare to purchase staples such as gasoline, ammunition, and foodstuffs. He repeatedly refers to their unhappiness with this economic dependency and explains that Inuit expected the education of their children to provide a more self-sufficient future. As a result, parents accepted the role of the school in their community, but some remained unsatisfied with the return on their investment:

> One obvious point to be made is that the parents in Eskimo Harbour have difficulty in seeing any immediate returns from education. The adults state that the only thing which the children have learned which is of value to the Island society are the chores which are performed as part of hostel living.
>
> This impatience for some tangible return is supported somewhat indirectly by traditional Eskimo world view which, based on the uncertainties of Arctic life, has never encouraged the luxury of gambling on something several months, let alone years, in the future. The process of formal education requires just such a gamble.[79]

Born highlights the fundamental discrepancy between the goal of Qallunaat education and the practical realities of everyday life in the Belcher Islands. Not only did schools teach skills that were foreign to parents, and incompatible with the way they had traditionally lived, but also the wage economy had not yet come about, so the benefits of education remained unclear. Born states, "The consequence of this is that the children are not entirely sure with which society they should affiliate themselves, and they are even less sure of their ability to fulfill the requirements of either society."[80]

Born expands on the greatest concerns about education expressed by parents, citing the children's loss of traditional skills such as hunting and sewing as well as the: "Loss of parental control and the subsequent problems of child discipline that arise from the present school situation."[81] Born explains this loss of parental control as resulting from the assimilative influence of school: "The children have learned that if they are to be successful in Euro-Canadian society they must 'be like the white man,' and such imitation requires that they value work activities and other social patterns which are not practiced or particularly valued by their parents."[82] Therefore, Born argues, the school program did not yet coincide effectively with Inuit needs. To increase the success of the education system, Born suggests improving adult understanding of education through adult education programs and increased parental participation in classrooms;

renewing emphasis on Inuit culture; carefully selecting teachers to act as social models; training teachers in Inuktitut to facilitate better communication with parents and community; improving the attractiveness of teaching in the Arctic; promoting Inuit participation in school governance through civic councils; and providing psychological services to the community. These suggestions were drawn independently by Born and should not be confused with the suggestions of Inuit parents; however, it is interesting to note that his insights align closely with the definition of Inuit education, which does seem to be his intention. For the education system to be successful, Born argues, it must be "intermediate adaptive" rather than assimilative, which means it should: "Be a program which involves both the Eskimo adapting to the western socio-economic world and the Euro-Canadian government administrators adapting their plans and policy to the Eskimo world wherever possible."[83]

This study reveals that in the early stages of formal education, many Inuit were in agreement that their children should learn English and wanted to see their children employed in jobs provided by the Qallunaat economic system. This desire, however, was brought about by feelings of inadequacy and a lack of economic self-sufficiency through incomplete integration in the capitalist system. In addition, it was accompanied by ongoing alienation by parents who did not model the social, cultural, and economic expectations of Qallunaat society, which children were being taught in schools. This alienation is echoed by an observer in Cape Dorset, a Catholic priest who took it on himself to represent the views of Inuit parents through a Catholic publication:

> The adults of Cape Dorset see the school as an institution which is to train their children in understanding how to do things like a Kadlunak [Qallunaat]. How to acquire some of those enviable characteristics of the Kadlunak which give him a good deal of power and wealth. In short, we have proposed an education system (and the Inuit seem to have accepted it) which divides the young from their parents; which makes the continuity of community impossible. Perhaps the enormous difficulties that teachers encounter in the classroom have nothing to do with a lack of aptitude for academic studies among the Inuit – but have to do with a deep instinctive resistance to the fragmentation of personality and community.[84]

With this comment, it is clear that Born was not alone in arguing that Inuit parents were supportive of the formal education system in principle but that it held little meaning for them in practice and, indeed, proved detrimental to their family relationships. John J. Honigmann and Irma Honigmann provide supporting evidence from Frobisher Bay that although students were interested in finding jobs, they did not find the pursuit of a formal education satisfying in itself and thus often dropped out:

> By age 12, school becomes an impossible chore for many children, who not only look for excuses to be absent but plead for the chance to withdraw and hopefully get a job. But hunting isn't something that a 12 or 13 year old boy can do daily, particularly if he belongs to a working man's family, and teen-agers can't find steady jobs. The town's economy, as we have pointed out, can't accommodate all of its 261 men aged between 15 and 69, so the younger men mostly suffer.[85]

The memories of students who attended Churchill Vocational Centre (CVC) offer another opportunity to investigate the role of schooling in the lives of Inuit, particularly as they grew into adulthood. CVC was the residential institution attended by most Inuit who stayed in school through their senior years during the late 1960s and, not coincidentally, by the generation that began the movement for political autonomy and the Nunavut land claim. CVC is generally remembered fondly by former students; few, if any, reports of abuse or misconduct exist.[86] Although James Arvaluk, a CVC student who later became a political leader, describes that period of his life as "very interesting for me" and points out that the teachers and supervisors treated students well, he also remembers some of the aspects of attending CVC that were less than ideal: "We couldn't call home because there were no telephones. There were no scheduled flights to our communities, so we never got letters from our parents all year round when we were there ... We had to dress the same. We weren't allowed to use our own clothes."[87]

However, the school played an important role in bringing together Inuit from across the Eastern Arctic and Northern Quebec. CVC was also in operation during a time when civil rights and postcolonial movements across the globe were attracting attention. John Amagoalik credits these events with offering Inuit insight into the struggles of other colonized peoples: "We were inspired by outside forces, by individuals like Martin Luther King Jr., John F. Kennedy, and Pierre Trudeau. We were living through very exciting times. I think that's part of the reason we became a bit bolder in pursuing our rights."[88] Amagoalik goes on to point out that many of the teachers were more open-minded than Qallunaat he had known before: "We had never experienced this sort of attitude before, and it was, in a way, liberating to be with new teachers that treated you as their equal."[89] According to Amagoalik, all of these circumstances at CVC conspired to offer Inuit students the opportunity to envision a different future and the path toward change: "We spent a lot of time discussing how we were going to change the Arctic."[90] Arvaluk concurs that what students learned and talked about in Churchill invested them with an awareness of the future: "They were given a dream to be well educated and to work with the government."[91]

A view on education that can be considered widely representative is accessible through transcripts of discussion at the Coppermine Conference in 1970. Questions and concerns were raised regarding the education of Inuit youth by participants who came from more than twenty communities to a meeting of Inuit representatives that directly preceeded the creation of Inuit Tapirisat of Canada. Their remarks about education centred on parents' dislike of seeing their children travel outside of home communities for vocational training; a desire that hunting and living on the land be included in the curriculum; the conflict between mandatory school attendance and participation in family hunting trips; the potential for loss of language; and parent involvement in schools. These issues were summarized in a resolution calling for action to better ensure that education for Inuit would be meaningful and relevant, which was sent to B.C. Gillie, director of education for the territorial government, and to R.F. Battle, deputy minister of social development in the federal Department of Indian Affairs and Northern Development. Specific requests made in the resolution include: that communities be involved in curriculum content to ensure that Aboriginal history, culture, and skills are included as credit courses; that each community be permitted to decide its own annual school calendar, as vacation in July and August is not preferable; that more schools be provided to keep children in their home communities; that instruction be provided in Aboriginal languages in the primary grades; and, that employment of Aboriginal teachers and aides be expanded.[92]

In 1979 the Inuit Cultural Institute published a special issue of its magazine, *Ajurnarmat,* devoted to the issue of Inuit education.[93] It speaks to parents' feelings about education in the later territorial period. The title article asserts, with respect to the education system, "It has become more and more obvious to everyone in the north, Qallunaat and Inuit alike, that the current system is just not working."[94] The significant points of discrepancy between the education system and Inuit culture highlighted by the article include conflict in basic goals of education, contradictions with Inuit values such as family unity, the gap between the promise of jobs and the reality of completing education, and a neglect to incorporate aspects of Inuit education.

With regard to the first point of discrepancy, the Inuit Cultural Institute article explains that the lifestyle most Inuit pursue does not necessitate education for its own sake and that Inuit have not necessarily fully accepted the wage economy but use it as a way to supplement hunting and living off the land. Therefore, many Inuit parents do not feel it is crucial for their children to finish school: "In the north Inuit feel it is unreasonable to think that all of their children will finish grade twelve and get a job."[95] This observation leads to the second conflict, which relates to the value of family unity, seen to be disregarded by the education system. The article suggests that parents may feel the family can be more successful if one member works while another member hunts, with both continuing to support each other. In other words, the same educational standard need not be applied to every individual. Further, the Inuit Cultural Institute points out that the "Officials" who devised education programs made too many presumptions about Inuit culture, particularly that "Inuit were not supposed to have any idea of what 'education' was about."[96] The examples of such presumptions or failures to understand Inuit culture that are offered by the article are not particularly relevant to fundamentals of education (one example the article raises is the difference in clothing conventions between Qallunaat and Inuit cultures), but the overall point is not lost: "Educators must have the sensitivity to realize that the 'Inuit educational concept' exists. This concept must be respected and recognized if formal education is to be successful in the north."[97]

The article next emphasizes the discrepancy between what Inuit were promised they would get out of school, such as a job as a settlement manager or a job in a professional occupation like teaching or nursing, and the reality of the time involved in achieving that outcome. In particular, the requirement that students attend high school outside of their home communities is a significant parental complaint:

> Inuit parents find that when a child returns, his realities have changed so much that they are discontent with their family and settlement life. They have lost their ability to be comfortable on the land, unsure what their future will be in the settlement, and insecure about their own cultural heritage ... It is not that they don't want their children to have a good education ... it is just that the price in most cases is just too high.[98]

Lastly, and most importantly, the Inuit Cultural Institute argued that Inuit knowledge and ways of education are either not incorporated into the education system at all or are incorporated superficially. Using examples such as studying Inuktitut names for constellations and learning Inuit ways of cooking or storing food, the article highlights topics that should be taught in a manner consistent with Inuit culture so as to achieve a better balance between offering students the best of Qallunaat ways and the best of Inuit ways:

> A northern school should have a curriculum which reflects the basic goals of the local residents and the realities of northern living. This system is not void of

> southern methods and technology. This is also part of the reality of the modern arctic. The two can be incorporated but at a pace and balance which makes sense for the north. Schools must prepare children in the north to be an Inuk living in the north; in their own home community with their family.[99]

As was the case with Born's study, these comments must be regarded as generalizations, not as representations of every individual's feelings toward education. Nonetheless, they offer us insight into Inuit perspectives, further emphasizing the variance between the formal education system introduced by Qallunaat and the Inuit view of their own needs and interests.

By the mid- to late 1970s, the education system in the NWT had expanded significantly, not only to ensure that all children had access to schooling up to grade 9 but also to include adult education and vocational programs. The following statistics from mid-decade paint a picture of the formal system in the territory:

> In the 1974-75 school term, territorial schools enrolled 12,803 children, of whom 4,951 were Eskimo, 1,921 were Indian, and 5,943 were "other." Another 177 were attending universities outside the Territories, 40 were training as teachers in the Northwest Territories, 310 were apprenticing at various points in the Territories, and 147 were in various vocational training programs in the provinces to the south.[100]

Despite these numbers, many students did not stay in the system long enough to complete their high school diploma. Frank Vallee touches on many of the reasons why the formal education system remained ineffective in reaching Inuit and other Aboriginal students:

> A third point has to do with incongruence and its consequences. By incongruence we mean lack of fit between parts of something. In the Arctic situation there are many examples of lack of fit, some of which are listed here: between the goals youngsters are encouraged to entertain and the lack of means to achieve these goals; between role demands from the Kabloona [Qallunaat] system and conflicting demands from the Eskimo one; between one status identity and another that a person is expected to adopt. These and other examples of incongruence arising from the rapid changes discussed earlier are described and analyzed in the literature. Associated with incongruence is the phenomenon of marginality. Personal marginality refers to the condition of belonging partly to one and partly to another group, without being fully engaged in either, and is generally regarded as a condition of considerable strain. Group marginality refers to the position of a whole

> category of persons, a category which is usually in a kind of middleman position between two distinct groups.[101]

The desire to transform the education system into one that affirms the way of life of Aboriginal students is reinforced repeatedly in official documents from this period. However, it is also evident that the Department of Education continued to rely on its own judgment of how and when such efforts should be made in the best interests of the students rather than involving or turning over such decision making to the students themselves, their parents, and their communities. Although the department was successful in opening the minds of its teachers and administrators to the importance of cultural recognition, the reflection of local realities, and the preservation of Aboriginal cultures and languages, most of its efforts still perpetuated a tone of condescension and tokenism. Thus, no matter how forward-thinking the recommendations of the department, the system remained one of a colonial origin that did not significantly empower Inuit and did not allow them to view schooling as a tool for their own ends. References to multiculturalism and bilingualism do not reveal the complexities of cultural negotiation in the classroom, and they do not identify the underlying values and assumptions inherent in the education system that are incompatible with Inuit culture. These documents do little to support changes to the pedagogical and structural barriers that remained in classrooms, firmly rooted in Qallunaat perspectives and approaches to education.

The system of education took great strides toward philosophical and curricular change in a relatively short amount of time. The introduction both of Aboriginal-language programs in the early elementary years and of certified Inuit teachers smoothed the Inuit students' path to formal Qallunaat education. Northern and culturally appropriate classroom materials and activities were encouraged, but these remained largely dependent on the initiative of the teacher and were not consistently applied or supported across the territory. In practice, there were likely fewer changes to the daily classroom experience than the Department of Education would have hoped as a result of the *Red Book* and *Green Book*. As community schools began to offer higher grades and to allow children to attend school in their home community, more Inuit stayed in school longer. But for the most part, Inuit were not graduating from high school, or proceeding to post-secondary education, or even using the education that they did receive to secure employment. The education system fell far short of supporting Inuit in knowing, being, and doing in accordance with their traditions, ancestors, and culture. Nor did it offer them the cultural capital to succeed economically in the Qallunaat way. Read in terms of the path toward self-determination, the story of education in the 1970s reveals a great deal of vision and hope, but it had not yet produced enough practical change. Decision making and control of education remained centrally located in the hands of Qallunaat administrators until the Education Ordinance of 1977 legalized local education authorities. The legislated right to create boards of education that could secure relatively high powers in the hands of Inuit parents and community members created an opportunity to move the formal education system in a new direction. Concurrently, a drive for political autonomy and land claims was growing among Inuit. As the first generation of Inuit educated in the Qallunaat way began to take greater strides toward making their people heard by the territorial and federal governments, the education system increasingly had to answer to parents and communities. By the early 1980s it was clear that Inuit wanted to regain control over the education of their children.

5
Reclaiming the Schools: Inuit Involvement in the Local Period

Today, as twenty years ago, answers to the questions of how much emphasis should be placed on those education programs that contribute to cultural continuity and how much emphasis should be placed on programs that lead to cultural replacement are uncertain. But now when these questions are raised, there is one important difference between the present and twenty years ago: the search to find the best answers is being carried on by the Native peoples themselves, a condition that simply did not exist until recently.

– Frank Darnell, "Education and the Circumpolar Nativistic Movement: Twenty Years of Change for the Better"

Since the school has become one of the fundamental influences in the lives of our children we have to ensure that it contributes effectively to the development of positive values and attitudes which are consistent with our culture.

– Baffin Divisional Board of Education, Our Future Is Now: Directions for Education in the Baffin

The year 1982 marks the beginning of a new chapter in the history of education in the Eastern Arctic, what I refer to as the "local period," so called because the Department of Education committed itself through both policy and practice to the delegation of responsibility to local education authorities. Between 1982 and 1999 three regional boards of education were created and came to facilitate local control over educational decision making in the Eastern Arctic.[1] The first board to be incorporated was the Baffin Divisional Board of Education (BDBE), which became a leader in the integration of Inuit education into school programs. Its initiatives included the enhanced provision of Inuktitut-language instruction in programs, the production of Inuktitut learning materials, increased recruitment and support for Inuit educators, the integration of Inuit culture into the curriculum, the employment of Elders, and most importantly, community and parental involvement in education, which had not existed since the traditional period. This chapter demonstrates that schooling under the BDBE administration best identified, reintroduced, and practised aspects of

Figure 5 Students encouraged to build igloos during an outdoor school activity. Taloyoak, 1974. *Source:* McGregor Collection.

Inuit education. Its greatest remaining challenge was pedagogical reform, or "doing" education as Inuit did, within the confines of formal schooling.

The Baffin region was chosen as the focus of this analysis of local educational decision making partly because the BDBE was the first board to be incorporated, and it took on a leadership role in establishing policy and programs in support of Inuit education from the centre of education in Iqaluit.[2] The Baffin region is also the biggest region of the Eastern Arctic in terms of geography and population. Documentary evidence from the BDBE and the Department of Education,[3] such as curriculum guides and annual reports, is used to inform this examination. Newspaper and magazine articles as well as meeting transcripts represent Inuit perspectives. I have looked specifically for evidence of Inuit articulating the desires and needs that they identify as crucial to an effective education system reflective of their identity and worldview. In terms of secondary sources, I delve into the growing body of academic research on education in Nunavut, including published works and unpublished sources such as masters and doctoral dissertations. These include studies primarily in the field of education, rather than history.

Community Consultations on Education

The education system in the NWT underwent a significant transition after 1982 when the report *Learning, Tradition and Change in the Northwest Territories* was produced by a Special Committee on Education for the Legislative Assembly. The political importance of this work is crucial to consider. The year 1975 marked the first official Legislative Assembly, with no federally appointed members and a majority of Dene, Métis, and Inuit elected representatives.[4] One representative of the Eastern Arctic (Keewatin South), Tagak Curley, also the founding president of Inuit Tapirisat of Canada, spearheaded the committee's work, which began in 1980. *Learning, Tradition and Change* is a landmark report because of the extensive consultations conducted with Inuit and other Aboriginal peoples across the NWT. This was the first time parents were formally consulted on their children's education. Frank Darnell and Anton Hoem point out the linkage between Inuit political mobilization and education demonstrated by this report:

> The awakening of Native activists in the 1960s and 1970s came to fruition in the decade of the 1980s. Curriculum reforms made possible through acquisition of policy-making authority during this period were extraordinary. The resolution in the Legislative Assembly of the Northwest Territories authored by Tagak Curley, an Inuit member of the Northwest Territories Legislative Assembly, that called for a Special Committee on Education, and the Education Act of 1983 that followed the committee's work, were the critical events that gave momentum to the movement.[5]

The "awakening" to which Darnell and Hoem refer was partly a result of the first generation of formally schooled Inuit coming of age only to realize the contradictions of their own position: they were educated enough to communicate well and to expect jobs, but they lacked the political or economic power to effect change in their communities. Curley's involvement in the examination of educational effectiveness through *Learning, Tradition and Change* indicates that Inuit were becoming politically engaged, and one of the first Qallunaat institutions they took on was the school system.[6]

The aims and methods employed by this Special Committee on Education differed greatly from the committee that had responded to the *Survey of Education* in 1973.[7] It was formed largely in response to public concerns about low graduation rates among Aboriginal students. The report cites the following statistics: "In 1980, in a system where over 12,000 students were enrolled, 192 students graduated from territorial high schools. Of this number 91 students qualified to enter university, with 6 Métis, 4 Inuit and 3 Dene students qualifying."[8] This time, the recommendations for improving the education system were to come from students, parents, and community members across the NWT. This consultative and decision-making role was envisioned as occurring not only in support of the Special Committee but also on an ongoing basis. As noted in the previous chapter, the roots of local and community involvement in education can be traced back to the period preceding the Education Ordinance of 1977. The ordinance legitimized the custom, already in practice in some communities, of establishing local education authorities to act in an advisory capacity to school principals or regional superintendents.[9] However, Darnell and Hoem point out the limitations experienced by these groups: "Without an adequate understanding of the political dimension of school governance, such as was provided by the Baffin Region Education Society (later to become the Baffin Divisional Board) in the mid-1980s, the likelihood of sought-after local considerations finding their way into the education system is unlikely."[10]

Rather than perpetuate the consultative role of the local education authorities, the Special Committee sought to enact legislation that would transfer administrative authority and responsibility to regional boards of education. On the board would sit one representative from each community or each district education council – the new name for local education authorities – in that region.[11] The responsibilities acquired by the divisional boards would involve grades K to 10, including programs,[12] language policy, staff recruitment and employment, and other aspects of education. Therefore, the most significant outcome of *Learning, Tradition and Change* was that local involvement in, and responsibility for, education came to be enshrined as the basis of the future school system:

> The Special Committee believes that the agreement between the people of the community and the school system regarding the aims and objectives of education is the crucial variable in the 'success' of the school in the NWT. Where this agreement exists, the school will be able to provide students with the necessary knowledge, skills, and attitudes. Also, parental support encourages both student participation and teacher initiative.[13]

With increased Inuit involvement in government and administrative bodies at the local and territorial levels, the call for, and meaningful practice of, local educational decision making were made possible.

Learning, Tradition and Change indicates that the focus of educational change in the NWT had temporarily shifted away from territory-wide "multiculturalism" and language programs and, for a short time, had even eclipsed concerns such as culturally appropriate curriculum. *Learning, Tradition and Change* says very little about creating a system that reflects traditional education and culture or that meets the needs of Inuit students specifically. Rather, its stated goal is to "transform our classrooms into friendly and comfortable places where well-trained staff can help learners of every age to find out what they need to know."[14] This vision of the schools seems to be under-defined in the context of northern education, particularly in comparison to the work started in the 1970s to increase cultural content and to identify the needs of Inuit learners. However, it is indicative of the growing political voice of Aboriginal groups in the NWT. Presumably the Special Committee felt it was most appropriate to leave the characteristics of successful schools to be decided at the local level. This vision also reflects the committee's difficulty making recommendations that would suit the numerous Aboriginal and non-Aboriginal populations that were becoming more vocal across the NWT. For Inuit, who formed a minority in the territory but a majority in the Eastern Arctic, it made a great deal more sense to demand local control than to carry on negotiating with the Department of Education about meeting their specific cultural and linguistic needs.

The Inuit of the NWT were not breaking new ground with this move toward local control. The James Bay and Northern Quebec Agreement of 1975 had ensured local administration of education for the Inuit of Northern Quebec through their own school board.[15] Scholars of Aboriginal education have explained that this shift was occurring among Aboriginal groups across Canada during the early 1980s:

> The principles of parental responsibility and local control were also prominent in the documents released by Aboriginal organizations [during the 1980s]. In this case, the discourse was centered on the need to transfer decision-making authority over education to the local or community level in order to give parents and communities greater control over the education of their children. These principles were repeatedly supported, and a broad consensus emerged at this early stage of the discourse: it was agreed that greater control for communities and parents would make Indian education more effective.[16]

The timing of this movement in education and in Aboriginal self-determination could not have been better: it coincided exactly with the first generation of educated Inuit leaders who were willing, able, and motivated to represent their people's needs and desires to the Qallunaat. Indeed, by 1987 Inuit were taking opportunities to point out the shortcomings of the school system in an international setting. Circumpolar initiatives to identify common challenges and to share best practices became increasingly common in the 1980s, and Inuit in Canada took a lead role in facilitating circumpolar solidarity. In 1987 Mary Cousins, an Inuk, outlined a proposed agenda for educational change in the Eastern Arctic according to the school system's "severe shortcomings as seen by the Inuit":

- The southern domination of Native education is unacceptable;
- The emphasis on our two official languages (English and French) without recognition of the Inuktitut language is unacceptable;
- The lack of Inuit involvement in and support of the present educational system is a symptom that must be recognized and dealt with;
- Any new and effective educational system must recognize that the Native northern societies have different values than those in the south and that the Native relationship with nature (the land and the animals) is significantly different than the non-Natives'.[17]

As discussed in previous chapters, opinions such as these had been expressed by Qallunaat educators as much as twenty years prior. However, the importance of Cousins' account should not be missed. First, it is unusual in Inuit culture to make such strong criticisms in a public way, indicating that Cousins had decided either that this issue was extremely important or that silence on the part of Inuit had not been effective. Second, that these opinions came directly from an Inuk and were expressed to other Aboriginal populations struggling with the same challenges indicates a new level of empowerment. And third, Cousins expressed these views at a time when Inuit had actually gained enough control over their school system to effect change.

Local Education Authorities

A 1986 article by Geoffrey Sherwood and Knute Sorensen, professors of education at McGill University, in collaboration with Eric Colbourne, then superintendent of schools for the Baffin region, sheds light on the process of moving from a centralized, bureaucratic administration run by educational specialists to one run by community leaders. They also point out that local control of education had become a major concern for First Nations groups across Canada.[18] They tell how, prior to the creation of the BDBE, there was a robust Baffin Regional Education Society (BRES), which had been in operation since 1979 and from which many of the first BDBE members were drawn. In 1984 fifteen BRES members were invited to participate in a training program through McGill

University, which helped them to determine how the school board would be organized and how it would establish policy.[19] Two sessions held in Frobisher Bay and one in Montreal allowed participants to become oriented to the management of a school board and to study the practices of the Kativik School Board in Northern Quebec and two First Nations boards in the Montreal area.[20] This article demonstrates that although the Inuit of the Eastern Arctic were the first in the NWT to gain local control over education, they were participants in a larger movement and benefited from the sharing of best practices and experiences in other Inuit and First Nations communities.

On 14 May 1982 *An Ordinance to Amend the Education Ordinance* was tabled in the Legislative Assembly with the intent to implement many of the recommendations included in *Learning, Tradition and Change.*[21] Reorganization of the administrative structure of the school system into ten education divisions, each to operate under a board of education answering to the local district education councils, was the most significant change included. As a result, the Baffin Divisional Board of Education was incorporated in 1985 as the first board of education outside of the territory's capital city of Yellowknife. It consisted of a chairperson and fifteen members, one representing each community, who met three times a year, and it had an executive committee that met six times a year.[22] Darnell and Hoem refer to this as the "First Inuit-controlled education system to come into existence in the Northwest Territories."[23] The establishment of Inuit control over the school system in the Eastern Arctic is highly significant given the state of Inuit education and Inuit self-determination shortly after the experience of colonization. Inuit used their new-found political voice, which coincided with a movement toward Aboriginal self-government and local control over education in the rest of Canada, to become stewards of their own futures through local educational decision making. Even though a generation of Inuit had been constantly reminded by Arctic administrators that Qallunaat ways are more effective, more important, more profitable, and the key to their future prosperity, Inuit became capable of responding, "That is for us to decide."

However, it is not simply the establishment of local control over education that makes this history important; it is the work that was prioritized and overseen by the Baffin Divisional Board of Education. Over its fifteen years in operation, the BDBE directly produced or supported the production of countless resources, including several hundred books in Inuktitut, teaching units in Inuktitut across many subjects, resource units on northern subjects, and culturally based programming. It continued to work closely with the Teacher Education Program toward the goal of 50 percent of Baffin classrooms having Inuit teachers who could teach in Inuktitut. The BDBE also oversaw the establishment of grades 11 and 12 in every community throughout the region, thus ending the necessity for residential schooling by 1998.

Although many of the BDBE's initiatives and accomplishments relate closely to the integration of aspects of Inuit education into the formal system, it would be impossible to effectively evaluate all of them in this chapter. Therefore, my analysis of the BDBE's impact on formal schooling in the Eastern Arctic focuses on the development of curriculum and on the relationship between the school and community. In 1987 the Baffin Divisional Board of Education produced *Our Future Is Now: Directions for Education in the Baffin,* which recognizes the significant level of change experienced by Inuit and the importance of clarifying the purpose of schooling to meet those changing needs.[24] The BDBE identifies the following roles for schooling: to lay the foundation for lifelong education, to complement the family as a place where the child learns to become an individual and a responsible person; to develop and expand the intellectual capacity of the child; to offer a place where young people can develop an identity; and, to transmit the cultural heritage from one generation to the next. With regard to this last role, the BDBE also states, "Because schools play this fundamental role in cultural transmission and change we must ensure that the school reflects the culture of the child."[25] The document goes on to set specific goals in terms of parental expectations, the purposes of schooling, and so on. Perhaps the most striking aspect of this document in comparison to those that came before are the specific references to Inuit culture, Inuktitut, and the needs of communities and individuals in the Baffin region. This represents a significant departure from the previous compromise necessitated at the territorial level to meet the needs of a multiplicity of cultures and communities.

Curriculum Development by the Baffin Divisional Board of Education

Two curriculum frameworks developed by the BDBE and the Department of Education – *Piniaqtavut* and *Inuuqatigiit* – are particularly important to examine in determining the purpose of education envisioned during this period, and the extent to which that vision was made real through practice in the classroom. In analyzing all available curriculum documents, I kept the following questions in mind: Do the documents indicate an effort to incorporate aspects of Inuit education? Are those aspects employed *because* they reflect Inuit education of the past? Or have these beliefs about education arisen independently, only coincidentally correlating with Inuit education? Did the associated decision making occur at the local level?

In 1989 the BDBE published *Piniaqtavut,* a framework document for grades K to 9 designed to support the development of an integrated program.[26] This analysis covers only *Piniaqtavut,* which preceded work to create a number of teaching units and resources for the program. *Piniaqtavut* was developed in response to *Our Future Is Now* and what the BDBE considered to be "clear direction" from parents in the region that education should centre on topics related to the North, respect for Elders, and maintenance of traditional skills.[27] To achieve this, the *Piniaqtavut* development committee involved a great number of Inuit educators, working bilingually, an important milestone on the path toward Inuit-led curriculum development. This group articulated teachers' growing concerns about the southern perspective embedded in most of the curriculum, the large volume and fast pace of mandatory content, and the lack of resource materials for teaching in Inuktitut.[28] To further determine what knowledge and skills schools should teach according to Inuit, most households in every Baffin community were surveyed.[29] Also in keeping with the practice of local consultation, a draft of the BDBE document was circulated to all of the division's district education councils, and their suggestions for changes were considered.[30] By carrying out processes of consultation like this and referencing them in its publications, the BDBE demonstrated its commitment to local involvement in educational decision making.

The BDBE describes the integrated framework presented in *Piniaqtavut* as providing: "Learning experiences which reflect the cultural and linguistic strength of the Inuit."[31] The three major goals of education to be realized are listed as: bilingual communication skills, pride in cultural identity, and responsibility and independence. The first goal immediately reveals that bilingualism was at the heart of the Inuit vision for education expressed by *Piniaqtavut,* and that it characterized much of the BDBE's work. Joe Enook, then chairperson of the board, described its vision for bilingual education as not merely intended to protect the erosion of Aboriginal languages but also: "Founded on our belief that higher order thinking needs to take place in our mother tongue before it can occur effectively in a second language."[32] *Piniaqtavut* represents the first step by the BDBE to fulfill its commitment to Inuktitut as a language of instruction across subjects and grade levels.

The last goal cited in *Piniaqtavut,* responsibility and independence, echoes the purposes often attributed to traditional Inuit education, but could also be considered culturally generic, and there is no specific indication that it reflects a distinctly Inuit approach. However, the second goal – pride in cultural identity – suggests an effort to accomplish something specific and unique. The narrative in *Piniaqtavut* around future development of education resources establishes the BDBE's interest in reinforcing Inuit values through program development: "Whenever possible, units and supporting resource material will be developed from an Inuit perspective, that is, by Inuit in Inuktitut, and translated into

English so that teachers who do not speak Inuktitut will be able to use the material. Inuit beliefs will permeate every unit so that the values of Inuit culture will be reinforced."[33] Unfortunately, these "values of Inuit culture" are not listed in *Piniaqtavut*. The suggested process of program development sounds ideal in terms of grounding the curriculum in Inuit ways of knowing, being, and doing, but since Inuit values are not identified and described fully, the implications of this process and of the entire program remain unclear.

The lack of specificity offered by the BDBE regarding Inuit values is an unfortunate hindrance that limits the capacity to support relevant classroom practice. The layout of the rest of *Piniaqtavut* only makes this point more damaging. The document begins with a diagram titled "Piniaqtavut Philosophical Base," which includes a large circle in which the words "Sky," "Land," "Community," and "Sea" appear at twelve through nine o'clock, and the following words appear down the middle: "Cultural Identity and Social Customs," "Seasonal," "Past/Present/Future," and "Local/Regional/NWT/Canada/World."[34] None of these words is labelled as an Inuit value or cultural tenet, and it is unclear what part of the program they represent. The layout then proceeds with a diagram page for each grade level (i.e., K to 9) in which a circle, or core, connects four rectangular sections of the page, each labelled with one of the four headings "Sky," "Land," "Community," and "Sea," under each of which are the subheadings of the thematic units.[35] For example, under the heading "Land" at the kindergarten level, the following thematic units are suggested: "Plants – What kind of plants can we find in our community?"; "Winter Play – What kinds of activities take place in our community in the winter?"; and "Animal Babies – what kinds of baby animals are born near where we live?"[36] For each grade level, the thematic units suggested are consistently northern-oriented. The circle, or core, of each diagram between kindergarten and grade 3 is labelled "Experiencing Inuit Beliefs," between grades 4 and 6 "Learning Inuit Beliefs," and between grades 7 and 9 "Living Inuit Beliefs." It still remains unclear what these beliefs are.

Piniaqtavut also advocates particular pedagogical practices in support of this program, such as guidance and facilitation rather than control of student learning by the teacher, encouragement of student-student talk in a collaborative learning context, and a focus on developing higher-level cognitive skills rather than on factual recall.[37] It advocates for student-centred learning, with statements such as, "Students will progress at different rates and acquire different skills at particular times."[38] Lastly, as noted, *Piniaqtavut* is structured around thematic learning in which separate subjects are integrated to provide what the BDBE calls: "A more complete and realistic view of the world than is possible

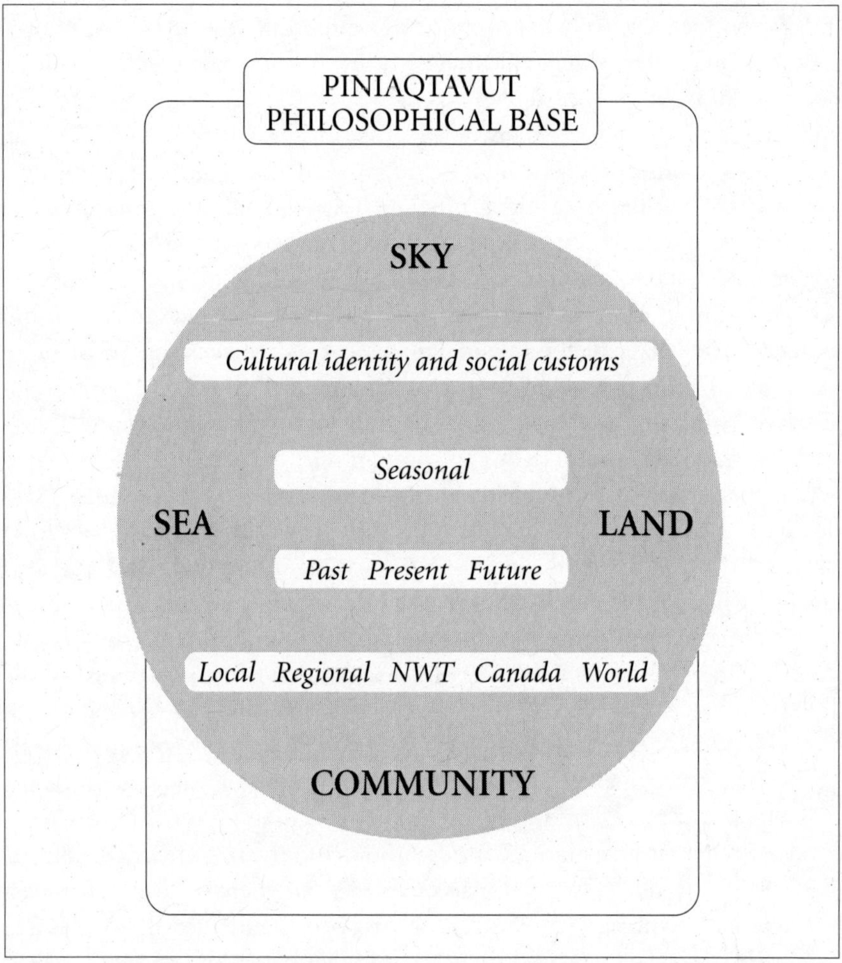

Figure 6 *Piniaqtavut* Philosophical Base. *Source:* Diagram reproduction authorized by Department of Education, Government of Nunavut.

when teaching discrete subject areas."[39] Implementation of the education program set out in *Piniaqtavut* involved a significant in-service training effort to bring the program to teachers and help them become comfortable with it in their classrooms. This process offered the BDBE and educators additional opportunity to address pedagogical approaches:

> Every staff received inservice on the program. The first three months of the school year was commenced with a "traveling road show" of consultants and supervisors who visited every school, or combination of staffs brought to one site. The program

was discussed and staff demonstrated what "themes," "whole language," and "culturally relevant programming" mean in the context of this region.[40]

Piniaqtavut is successful in demonstrating a commitment to the development of programs that are not only northern-oriented but also locally oriented and Inuit-oriented in content. It offers teachers a guide by which to approach subject-integrated teaching and learning, centred on themes that are more reflective of Inuit knowledge (although the document does not refer to the themes as being so). *Piniaqtavut* identifies many of the ingredients that must go into a system of schooling in order for it to achieve culturally appropriate ways of knowing, being, and doing, such as the development of programs by Inuit in Inuktitut, employing teaching methods like hands-on learning, and encouraging a student-centred rather than standard-centred approach to achievement.[41] I cannot fully evaluate to what extent *Piniaqtavut* is successful in offering a model of bilingual education, but the ingredients that it incorporates to make the English programs more relevant, such as a local focus in content, should serve to ease the task of offering equivalent Inuktitut programs. The intention to build a program around a core of Inuit-specific values, rather than around assimilative, multicultural, or universal ways of engaging with the world, indicates the vast difference between the BDBE's approach to formal schooling and what students had experienced previously. The stated intention to involve parents, Elders, and community members in the development of culturally relevant learning experiences reinforces the opportunity for local control. However, the BDBE's oversight in not specifying those Inuit values largely undermines *Piniaqtavut*'s effectiveness, leading me to question how successful it could have been in creating change in the classroom.

The activities of the BDBE were not entirely independent; they continued to be shaped by the Department of Education. The department's 1988 philosophy statement *Education in the NWT* emphasizes the concept of partnership between the principals, the department, education authorities, parents, children, and teachers in facilitating northern education. The document proceeds to lay out the responsibilities of each partner in fulfilling this goal, under five guiding principles:

1 Educational activity should recognize and respect the cultural background, language, and learning styles of each student.
2 Educational activity should reflect the valuable learning experiences available to students in the community and the wider environment.
3 Education should provide opportunities for students to experience success and failure and to develop a positive self-concept.

4 Education should be an interactive process involving students, families, communities, and the school system.
5 Education should provide opportunities for students to develop thinking, problem-solving, and communication skills to help them make sound decisions for themselves and their environment.[42]

By 1991 the Department of Education had translated these principles into a framework for education titled *Our Students, Our Future*. As a result of the entrenchment of meaningful local control through the divisional boards, the department was able to reach beyond its former emphasis on multiculturalism. Rather than striving to avoid cultural specificity, *Our Students, Our Future* places an unprecedented importance on the reinforcement of cultural identity, referring to the vision of the system as "culture-based" schooling:

> In order for schooling to be relevant for students, it should recognize who the learners are and build on the experiences and strengths which they bring with them; it should understand all of their needs, including those which will be required for the world in which they live as adults. Foremost, however, it should reflect their worldview, thus enabling them to make connections between home and school. Schooling, therefore should incorporate and be shaped by the culture of the individual communities, that is, it should be culture-based.[43]

To facilitate culture-based schooling, *Our Students, Our Future* also details the approach to education that the department expected of teachers. Several characteristics of this approach closely reflect aspects of Inuit education that were elusive in the documentation discussed thus far. Under a section titled "The Learning Process," the department advocates a learner-centred focus, experiential (or in-context) learning opportunities, and independent problem solving.[44] For example, the department emphasizes that "interactive learning reinforces important processes, such as communicating and problem solving."[45]

Overall, this framework document responds to the legacy of mission schools, residential schools, and the exclusion of parents from the formal education process for many years, suggesting that as a result of this legacy some parents did not realize the importance of their role in supporting their children through school.[46] It identifies connections with culture, community, and the "traditional roots" of a family's past as critical to the development of a self-determined student. In the introduction to this document, under a section titled "Environment and Culture of the Learner," the Department of Education explains, "Today, young people often find themselves caught between the 'old ways' and the demands of modern society. Their connections with their past and, hence, their sense of identity, are sometimes tenuous; they are often separated from both worldviews."[47] The department reveals itself to be making strides in coming to terms with its past as it recreates its relationship to schools through the lens of partnership. The following analysis of the BDBE offers evidence of this partnership in practice as seen in numerous instances of consultation on education with parents, communities, and Elders.

Inuuqatigiit is the title of a curriculum issued by the Department of Education in 1996 based on collaboration with Inuit groups across the NWT,[48] although the project was initially spearheaded by staff of the Baffin Divisional Board of Education. There are three documents associated with *Inuuqatigiit*. The first, *Inuuqatigiit: The Curriculum from the Inuit Perspective*, lays out the curriculum itself, outlining the objectives, knowledge, and experiences deemed essential to each set of grades (i.e., K to 3, 4 to 6, 7 to 9, and 10 to 12) in fulfilling a curriculum reflective of Inuit culture and values. To determine how *Inuuqatigiit* operated at the regional level, I have examined two BDBE-specific documents. They reflect a multiyear process to link *Inuuqatigiit* with a vision for education in the Baffin region developed at the local level. The first, *Our Future Is Now ... Implementing Inuuqatigiit*, is a long-term plan for education developed to shape the work of the BDBE until the creation of Nunavut in 1999. The second, *Our Future Is Now ... Implementing Inuuqatigiit: Goals, Strategies and Actions 1995-2000*, is a guide to developing a local "work plan" that was provided to schools and community education councils as a more detailed supplement.

The introductory section of *Inuuqatigiit: The Curriculum from the Inuit Perspective* provides a great deal of context for the vision of schooling articulated through *Inuuqatigiit*. This curriculum document unapologetically explains, first, that *Inuuqatigiit* was developed precisely to reinforce the Inuit identity in future generations and, second, that much of this work came about as a solution to the loss of Inuktitut and Inuit ways of knowing, being, and doing: "Traditional beliefs and values are still felt to be important to the communities and the elders would like to see them revived through the schools."[49] The document provides clear evidence of the direct linkages between education and what we now call *Inuit Qaujimajatuqangit*, and the intent to incorporate Inuit traditions into schooling. At least fifty-five Elders and many more Inuit are named in the credits of this document, and it abounds with quotations from those participants.

Prior to setting out the curriculum itself, the document includes a discussion of the goals of education, an orientation to the Inuit values and beliefs, a description of traditional Inuit education, a vision of learning and development, a justification for bilingual education, an approach to pedagogy and evaluation, and the philosophical foundation of the curriculum. Several of these points of context are important to consider in investigating the extent to which this curriculum intentionally revives aspects of Inuit education within the formal school system. The goals of *Inuuqatigiit* as listed, which are derived from "what Inuit say is important for children now and for the future," include:

- maintain, strengthen, recall, and enhance Inuit language and culture in the community and in the school
- enhance unity within Inuit groups
- create a link between the past and present
- encourage the practice of Inuit values and beliefs
- encourage pride in Inuit identity to enhance personal identity.[50]

These goals indicate a desire to reflect Inuit ways of knowing ("enhance Inuit language and culture"), being ("pride in Inuit identity"), and doing ("practice of Inuit values"), which were traditionally achieved through Inuit education. These aspects of Inuit education are all interrelated, and within the curriculum document they are not addressed separately. In keeping with that holistic approach, the following analysis touches on each through a discussion of the entire document.

For the most part, the introductory portion of the document is laid out according to topics such as language or evaluation. Each includes a summary of the traditional approach to, or belief about, that topic, followed by a short recommendation regarding how it may be applicable to the school environment. Following the discussion of the goals of education, there is a brief but informative orientation to the general values and beliefs espoused by Inuit Elders and consequently by this document. Although not listed as such, throughout the narrative the following values appear: respect for ourselves and for others, especially Elders; respect for animals and for the environment; unity of the family and community; caring relationships between family members; sharing and generosity; treating others equally; and, valuing life regardless of obstacles. This general description is followed by an account of the Inuit view of childrearing and parenting, in which the values are extrapolated to establish relevance to the school setting. For example, under the heading "What Are Our Values about Parenting?" the following direction is offered regarding the discipline of children: "Many 'southern' methods of disciplining are not considered appropriate by Inuit and these differences should be understood by teachers."[51] Points such as this indicate awareness of the cultural negotiation that constantly occurs in northern schools, even after a commitment to reflect Inuit culture has been established by educational leaders. *Inuuqatigiit* attempts to inform teachers

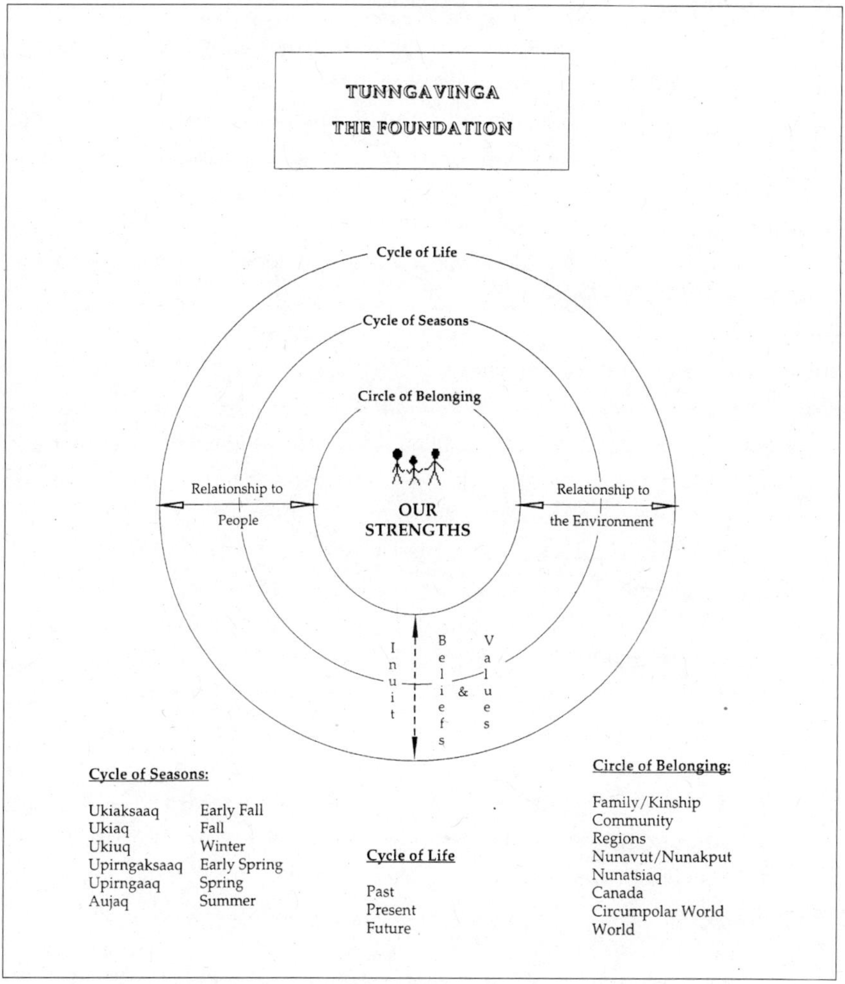

Figure 7 *Innuqatigiit* The Foundation. *Source:* Diagram reproduction authorized by Department of Education, Culture and Employment, Government of Northwest Territories.

about Inuit education and to provide them with the means to adapt it to the modern school setting. Therefore, this curriculum can be considered an effort to cast Inuit ways of knowing, being, and doing into a framework for education, rather than copying them exactly.

The curriculum itself is divided into two sections: "Relationship to People" and "Relationship to the Environment." Each of the topics within these two sections includes a summary according to Inuit and at least one direct quotation from an Elder about the topic. This is followed by a description of what should be accomplished to cover the topic in grades K to 3, 4 to 6, 7 to 9, and 10 to 12. "Relationship to People" includes such topics as "The Family," "Responsibilities of Women," "Traditional Responsibilities of Boys," "Medicine and Healing," and "Laws and Leadership." "Relationship to the Environment" includes "Land," "Water," "Weather and Weather Predicting," "Seals," "Birds," and "Plants." Each of these two sections is also built around a threefold foundation that Inuit have identified as critical to their philosophy: "Cycle of Life," "Cycle of Seasons," and "Circle of Belonging." In the description of the curriculum, or what should be achieved in the classroom, these foundational bases do not play a clear role, but perhaps they serve as a reminder of perspectives from which to approach the material according to Inuit philosophy.

In the summary for each topic, *Inuuqatigiit* offers a rationale for why the topic has been included, the values around the topic, the beliefs held by Inuit, the major understandings expected of children, and the attitudes that should be developed. For example, under the topic of "Whales," some of the values identified are: "The whales have sustained families and camps for generations"; and "The whale was shared with others after a successful hunt."[52] Listed as a belief about whales is: "Never show joy when a water animal is near death, otherwise the animal will come alive and swim away." Major understandings concerning whales include things like: "There are names for different parts of the whale and their internal organs"; "The whalers from the south came to the north because of the bowhead whales"; and "There are specific whale hunting techniques." Finally, the attitudes to be adopted with regard to whales are: "Respect and understand the modern regulations placed on whale hunting"; and "Realize that people are working hard to make sure that whales are not over-hunted."[53]

Following this summary, each topic is broken down by grade set, and as mentioned above, the objectives, knowledge and traditions, as well as key experiences and activities are outlined in point form for each. For grades K to 3, objectives for the study of whales include hearing stories about whales and whale hunting as well as learning the names of whale species that live in the Arctic. By grades 10 to 12, students should be learning about traditional and modern techniques for whale hunting and about the international aspects of modern commercial whaling, including how it affects northern hunting. References to knowledge and traditions relevant to the topic of whales range from "Inuit shared many whaling stories after a successful whale hunt" at the K to 3 level to "The stomach and gullet were used as oil bags" at the highest grade level. Key experiences and activities recommended by *Inuuqatigiit* often involve invitations to community members to address the class. In the case of the topic of whales, this might be an Elder who knows about whales or how to prepare whale meat, or it could be a wildlife officer who knows about the whale populations in the area. For grades 10 to 12, *Inuuqatigiit* recommends encouraging students to participate in a whale hunt or butchering and to report on it to the class. Research topics and class discussions are also suggested.

The curriculum provides teachers, especially Qallunaat and young Inuit teachers, with the background information and broad context necessary to begin developing classroom activities that reflect culturally appropriate content and values. The information offered regarding each topic not only incorporates northern content but also consistently reflects an orientation to Inuit ways of knowing, being, and doing. The following is one of the most concise articulations of the vision of education promoted by *Inuuqatigiit:*

> Instruction must incorporate not only a sensitivity to the Inuit perspective, but actual learning experience in Inuit language and culture. Instruction should always relate subjects to Inuit history, knowledge and experience. Every school, ideally, every classroom, should have elders adding their living wisdom and skills to our children's education. Positive learning can happen whenever there is an educational partnership between the child's family, the community, educators, and the school system.[54]

Here again, the emphasis is on the role of the local community and on an education driven by the local culture and language rather than on an abstract construction of multiculturalism. This is evidence of an intentional effort to revitalize aspects of Inuit education through formal schooling.

In terms of pedagogy, *Inuuqatigiit* repeatedly promotes the use of Inuktitut, the involvement of Elders in the classroom, and the practice of Inuit values. Throughout *Inuuqatigiit* there is an emphasis on flexibility in responding to local community or school needs and wishes. For example, even with reference to the goals of the curriculum, the document stipulates that "individuals in their setting will ultimately identify how best to promote them. Some ideas are written for you as examples, but again, there are many more you and your school can identify."[55] This emphasis demonstrates an ongoing commitment by administrators to local educational decision making. *Inuuqatigiit* also strongly promotes bilingual education and speaks to the importance of sustaining oral tradition through storytelling in the classroom.[56] The use of meaningful, relevant materials is also repeatedly suggested. The descriptions of key activities and experiences that appear throughout the curriculum itself often promote hands-on, or experiential, learning.

The implementation of *Inuuqatigiit* in Baffin schools involved a crucial regional and local component, and this involvement offers an opportunity to determine how Inuit viewed an ideal education system for their children. Although the Baffin Divisional Board of Education participated with the Department of Education in developing *Inuuqatigiit,* it also developed, as noted above, two BDBE-specific implementation documents in anticipation of additional support required by educators in their schools. The basis of the planning for implementation of *Inuuqatigiit* is cited as resulting from local consultations, or "community visioning" meetings, with teachers, principals, district education council members, parents, community members, students, and Elders. These consultations were used "to determine what each school should be teaching and the characteristics of the school that could promote that knowledge."[57] The first resulting document, *Our Future Is Now ... Implementing Inuuqatigiit,* describes the BDBE's beliefs about learning, specifically that it should be community-based, culturally relevant, student-centred, activity-oriented, balanced, integrated, collaborative, and process-oriented. What is significant to note about this list of characteristics is that it closely reflects Inuit education during the traditional period, as described in Chapter 2. Indeed, the high level of local input regarding the implementation of *Inuuqatigiit* contributed to a vision of education that not only reintegrates distinct aspects of Inuit education but also promotes Inuit education as an end in itself. *Implementing Inuuaqtigiit* briefly touches on the explicit desire to recreate an Inuit education using the tools of formal schooling: "*Inuuqatigiit* further articulates the challenge to translate traditional Inuit ways of teaching and learning into the contemporary context of the school."[58]

However, apart from short references to local input in the introduction of both BDBE implementation documents, it is difficult to determine precisely the source behind many of their recommendations. Indeed, unlike the curriculum document, there are few overt linkages between school practice and Inuit tradition. For example, *Implementing Inuuqatigiit* articulates a vision of the "BDBE student" and how he or she should develop in three areas: (1) as individuals; (2) in relation to others; and (3) in terms of the knowledge, skills, and attitudes they need to prepare them as adults in the Arctic, Canada, and the world. It also describes the "BDBE school," which has been envisioned as one that provides shared purpose, partnerships with the community, relevant programs, appropriate learning resources, knowledgeable staff and leaders, and a caring and supportive environment. The second BDBE-specific document, *Our Future Is Now ... Implementing Inuuqatigiit: Goals, Strategies and Actions 1995-2000,* elaborates on each of these goals to identify more detailed activities that each school should practice.[59] The lists for the "BDBE Student" and the "BDBE School" include examples that do correlate with Inuit ways of doing and being, but they are not identified as having that particular origin in the document. Apart from references to northern elements such as hunting and survival skills, it is left to the reader to assume that the recommendations are drawn from a foundation of Inuit culture and community consultations. As pointed out with regard to *Piniaqtavut,* the integrity of the BDBE documents is compromised by the fact that they do not make clear enough the values and beliefs that they are promoting.

Even with the supplement of the implementation documents by the BDBE, the weakness of *Inuuqatigiit* overall lies primarily in the great deal of further work needed to provide teachers with sufficient classroom resources. Because the curriculum provides an overview of the knowledge and skills for every grade set and covers a wide range of topics, it does not provide the level of detail required by teachers, nor does it provide specific teaching tools. The development of resource packages for each topic to support this overview would be necessary to avoid teachers reverting to the southern curriculum, which is likely more familiar to them or covered in more detail. It is also unclear from this document what knowledge and competencies are considered mandatory as part of the curriculum and which topics are more important than others at each level. Lastly, the articulation of the relationship between students and teachers and the ways that teachers can create student-centred learning experiences are underdeveloped in this document. In other words, it does not articulate how an environment is created within the formal school setting that reflects Inuit ways.

Inuuqatigiit offered the closest observation, articulation, and reinforcement of Inuit education found in any document produced for the Eastern Arctic schools by this time. However, as argued by Lynn Aylward, a former employee of the NWT Teacher Education Program and a current educational scholar, a great deal of work remains to be done in terms of implementation:

> This valuing of *Inuit Qaujimajatuqangit* is a necessary first step to what the authors of the curriculum from the Inuit perspective – *Inuuqatigiit* – hoped for when they began its implementation in Nunavut schools in 1996. The Inuuqatigiit authors promoted a sociocultural and sociostructural view of community-based education such that Inuit culture was given status and power in curriculum development ... Efforts to implement the Inuuqatigiit curriculum and reorient Nunavut schooling towards an Inuit worldview and away from bicultural or "both ways" ... schooling are presently part of an ongoing complex negotiation by Nunavut educators.[60]

Educators must successfully adapt aspects of Inuit education to the formal school system without letting the formal system or Qallunaat structures change those ways so much that they lose their meaning. At the same time, they must prepare children to attain a standard level of education at the grade 12 level. Although *Inuuqatigiit* offered a robust effort to facilitate this process, achieving balance remains a significant challenge to educators and administrators.

Schools and Communities

In addition to examining curriculum and programming documents that were initiated by the BDBE, it is important to seek other insights into how Inuit education was incorporated into the formal school system during this period. A consistent effort to bring parents, community members, and Elders into the schools was a high priority undertaken by the BDBE. A sample of the headlines from a 1994 BDBE-published newspaper insert gives an impression of the work being done to directly engage students, parents, and community members in accepting responsibility for Inuit education. All of the following articles in this insert refer to meetings, workshops, or initiatives employed to bring communities and schools closer together:

- "Students Design High Schools for Nunavut"
- "Student Visioning Workshop Looks for Links"
- "Bringing High School Programs to the Communities"
- "Reaching Our Goal: 50 percent Inuit Teachers by the Year 2000"
- "Visioning Meetings in Pangnirtung, Broughton Island, Clyde River and Pond Inlet"
- "What Do You Want Your Children to Learn?"
- "What Should My Child Be Able to Write in Grade One?"
- "What Is Student Support?"[61]

Another initiative undertaken to increase engagement between communities and schools was the employment or involvement of Elders in teaching traditional skills. A total of $1.2 million was spent on the employment of Elders in BDBE schools over a six-year period.[62]

My own experience in school, detailed in the Introduction to this book, illustrates that bringing Inuit Elders into the classroom in relevant and vital ways has remained a challenge for educators. One resource book that is particularly helpful for improving connections between Elders or community members and schools is titled *Working Together – Your Community and Your School.* It was published by the BDBE in 1997 precisely to promote interaction of the schools and their communities. According to its introduction, "This interaction is of primary importance if the school is to reflect the culture and values of the community. This booklet contains a collection of practical activities used in communities and schools to enhance this interaction."[63] The book provides short (one- or two-sentence) ideas or activities that have been carried out by specific schools, all of which are organized around specific themes. For example, under the theme "Elders and Cultural Activities," the following suggestion is made by the two schools in Pangnirtung: "Classes attend meetings in the afternoon at the elders' centre in Pangnirtung. Students take baking they have prepared. String games and story telling take place. Museum objects are discussed, as are historic photographs."[64] Some schools have expanded their programs regarding a particular topic and thus include greater detail. Other themes around which ideas are arranged include "On the Land," "Community Resources," "Seasonal Activities and Special Events," "Getting the News Out," "Assemblies," "Theme and Class Celebrations," "The Community and the High School," "Literacy," and "Fundraising." This fifty-four-page booklet, which includes a number of pictures of school-community events from around the region, is an extremely useful resource. Its strength lies not only in the number of practical activities suggested but also in creating connections between schools across the region, sharing news about what is being done to realize the same goals in various locations known to the readers.

Although it happens less frequently, taking children out of the classroom to experience traditional education, in the environment in which it was designed to take place, often proves more successful than classroom instruction. Educational initiatives outside the classroom are usually referred to as "land programs" or "land trips." Such programs have occurred on a variable basis in different communities, largely depending on the initiative of local teachers and community members. For example, Caleb Apak of Igloolik was interviewed in 1981 about the land program he ran for school children. Although this example comes from the years prior to the BDBE, it reveals the accomplishments of some individuals and individual communities in providing students with experiences that approximate Inuit education. Apak explains that he taught both in and out of the school, taking children out on the land on a rotating basis. His role was to introduce them to hunting and survival skills, some for the first time, and he did so in accordance with the way parents traditionally taught their children: "The technique I use is almost the same as what our parents used to use. Now-a-days we parents no longer educate our children in the traditional way. While we are out camping, I use the traditional method of teaching the children. We sleep in igloos lit with Inuit stone lamps, for instance."[65] When asked about his goal or purpose in becoming a land skills teacher, Apak explained,

> We have been concerned about the lack of traditional Inuit educators for many years now. The climate in the North is not going to get any warmer. It will always get cold during the winter season. We are now hearing more and more about young people dying while they are out on the land and in different places in the North. This is due to their lack of knowledge of survival skills out-of-doors. This was our main concern.[66]

During the BDBE years, local initiatives such as this were documented and turned into units with resources, objectives, and outcomes that were circulated throughout the region to support teachers in carrying out land programs. For example, the BDBE issued modules on traditional skills that could be used for credit at the high school level under the umbrella of the Alberta curriculum's course in career and technology studies.[67] Land programs could be considered an integrated learning opportunity that would cover many subjects and concurrently facilitate an approximation of Inuit education.

What remains is to determine the views of students concerning the delivery of Inuit educational experiences such as land programs. The views and experiences of students participating in the school system have proven difficult to capture throughout this investigation, but one key study provides insight into this very question. In the late 1990s Alexander Tufts, a Qallunaat teacher who has worked in the Eastern Arctic for many years, studied the perceptions of Inuit students regarding the relationship between their culture and high school science. His findings provide invaluable evidence of the barriers to cohesive integration of Inuit education into the formal school system, particularly at the high school level.

Tufts tells the story of taking a group of students in grades 9 to 12 on a "land trip" by snowmobile and *qamutiik*[68] during which an Inuit hunter who accompanied them caught a beluga whale. Tufts notes that this was, for a number of his Inuit students, the first time they had seen a beluga. He describes the way the hunter explained many things about the whale to the students while he was butchering it, conveying traditional knowledge. There was conversation about the pregnant whale's fetus, speculation about the reason for one of its deformed fins, and ongoing enthusiastic conversations in Inuktitut between the students and hunter (in which Tufts largely could not participate). He then tells of how the students brought the beluga fetus back to the high school, showed it to fellow students, dissected it, and continued to study both traditional and modern knowledge associated with its biology. Tufts says, "I had never witnessed such student enthusiasm and interest in science. These experiences demonstrated the effectiveness for Inuit learners of active participation, student-initiated exploration of culturally relevant material and subject matter, and student-teacher collaborations in science education."[69] However, this enthusiasm, participation, and integration of traditional educational experiences are not standard in science education in the Eastern Arctic. Tufts notes that "most of our students spend most of their science periods at school reading and writing at their desks by themselves or listening to lectures. There are dismally few Inuit students enrolled in academic, college preparatory science courses."[70] Tufts attributes the ineffectiveness of science education to a number of factors, including the significantly different worldview possessed by Inuit, and Aboriginal peoples in general, in comparison to that of the Qallunaat, on which the science curriculum is based. Another factor is the historical neglect of Inuit traditional knowledge and skills in the formal school system. He says that acknowledgment of these shortfalls in the late 1980s and early 1990s led to some efforts at mitigation, such as land trips.[71]

This particular land trip inspired Tufts to determine and highlight the views of Inuit students in terms of developing culturally appropriate science education. To this end, he conducted several talking circles with grade 12 students and recent graduates in one community. He asked them to express their perceptions of the connections, or lack thereof, between Inuit culture and science education as they experienced it in school. Their responses reveal a gulf between schooling and culture, which the students themselves feel they must bridge with little support from their teachers: "All the graduates reported that they did not feel their school science reflected their culture to any measurable extent. Yet, despite this claim, the graduates spoke of being able to make connections between their culture and Western science, but they maintained that this ability was something they developed and not the result of teacher or other assistance."[72] The following list is a summary of Tufts's findings about the perspectives of students and recent graduates:

- Capturing traditional Inuit knowledge through observation skills, hands-on activities, and oral history all played a role in their learning at home or prior to entering school.
- School science seldom deals with "real things" and activities but with drawings and pictures, which makes it more difficult to understand.
- They recognize that science and technology were practised by their ancestors in pursuit of survival, but it was not referred to or thought of as science.
- Schools should acknowledge the validity of Inuit "science" or traditional knowledge, not merely as an alternative to Western science but also as the basis for science education.

- Some students who had taken an archeological field trip during high school felt it was their "most meaningful school science experience."[73]

Revealed here is a vision for greater recognition of *Inuit Qaujimajatuqangit* by school science and teachers, as well as greater opportunities for students to bring their knowledge and experience from home into the classroom. It also shows a strong preference for experiential and in-context learning. Tufts points out that the recent graduates all felt strongly that Inuit science should be integrated with Qallunaat science so that students can have the best overall understanding. Tufts says they also understood the barriers to fully realizing Inuit science in the classroom, which can be summarized as follows: traditional Inuit science was not taught in a structured or formal way; experience, which often cannot be gained in the classroom, is essential; traditional Inuit science involves values and beliefs that most Qallunaat teachers do not accept or hold themselves; and, most science teachers do not have experience in traditional Inuit science. In his conclusion, Tufts agrees with the students that Inuit science should form part of the curriculum for high school students but that it cannot and should not be integrated with Qallunaat science because the content and method largely cannot be accommodated by the formal school system as it stands. He argues: "As the graduates in this study noted, many aspects of Inuit science could not and should not be taught within a school setting. Bringing culture into the school under non-Inuit control and in a non-Inuit context trivializes and devalues Inuit culture."[74] This study reveals the lasting discontinuities between two systems of knowing and doing that continue to be experienced by Inuit students. Even when increased local control and unprecedented cultural integration were being realized, opportunities to practise Inuit education according to its traditional methodology were exceptional, despite the success of such practice in engaging students.

Examining the views of Inuit educators may serve to complement the perspective of students in this evaluation of the local period of educational administration in the Eastern Arctic. Did Inuit teachers see themselves fulfilling the vision of education espoused by the BDBE? Unfortunately, I have found few documentary sources that can provide answers to this question. However, there are two sources that provide insight into the views of educators; one represents the early years of the BDBE, and the other offers a retrospective on the overall impact of the BDBE.

In June 1987 the Steering Committee for the International Cross-Cultural Education Seminar Series held a conference in Iqaluit. The theme of the conference was "Inuit Control of Inuit Education," and it offered Inuit educators the opportunity to raise concerns or highlight goals for the school system in a context external to the BDBE. The report of the proceedings of this conference includes extensive quotations and excerpts by Inuit participants. Discussion during the conference indicates that although Inuit had accomplished some of their major goals – Inuit teachers in the classroom, local control of educational decision making, and administrative support for the integration of aspects of traditional education – they felt subtle differences between Qallunaat and Inuit approaches to education were becoming more evident. Meeka Arnakaq explains the extent to which, even with increasing numbers of Inuit teachers taking over classrooms, traditional knowledge, values, and methods were still underused and undervalued:

> In observing their [new Inuit teachers'] classrooms, I do not see the promotion or the emphasis of Inuit culture. I wonder if it is possible for the teachers to have older Inuit or elders, the experts in providing the knowledge of Inuktitut and Inuit ways, to assist them in their classrooms. We are not using our Inuit people as resources. For example, we hear people saying that Inuit elders do not teach us any more about our culture and that is why we are forgetting our ways. But the fact is, time and time again, the elders bring up questions and issues, concerns and solutions. The answer that they get from the school is always, "Well, we have policies that we have to abide by." Because of such policies, the elders are prevented from the opportunity to participate in the school programs. This obstacle to elders' participation and involvement restricts our ability to make improvements in the senior Inuktitut programming.[75]

Another Inuit educator, David Serkoak, also highlighted challenges to incorporating subjects and activities into the formal school environment by an Elder or traditional specialist: "Often the instructors, who have much cultural knowledge and expertise to share, feel incompetent and ineffective in the school setting. They lack adequate training in teaching methodology and classroom management. In many cases they are provided with a skeletal guideline instead of a curriculum developed with proper scope and sequence."[76] The difficulty of compromise between meeting Qallunaat standards of schooling and integrating Inuit approaches to education is valid and important. However, Serkoak's suggestion that Elders be provided with a curriculum may not be a culturally appropriate solution to the conundrum of their lack of experience with classroom management. Rather, rotating the class to work with the Elder in small groups, as opposed to the entire class of twenty students, could offer a more effective context that is also a closer approximation of the Inuit approach to education.

These comments reveal that characteristics of the pedagogy and practice of Inuit education remained a significant barrier to the school system's ability to respond to the needs of Inuit.

The second document of note concerning the views of educators details the initial stages of a study, undertaken in Iqaluit in 2005, to collect best practices in education as carried out during the administration of schools by the BDBE. Fiona O'Donoghue, Joanne Tompkins, and Sandy McAuley, all former northern teachers or educational administrators who have become university professors, collaborated with Lena Metuq, a principal in Pangnirtung, and with Nunia Qanatsiaq of the Nunavut Department of Education in Arviat, supported by Elizabeth Fortes, to interview six experienced Inuit educators (referred to as "educational leaders") and some non-Inuit administrators. Their goal was to: "Investigate the possibilities for establishing a long-term research agenda to document best practices in Inuit education in the Qikiqtani Region from 1980-1999."[77] Titled *Pursuing a Dream,* this study's focus is primarily on the impact of colonial power relationships and, conversely, on the decolonizing practices that enabled Inuit education to change. Its conclusions also offer several general insights into the work of the BDBE.

The initial stage of the study collected a number of direct quotations, such as the following, that reveal positive perceptions by Inuit regarding their experience working under the administration of the BDBE:

> When it was the BDBE we looked at kids and how they grew and what's the meaning of going into a classroom with second language learners, what's their culture, what's important to the parents ... all these were being taught ... were goals of what we wanted to achieve in education.[78]

> And they were willing to listen to what was important to us ... When I went to BDBE I think it was the first consultation for Our Future is Now ... I was told to speak what was important for me. I never had felt that before. Like in school our principal said "do this," "do that," and then I went to BDBE and was told "what's important to you" ... "what's important for your children"? I felt empowered.[79]

The authors also collected examples of BDBE initiatives identified by Inuit educators that "provided opportunities for their leadership to develop and evolve in ways that were contextualized and meaningful,"[80] such as courses offered by the Teacher Education Program, the development of the documents *Piniaqtavut* and *Inuuqatigiit,* writing and illustrating Inuktitut books, and teaching that is culturally based and draws on traditional Inuit knowledge. Another comment by an Inuit participant regarding these initiatives reiterates positive memories of this period: "[We] had a common goal that everyone was trying to reach and being an Inuk was valued ... being able to speak Inuktitut was valued ... being able to teach in Inuktitut was valued ... that's one of the high points ... and a lot of the workshops were done by Inuit. People at the session were [all] Inuit."[81] *Pursuing a Dream* identifies two other factors of particular note in supporting Inuit education in the formal school system. The first is the role of Elders in schools and in educational decision making, the importance of which is so strongly emphasized in the *Inuuqatigiit* curriculum. Elder involvement continued to be seen in 2005 as a key to the revitalization of Inuit education. The second factor is that Nunavut-wide initiatives became the norm in the post-1999 period of educational administration under the Government of Nunavut. Nevertheless, *Pursuing a Dream* also advocates for the return to an emphasis on regional initiatives as a more effective approach to programs and policy:

> While Nunavut-wide shared philosophy is vital, the researchers believe that the process of revitalization also needs to take place within each region, as the respective histories and challenges differ. The strength of each region needs to be encouraged. Complex, expensive, Nunavut-wide initiatives take a great deal of time to organize and complete. In any successful change process, the energy of those who share local or regional goals is crucial. The costs of bringing groups together on a Nunavut-wide level may have prevented some creative developmental processes from taking place and loss of institutional memory is also a factor.[82]

Although this study is brief and preliminary, it suggests that Inuit educators were offered unprecedented and largely successful opportunities during the administration of the BDBE to participate in educational initiatives and decision making. It suggests that Inuit educators felt empowered by local control and the commitment to Inuit culture and language in classrooms.

The evidence thus far has indicated that the BDBE created a system that was more successful at incorporating aspects of Inuit education. How can we determine whether these efforts made the system more successful in producing graduates and directly led to employment? One indicator of educational success is graduation rates, which steadily rose throughout the tenure of the BDBE. In 1984-85 there were 14 graduates (with 2,663 students enrolled), 1988-89 showed an impressive increase to 34 graduates (out of 2,999 students), and then rates levelled out at around 22 students per year, until 1993-94, when 48 students graduated (out of 3,454).[83] In other words, in 1993-94 the BDBE doubled the 1984-85 graduation rate. The school year 1994-95 saw a drop to 24 graduates, but in 1996-97 the graduation rate rose again to 41.[84] It is difficult to determine

Figure 8 Example of student's language arts work, depicting her life. Eastern Arctic, early 1980s. *Source:* McGregor Collection.

direct causes for the increase in graduation rates during the BDBE's administration. However, one important factor is the access to all secondary grades in each community across the Eastern Arctic. Although the form of residential schooling offered to students in grades 10 to 12 in the 1980s and 1990s may have been less difficult than the residential system of the 1950s and 1960s, leaving home to live in a hostel in Iqaluit was a significant deterrent for many students. Only Iqaluit and one other community in the Baffin region offered secondary programs in 1982-83, but by 1990-91 the number had grown to eight (although some of those offered courses only up to grade 10 or 11).[85] Access to grade 12 in each community (except Apex, which is situated within a few kilometres of Iqaluit), was finally achieved by the BDBE in 1997-98.[86]

Despite improvement in Inuit education during the tenure of the BDBE, graduation rates were a challenge for the formal school system under the Government of the Northwest Territories throughout its history in the Eastern Arctic, and under the Government of Nunavut they are still dismally low in comparison to most Canadian jurisdictions.[87] In very brief terms, this challenge is primarily a result of two discrepancies. The first discrepancy exists between the daily experience of schooling, which may be designed to accommodate local and cultural needs through a northern-developed curriculum, and the expectations of standardized high school leaving exams originating from the Alberta curriculum.[88] This discrepancy is an ironic by-product of the integration of Inuit education into the formal school system; despite bringing students closer to their culture and identity, these efforts often take them further away from southern standards, which must still be met for them to graduate. Although her comments are set in the context of post-1999 Nunavut, Lynn Aylward speaks to the same complex issue for curriculum developers and educators at the secondary level:

> Based on some of the policy positions of the Government of Nunavut and the opinions of the secondary educators ... curricular and policy changes that consider cultural relevance may only be acceptable within Nunavut education if they translate into equivalencies judged to meet southern Canadian educational institutions definitions of academic excellence. Immediately, one has to wonder how different or culturally relevant the Nunavut education experience can be while intertwined with these discursive formations of standardization and homogenization.[89]

Unfortunately, there are examples of Inuit students who have chosen and have been supported to stay in school through the secondary grades, only to be disappointed by failing marks on their leaving exams.[90]

The second discrepancy exists between the students' perceived benefits of staying in school with the intent to get a "better" job at graduation and the actual availability of those jobs or the extent to which they are experienced as "better" by those students. In other words, the preparation for the establishment of the Nunavut government did create many new jobs across the territory, and a priority hiring policy favoured Inuit applicants. However, even with the increase in the number of jobs available, there was little increase in the types of jobs available.

The Creation of Nunavut

Just when access to the high school grades was secured across the Eastern Arctic and the curriculum from the Inuit perspective, *Inuuqatigiit,* was being implemented in classrooms, the momentum of educational change toward local control and the growing expertise of the BDBE were interrupted by the creation of Nunavut Territory on 1 April 1999. Soon afterward, the new Government of Nunavut Cabinet voted to dissolve the boards of education entirely. This dissolution came partly as a result of the reports *Footprints in New Snow 1* and *Footprints in New Snow 2,* published in 1995 and 1996 respectively by the Nunavut Implementation Commission. These reports include extensive recommendations to the federal Department of Indian Affairs and Northern Development, the Government of the Northwest Territories, and Nunavut Tunngavik Incorporated with regard to the establishment of the Nunavut government. *Footprints 1* raises a number of concerns both about the regional boards of education and about the boards of health and social services. The report notes that there is a lack of direct accountability comparable to elected officials, that development and effective delivery of programs and services had become complicated and time-consuming, that boards and agencies detract from the priority attached to programs and services being delivered at the community level, and that these bodies compete for funding that could be devoted to the delivery of programs and services.[91] *Footprints 1* articulates a new vision for administration of education – indeed, for public administration in general – that trumps the justification for regional representative bodies altogether:

> The key point is that education and health boards were established essentially in response to the early physical, social and political distance of GNWT [Government of the Northwest Territories] headquarters from Nunavut, and the manner in which they developed over the years was very much a function of pre-Nunavut political realities ... Nunavut will be a more homogenous society than the existing NWT. There will be a higher number of members in the Nunavut Legislative Assembly to represent the people of Nunavut than there are representatives from Nunavut in the current NWT Legislative Assembly in Yellowknife.[92]

The report also points to concerns about fiscal circumstances in the context of a new government and about the potential for overlapping, or "extra," management structures that may not be necessary. They argued that "sustaining the status quo is not, in itself, a convincing reason."[93]

The *Footprints* reports do, however, make the recommendation that the new government should maintain one territory-wide board of education. This board would include ten to twelve representatives elected directly from the territorial constituencies and would have a diminished mandate related to territory-wide policy and programming: "It would emphasize the common features of education and health policy issues affecting Nunavut as a whole, while allowing regional variations at the delivery level; it would preserve the long-standing tradition in Canada that parents and other electors have a direct say in the running of the schools."[94]

The Government of Nunavut did not accept the recommendations of the *Footprints* reports. Rather than amalgamate the boards into one territory-wide board of education, the new government decided that the boards should be dissolved altogether and that all programs and services should be transferred to the Nunavut Department of Education.[95] This decision was in accordance with the recommendation of a third-party consultation commissioned by the government in 1999, which reported that the accountability and cost-saving efficiency of having no boards outweighed the responsiveness to people's needs that could be accomplished with one territorial board.[96] These two explanations are publicized in the news release for this decision, which emphasizes that greater accountability can be achieved by investing Nunavut's elected officials with the responsibility for program and service delivery and that a savings of $4 million can be expected annually.[97] The "backgrounder" accompanying the news release refers to the concerns raised by the *Footprints* reports, notably "that the large number of regional boards across Nunavut promotes regionalism and lack of accountability" and that the boards may no longer be valid in the new political climate of Nunavut: "The boards were originally created to give the residents of the Eastern Arctic a voice in the Government of the Northwest Territories. With Nunavut, that concern no longer exists."[98] The backgrounder does not refer at all to the *Footprints* reports' recommendation for a territory-wide board.

The consultation on which the government based its decision applied the same criteria to the boards of health and social services as it did to the boards of education. Although it is impossible to speculate about what might have happened if each sector had been evaluated separately, it is important to note that the perspective of decision makers was shaped by the existence of six or more various boards in both sectors. The merit or accomplishments of the boards of education, and the precedent of educational control to which Inuit had become accustomed, may easily have been lost in the bird's eye view that this report demonstrates. Indeed, in the "Executive Summary" of the report recommending dissolution of the boards, there is no reference to sector-specific concerns or distinctly educational issues.

How did the BDBE and the general public respond to the board's dissolution? The board itself demonstrated resistance; the formal vote held on the dissolution was the first in at least eight years that was not unanimous.[99] However, some particularly powerful district education councils felt that dissolution was a positive change because it would allow them to communicate directly with the Nunavut Department of Education rather than through a divisional board that might sideline or diminish individual community needs. For example, the head of the District Education Authority (DEA) in Iqaluit, John Thomas, led an ongoing objection to the BDBE for not being responsive enough to needs in his community. In *Nunatsiaq News* Thomas refers to the board reform in preparation for Nunavut, expressing his support for reigning in the three divisional boards:

> Thomas likes the idea of having a single school board for the new territory, but he likes the thought of abolishing school boards altogether even more. "If you pump six million dollars a year into boards can't you cut that out and let the DEA in that community do all the work? For years and years we have talked about community empowerment. Let's see it realized."[100]

In the same article, John Maurice, a long-serving teacher, echoes Thomas' sentiments, stating his desire to see the DEAs invested with greater powers in the absence of school boards: "'Many of the DEAs are so politically active that they could take on the job of the boards,' Maurice said. 'The Iqaluit DEA is so proactive and organized that it is triplicating some services that the board and the department offers.'"[101] On the other hand, according to the assistant director of the BDBE, for communities that may not have such a strong voice, the advocacy offered by the BDBE played an important role. The article reports, "Lorne Levy, the assistant director at the Baffin Divisional Board of Education thinks that eliminating regional boards would be a terrific loss, especially for small Nunavut communities."[102] There is no doubt that the perspective of the Iqaluit District Education Authority usually differs from that of other communities due to its large size, multiple schools serving a more diverse community, and greater pool of active parents that form their constituents. Ultimately, it mattered little what BDBE employees or district council members felt was best. Much was expected to change in the political context of Nunavut, and the new vision of a territory where Inuit could establish consistent cultural policies outweighed priorities at the local level.

Integration of aspects of Inuit education into the formal school system was shown to be possible and to have some positive outcomes during the local period. Such work was particularly dependent on the condition of local parental or community control. During the local period, the district education councils that made up the BDBE provided a mechanism for Inuit teachers, parents, and community members outside of the school to become involved in educational decision making and to increase school-community linkages. Therefore, as a result of the policy responsibilities of the BDBE itself, as well as its ongoing work to sustain local control over education, Inuit became empowered to envision and effect educational change. The history of the BDBE, which includes several joint projects with the Keewatin and Kitikmeot boards, indicates that major initiatives were undertaken to reverse the assimilative direction of the school system that had characterized the colonial period. In turn, the school system became one that not only includes, but is also grounded in, Inuktitut and Inuit culture, identity, and ways of doing. The BDBE led the way both in providing bilingual education and in developing curriculum content consistent with northern and Inuit perspectives. In doing so, it was discovered that a great deal of negotiation was necessary to approximate the traditional aspects of Inuit education in the environment of a formal school system. In some cases, students were taken outside of the physical and structural confines of the school to experience Inuit education, and this proved both memorable and effective in engaging students, particularly in the subject of science.

Incorporating the methodology of Inuit education, which is experientially based, student-centred, and dependent on close relationships between teachers and students, was identified as a goal for the school system under the BDBE, but the extent to which this methodology was consistently employed is most difficult to establish. Indeed, the implementation and success of *Inuuqatigiit* – published in 1996 – in supporting change is difficult to evaluate because by 1999 Nunavut had chosen a new course of action for the administration of its school system. One significant and identifiable barrier to the success of the integration of Inuit education into formal schooling was the necessity of meeting the standards for graduation under the Alberta curriculum. The mandatory requirements for successfully completing one's education in the Eastern Arctic were never brought into alignment with the goals and priorities of education practised in classrooms on a daily basis. Therefore, despite the expansion of access to the senior grades, graduation levels remained low. Great strides were made during the tenure of the BDBE, to the extent that it should be recognized as the period in which the school system was most successful in integrating Inuit education. However, much work remained, and as the conclusion will demonstrate, the approach to education taken by the Government of Nunavut not only differed but also substantially interrupted the momentum of change supported during the local period.

Conclusion: The Integration of Inuit Education and Schools in Nunavut

If you have education you can do something. Our ideas were needed at that time, your ideas are needed today.

– Tagak Curley, former land claim negotiator, *Staking the Claim: Dreams, Democracy and Canadian Inuit*

Learning about your past, you build pride. Being proud of your past, you gain faith. Without faith, there is no hope. And without hope, there is nothing.

– P.J. Akeeagok, *Staking the Claim: Dreams, Democracy and Canadian Inuit*

This book endeavours to examine education within the Inuit families and communities of the Eastern Arctic during the twentieth century. In the early decades, during the traditional period, education occurred much as it had within hunter-gatherer societies in the Arctic for centuries. Education was integrated into the daily lives, daily responsibilities, and daily relationships of families. It was focused largely on preparing children for their future by providing them with the traditional Inuit knowledge and skills necessary to procure food, make tools, and sew clothes. Education was part of perpetuating the relationship between the environment, or *sila,* and the generations of Inuit – both past and future – to whom each person was connected. However, education was also shaped by the person who took it on themselves to act as teacher, the local particularities of the environment, and the special abilities and interests that each child demonstrated. This approach to education resulted in a competency, worldview, and knowledge base that have been distinguished as comprising traditional knowledge, *Inuit Qaujimajatuqangit,* and Inuit education. In the interest of simplifying a comparison with other approaches to education, Chapter 2 has identified the most critical aspects of Inuit education: environmental knowledge, experiential learning, caring between teacher and learner, and local control.

Colonization at mid-century, which occurred quickly and involved drastic change, devalued and dismissed the approaches and outcomes of Inuit education. During the colonial period, when Inuit were politically, socially, and economically paralyzed in their increasingly interventionist encounters with Qallunaat, it was believed by Qallunaat, and by many Inuit, that the future of Inuit children could be best secured if they learned to act, think, and do in the Qallunaat manner. The introduction of formal schooling by the federal government meant removing children from their homes, disrupting their relationships with family members, and teaching them that Inuit language, knowledge, and ways of doing belonged to the past and were dying out. In other words, none of the aspects of Inuit education were employed by the school system; it was an assimilationist system controlled by unknown Qallunaat far away in Ottawa. However, even though the timing of colonization in the Eastern Arctic left Inuit extremely vulnerable, it also offered them an opportunity. Approximately only twenty years – fewer for some – passed between the time of their permanent settlement and the beginning of their political mobilization toward self-determination, and their education in the meantime became an advantage in that pursuit. This was due partly to the changing beliefs of the colonizers. Many Qallunaat in the Arctic, and across the country, no longer viewed assimilation as an appropriate purpose for education and instead turned their eyes toward cultural protection.

The first major step toward reinventing the formal school system as one that could respond appropriately to the contingencies of life in the Eastern Arctic was the transfer of administrative responsibility to the NWT in 1970. The territorial period also marks the beginning of reintegration of aspects of Inuit education, such as the recognition and use of Inuktitut, the employment of Inuit in classrooms, and the development of a curriculum that would include culturally appropriate content. Knowing and doing as an Inuk were becoming acceptable again, but a great deal of compromise and negotiation were still necessary to navigate the two worlds of Qallunaat and Inuit in these small communities. The initiatives of the early territorial school system may appear superficial insofar as aspects of Inuit education were employed not necessarily *because* they reflected Inuit education but rather because they made the classroom more familiar to Inuit students. Change was still envisioned, driven, and carried out by Qallunaat according to their ideas of what was best for Inuit. Nonetheless, in comparison to the assimilationist federal system, this level of educational change was highly significant. Even more important, it was during the territorial period that Inuit began to be included in educational decision making.

The local period in the history of education in the Eastern Arctic is so named because control of education was returned to Inuit parents, community members, and students. Through legislation, the Government of the Northwest Territories established local education authorities with significant responsibilities, and in

1982 those local authorities were organized to form regional boards of education. The combination of parental and community control over local schools and representation of communities at the regional level to enable their participation in curriculum and programming offered Inuit the opportunity to envision their own system of education once more. In doing so, they largely chose to identify and reintegrate the most important aspects of Inuit education, such as traditional environmental knowledge, experiential learning opportunities, and Elders as teachers. Inuit and Qallunaat educators worked together with communities to develop a curriculum within a framework of Inuit values. The structural constraints of a formal education system, particularly the expectation that students meet national standards, remained. This mechanism of evaluation ultimately dictated student "success" or "failure" without regard for ideal goals that may have been chosen by Inuit, and it brought with it a great deal of ambiguity. However, Inuit responded to such challenges by discovering compromises that better matched their regional and local particularities.

The local period, examined in Chapter 5 through a study of the Baffin Divisional Board of Education, represents the closest realization of Inuit education within the formal school system in the Eastern Arctic. That this period came to an end with the creation of Nunavut Territory in 1999 is both a historical fact and an argument: not only did political reorganization of the Canadian Arctic redirect the history of Inuit education, but local and regional administration of education was also significantly diminished under the new public government. The creation of Nunavut was intended, and expected, to increase the level of Inuit control over their future. In terms of education, however, the changes introduced resulted in centralized power and diminished local and regional capacity.

Examining Tradition and Education

The story told in this book can be viewed as the story of a tradition, namely the Inuit tradition of education, and how it was affected by the continuity and change experienced by Inuit society during the twentieth century. This focus calls into question the definition of "tradition" as a theoretical concept, the way that it operates both in society and in the discipline of history, and the relationship between its theoretical definition and its expression in this specific historical context. I did not initiate this study with the goal of revealing the ways that the history of the Eastern Arctic can or cannot be said to reinforce theoretical frameworks such as are associated with the concepts of tradition and authenticity. I had trepidations about imposing a theoretical discourse (steeped in the culture of Qallunaat academia) on a historical account that is intended to draw out the Inuit perspective. However, I recognize that historiographic and theoretical discourse represents an important means of communication between historians and between histories. At the best of times, theoretical analysis has the capacity to bring seemingly disparate historical experiences closer through comparison and to organize them into maps that help us to find our way as a community of scholars. Therefore, the following comments from scholars regarding tradition and authenticity, which form one theoretical context in which to consider the preceding evidence, are examined as a necessary ingredient in the work of demystifying the history of the Canadian Arctic.

According to Mark Salber Phillips and Gordon Schochet, "tradition" has been underutilized and undertheorized recently in history and the social sciences as a result of its multiple meanings, many of which invoke political and ideological foundations: "The taint of *traditionalism,* in other words, has seemed to cling to almost any discussion of the idea of tradition, whatever its overt intention or political engagement."[1] Jan Vansina's comments echo the problems of these semantic nuances, particularly in the discipline of history:

> The popular use of the term in the sense of "lack of change" irritates historians whose avocation is to discover change. They rightly feel that the term has been used in this sense as an excuse to state a historical claim without analyzing its validity. In addition, "tradition" is often invoked to designate the historical consciousness of a particular group, and more often than not the term is just a flag of convenience to legitimate a position held on other grounds. Historians also often felt poorly equipped to cope with the enormous time-depths involved in such phenomena, and the often hopelessly vague, romantic and emotion-laden description of their content discouraged scholars from subjecting them to close scrutiny.[2]

A theoretical literature about the concept of tradition is nonetheless being revived in the field of history and is proving particularly important in the history of colonialism and postcolonialism in Canada. Heidi Bohaker, whose doctoral thesis examines Anishinaabe identities in the Great Lakes region, points out that where the concept of tradition has been applied, it often operates to hamper our view of Aboriginal history: "Scholars have used the idea of tradition as a litmus test for the integrity of Aboriginal societies in the centuries since contact."[3] According to Bohaker, "The 'litmus' test of tradition puts Aboriginal cultures in a bind."[4] It is precisely this danger of reducing Aboriginal culture and tradition by binding it to what is "primitive," "of the past," or "dead" that must be avoided.

In *Paths in the Rainforests: Toward a History of Political Tradition in Equatorial Africa,* Vansina describes the *process* of tradition among the Bantu peoples of equatorial Africa. The characteristics of tradition that emerge from Vansina's study provide a helpful definition of the concept, one applicable to cultures and societies around the world. Vansina identifies two elements inherent in tradition: (1) continuity of a set of basic principles but changeability and vitality in their practice and (2) the subjectivity and autonomy of the tradition's participants. Vansina says:

> In sum then traditions are self-regulating processes. They consist of a changing, inherited, collective body of cognitive and physical representations shared by their members. The cognitive representations are the core. They inform the understanding of the physical world and develop innovations to give meaning to changing circumstances in the physical realm and do so in terms of the guiding principles of the tradition.[5]

A number of important specifications emerge from this definition that counter our more common understanding and usage of the term "tradition." Tradition is not old, static, and unchanging, as is often assumed. Likewise, tradition is not a "thing" to be utilized or not utilized but a process constantly under development and influenced by the particularities of cognitive and physical experience within a societal context. Tradition must also be recognized for its dual existence insofar as it both resides within the minds of individuals and is shared among the individuals of a group. The practice of tradition, therefore, constantly demands a balance between individual interpretation and unchanging principles. Further clarification can be gleaned from Vansina's characterization of the death of tradition: "A tradition dies when its carriers abandon its fundamental principles to adopt those of another tradition. This happens only after a society has become aware of a state of major incongruence between the cognitive and the physical worlds of its tradition, and is also aware of an alternative paradigm."[6]

These conditions of incongruence, which may lead to the abandonment of tradition, are ripe in the experience of colonialism. Paige Raibmon reveals how the concepts of tradition and authenticity functioned in the colonial society of the late-nineteenth-century northwest coast. She points out that our colloquial understanding of tradition is mirrored by a simplistic perception of authenticity. According to white society, authenticity, especially in Aboriginal societies, perpetuates what is static and "old": "The notion that all things Aboriginal were of the past was a critical element of the colonial discourse of authenticity. By this definition, all things authentic were (and are) constantly receding into the past."[7] Raibmon illustrates the ubiquitous dichotomies of authenticity/inauthenticity and tradition/modernity in relations between Aboriginals and non-Aboriginals and how these conceptions have served colonial cosmology. She argues, "The refashioning of Aboriginal identity in the late nineteenth century would have been a challenging task even apart from the shifting ambivalences of non-Aboriginal people. Dominant society's refusal to acknowledge the possibility of fusing 'traditional' and 'modern,' 'uncivilized' and 'civilized,' 'Indian' and 'White' made it all the more difficult."[8] According to Raibmon, tradition is constrained when those with power (i.e., members of white colonial society) impose their beliefs about the essence of tradition and authenticity on those without power (i.e., the Aboriginal population being colonized) and prevent the tradition from growing and changing. As a result, a false dichotomy emerges whereby an individual can be only "white" or "Indian" and cannot bend the traditions of his or her past to meet the demands of a changing society. Raibmon does not characterize the Aboriginal players in this colonial scenario as lacking agency. Rather, like Vansina, she points out that they keep tradition alive through change: "They pruned elements of 'tradition' and 'modernity' from this tangle and fashioned self-identities that were authentic on Aboriginal terms. This practice has not changed."[9] Raibmon concludes by arguing, "Surely, any just notion of authenticity must be self-determined."[10]

Paige Raibmon and Jan Vansina reveal commonalities in how Aboriginal communities have navigated cross-cultural encounters imbued with colonialism as well as the role of tradition therein. If we consider the practice of Inuit education in the Eastern Arctic to be a "tradition" and identify the *Inuit Qaujimajatuqangit* principles as its unchanging cognitive core, then the history presented in this study has proven this tradition to be highly dynamic. If we agree with Vansina that the death of tradition is the abandonment of fundamental principles in favour of an alternative (i.e., Qallunaat) paradigm, then it is remarkable that Inuit succeeded in keeping their tradition of education alive in the face of assimilation during the colonial period. The importance of the work by Inuit Elders and educators to identify, describe, and model *IQ* is unquestionable. Although the *IQ* principles were identified retrospectively and may not operate tacitly as they once did, in accordance with Vansina's definition of "tradition," this change is what has kept *IQ* and Inuit education alive.

The tradition of Inuit education may no longer always be distinguishable by specificities such as the precise tools used, the location of transmission, and the skills acquired. Nonetheless, Raibmon convinces us that the melding of tradition and modernity that occurs in Inuit schools by no means renders Inuit education inauthentic. My experience as a student learning sewing skills from Elders in a school classroom, discussed in the Introduction, did not replicate what would

Figure 9 Display of Inuktitut numeracy learning materials, incorporating local, northern content. Eastern Arctic, early 1980s. *Source:* McGregor Collection.

have been experienced by a young Inuit girl forty years prior, but as this book establishes, the replication of old ways is not the marker of a "traditional" education. Qallunaat educators initiated the recognition of Inuit culture in the formal school system in the Canadian Arctic, but culturally relevant content, methods, and social values were integrated into Inuit education to their fullest extent only when ownership of the schools was turned over to Inuit parents and educators. Mariano Aupilaarjuk, one of the Elders employed by the Nunavut Department of Education to advise on the integration of *IQ* into the curriculum, says that teaching Inuit youth: "is only really knowing what the strengths of the traditional ways are, and with Inuit really understanding what the strengths of the Qablunaat ways are, that these two can be wholesomely joined. They will be very strong in combination, the way of the Inuit and the way of the Qablunaat."[11] If we accept that authenticity is self-determined, then we must recognize this educational work by Elders as tradition in process.

Unlike the Aboriginal people featured in Raibmon's late-nineteenth-century history, the Inuit of twentieth- and twenty-first-century Nunavut have shown more openness to collaboration between tradition and modernity. This is undoubtedly due both to the relatively late timing of colonization in the Eastern Arctic and to the fact that Qallunaat have remained a minority population. Not only is Inuit education a tradition being employed in schools, but it also offers an essential means to maintain other traditions – not by resurrecting static and irrelevant ways of living from the past but by consciously engaging in a dialogue that weighs the principles of Inuit culture against the alternative principles offered by the Qallunaat. Through local control of education, Inuit took advantage of the opportunity to integrate traditional and modern, or authentic and inauthentic, practices on their own terms, thereby diminishing these false dichotomies and shaping their schools in accordance with their own local cognitive and physical realities.

Education in Nunavut

The change that has occurred within the education system in the Eastern Arctic since 1999 is very recent history and outside the confines of most of the research presented in this book. Nevertheless, the trajectory of political change and how it led to the contemporary system of education resulted in some public reflection on the previous system, allowing for further investigation of the themes presented here. My hope is that this history can help to inform a formula for education that more fully reflects Inuit ways and *IQ* in the future. I hope it will serve as a reminder of the demanding context in which educators have strived for change and the lessons learned in the work of integrating Inuit education into the formal school system. This cannot be fully realized without some reference to the system instigated at the time of Nunavut's creation.[12]

The story of the downfall of the regional boards of education and the struggle of the Nunavut Department of Education to invent itself after the creation of Nunavut Territory has its roots in the negotiation of the Nunavut Land Claims Agreement (NLCA) in the early 1980s. In defining the rights and benefits claimed by Inuit, education was not considered a priority. The schools, which are the launching pad into adulthood for every child in Nunavut, were not identified in the NLCA as necessitating legislated financial investment, language and cultural content, or local control. The following evidence suggests that education may have been used as a bargaining chip in negotiations with the federal government and deprioritized in favour of other issues. In October 1981 *Nunatsiaq News* reported the attainment of an agreement-in-principle between Inuit Tapirisat of Canada (ITC) and the federal government. The agreement-in-principle addressed three issues: (1) Inuit rights to wildlife harvesting, (2) the management of those rights, and (3) Inuit participation in the development of the renewable-resource economy. This, according to the report, was the first critical stage of negotiations leading directly to the Land Claims Agreement (and, indeed, those issues have always been publicly considered to be of paramount importance). *Nunatsiaq News* reported the pride and excitement expressed by Thomas Suluk, the lead negotiator for ITC, at what had been accomplished in this stage of the negotiations. It was also revealed that Suluk believed the rest of the negotiation process would be far simpler: "Mr. Suluk said the next topics for negotiation will be communications, housing, health, education, archaeology and justice. 'These are short items,' he said, 'and are not going to take two months to do.'"[13] This report and Suluk's comment reveal two important points: first, that education was still on the table for negotiation and, second, that it was lumped in with topics such as health care and justice and attributed a low level of importance in relation to issues like wildlife and mineral-resource rights. As we know, the final version of the NLCA does not make any specific provision for education; at some point, it was dropped from the negotiations. How can this initial deprioritization, and ultimate dismissal, of education in the negotiations be explained? Without further research and interviews with Inuit leaders of the land claim negotiations, I cannot comment on the reasons for this discrepancy. Nonetheless, there is evidence that this decision was short-sighted on the part of Nunavut's leaders.

The lack of concern for education set the Inuit of Nunavut apart from the other First Nations in Canada, whose education is still overseen by the federal Department of Indian and Northern Affairs. It also set them apart from the Inuit of Nunavik or Northern Quebec, who made local control of education a cornerstone of their entire land claim. The James Bay and Northern Quebec Agreement of 1975 was the first major land claim settlement in Canada, and it addresses social development issues such as education, social services, and health rather than just land ownership and financial settlement issues.[14] Section 17, pertaining to Inuit education, ensures that one school board is responsible for elementary, secondary, and adult education of all persons north of the 55th parallel.[15] This school board is led by a council consisting of one representative from each community within the region, and the board holds broad powers in administration of education, comparable to those held by the boards of education in the NWT. The funding of this school board is split between the Quebec and federal governments, which are responsible for 75 percent and 25 percent of the funding respectively.[16] This school board not only facilitates local control but also supports the mandate of developing a school system with culturally appropriate programming. The Inuit of Nunavut, by comparison, did not follow in the footsteps of the Inuit of Northern Quebec in settling the terms of education through their agreement with the federal government.

"Nunavut today faces a moment of change, a moment of crisis. It is a crisis in Inuit education and employment, a crisis magnified by the advent of global warming in the Arctic and the challenge of Arctic sovereignty."[17] This characterization is offered by Justice Thomas R. Berger of the Nunavut Project in a 2006 letter to the minister of Indian affairs and northern development. Justice Berger commented on this predicament in his role as conciliator in the negotiations for a renewal of the agreement between the Government of Nunavut, Nunavut Tunngavik Incorporated,[18] and the Government of Canada. This agreement, for the period 2003-13, should replace the contract that supported the NLCA and the creation of Nunavut between 1993 and 2003. Berger's task was to review the outstanding issues contributing to the impasse in negotiations, which had produced no agreement on a single issue from 2002 to 2005.[19] He went about collecting information to inform his report through targeted (though perhaps not completely systematic) consultation with Nunavummiut; therefore his conclusions should be considered reflective of the views of at least some Inuit and Qallunaat in the Arctic. The two most important areas of dispute identified by Berger are determining the level of funding appropriate for the institutions of public government and establishing a representative public service in accordance with Article 23 of the NCLA. Berger explains the significance of Article 23:

> Article 23.2.1 sets out the objective: "To increase Inuit participation in government employment ... to a representative level." Under Article 23.1.1 this means a representative level of Inuit employment "within all occupational groupings and grade levels."

> In Nunavut employment in the public service, if it is to be employment at a representative level, must therefore be 85 per cent Inuit employment "within all occupational groupings and grade levels."
>
> Article 23 may bear a resemblance to a conventional equity clause of a type well known. Employment equity is not obviously a land and resources issue, to be included in a land claims agreement. But neither is a provision to establish a new Territory. If the one were included in the Nunavut Land Claims Agreement the other had to follow. It is in fact an equity clause for a majority.[20]

Berger goes on to argue that the failure to realize Nunavut's Inuit employment objectives can be explained only by the lack of adequate educational capital held by most Inuit. He explains that although the Government of Nunavut has put in place programs and employment opportunities for Inuit, they have not been properly prepared to fill the available positions:

> The problem is that the supply of qualified Inuit is exhausted. Only 25 percent of Inuit children graduate from high school, and by no means all of these graduates go on to post-secondary education. The types of jobs where the need for increased Inuit participation is most acute – such as the executive, management and professional categories – have inescapable educational requirements.[21]

In turn, to fulfill the mandate of Article 23 of the NLCA, Berger recommends a significant investment in a more robust system of bilingual education:

> You can't envisage any way of achieving the objective of Article 23 over the long term unless you start by increasing the number of high school graduates. So it all leads back to the schools, to education, for it is Inuit high school graduates and Inuit graduates of university and other post-secondary programs who will enter the public service. There will have to be major changes in the education system in order to vastly increase the number of Inuit high school graduates; in my view a new approach is required, a comprehensive program of bilingual education.[22]

Berger explains that Inuktitut is essential because it is the language used in most homes, because it is the only language used in some homes, because it is fundamentally connected to the Inuit identity, because the Inuit desire that it be the language of government in Nunavut, and because it will allow the Inuit to learn and speak English better: "Loss of language and educational underachievement are linked. The strengthening of Inuktitut in the school, the home and the community can bring improvement in achievement in both Inuktitut and

English."[23] Financial investment is not the only resource required to implement Berger's vision of bilingual education; implementation also requires the increased training and retention of Inuit teachers: "There is a shortage of Inuit teachers in Nunavut. Only 35 per cent of teachers speak Inuktitut, and their numbers are slipping due to attrition from retirement, the stresses of the job (particularly for women with families) and the temptations of other careers in the territory, since Inuit teachers are the largest cohort of qualified Inuit in any field."[24]

Another important component of Berger's report is the implication that the federal government bears some responsibility for investment in the education system in Nunavut. Although the Nunavut territorial government has experienced the growing pains of any new administration, he argues that the federal government has at least some responsibility to provide additional support. The Inuit of Nunavut still live in the most crowded homes in the nation, they still have the lowest average lifespan in Canada, and they struggle with a high rate of school dropouts, alcoholism, and suicide. Inuit are living with very low standards in one of the richest countries in the world, indicating that they are an underserviced population who require supplemental housing, social services, education, and health care.[25] There is no question that the cost of providing services in Nunavut is extremely high in comparison to the cost in all other Canadian jurisdictions. Much higher rates of per capita federal funding are required simply to keep the government running: $21,327 per capita in 2000-1 versus $1,277 per capita for the provinces.[26] Although Nunavut may appear to other Canadians to be a drain on federal resources, Jack Hicks and Graham White point out that the federal government has yet to make an investment in infrastructure and economic development that is comparable to the massive spending that other jurisdictions received in their early years.[27] Nunavut has offered detailed proposals and costing for initiatives such as bilingual education, as documented by Berger, but these initiatives continue to be neglected by the federal government, thus hampering change.

Berger draws attention to the connection between education and employment; lack of acknowledgment of this connection in the original agreement was a significant oversight and arguably the greatest hindrance to the success of Nunavut Territory. Just as language protection was an important motivator for educational change in the early 1970s, here too it is viewed as a cornerstone for a system of education that would most appropriately meet the needs of Inuit in Nunavut. Berger's argument is indispensable in its articulation of the responsibility of the parties involved in the implementation of the NLCA to manifest an education system that will facilitate improved Inuit employment and, by extension, improved Inuit representation and self-determination in Nunavut, xii

Every Canadian must be aware of Inuit achievements in art and sculpture, in film and performance arts, achievements for which the Inuit have won international renown. The Inuit are a bright tile in the Canadian mosaic. Why not Inuit bilingualism? Why not an Inuit literature?

I believe Canadians will support this project – the Nunavut Project. They realize that no affirmation of Canada's Arctic sovereignty will be complete unless the people of the Arctic – the Inuit – are partners in the task.

Our ideas of human rights, of strength in diversity, of a northern destiny merge in the promise of Nunavut. It is a promise that we must keep.

Thomas R. Berger
Conciliator
Vancouver, March 1st, 2006

Figure 10 Conclusion of Justice Thomas R. Berger's covering letter to "*Conciliator's Final Report: The Nunavut Project.*" *Source:* Justice Thomas R. Berger.

which was established for the Inuit majority. However, as demonstrated, there are other components of an education system that equally reflect and facilitate Inuit ways of knowing, being, and doing, and these components receive too little attention in Berger's analysis of education. The most important of these components is local control.

From the time of the dissolution of regional school boards during the first year of Nunavut, until the coming-into-force of Nunavut's Education Act in 2009, educational administration and decision making was occurring in a vacuous context in the Eastern Arctic. The public and policy makers could not reach consensus on what a school system in Nunavut should look like, and how it should be run. That is not to say that all work toward integration of Inuit education into the schools stood still. On the contrary, important strides in curriculum development and foundational direction for the schools were being made toward goals which were likely to be entrenched through the eventual passage of legislation. However, one of the most significant outstanding questions was: Who would be responsible for implementing, overseeing, and supporting these changes? During this challenging and protracted legislative development process light was shed on differing views of parents and politicians and how people felt about the work of the BDBE in hindsight.

Since at least 2002, Inuit outside the Department of Education said that their level of local control, and consequently their capacity to shape the education system, was higher prior to the creation of Nunavut. Indeed, the change in trajectory of educational administration during this time, with limited responsibility devolved to district education authorities and no regional school boards, caused a significant interruption to local and regional capacity and has not proven more effective in meeting the needs of Inuit students. This desire for reinstatement of local control partially explains the difficulty of the Government of Nunavut in passing its own education legislation.

Prior to the passage of the Education Act in 2008, the district education authorities (DEAs) in Nunavut consisted of elected individuals, usually parents, responsible for the school or schools in their community. Each DEA is allocated a budget largely based on student population by the Department of Education, to spend on school supplies, cultural activities in its school or schools, and running the DEA itself. The DEAs can be involved in hiring teachers but have no supervisory authority and no authority to fire staff. Policy development at the local level must fit into department parameters, and although the DEAs have some capacity to influence local education programs (such as by offering a locally developed unit of study that meets curriculum standards), they have not often exercised this ability. During the first ten years of Nunavut, the DEAs suffered from a lack of consistency because every two years each DEA was fully elected as opposed to a staggered approach. In theory, the opportunity for local control was available through the DEAs, but this control proved severely limited in practice by the lack of access to adequate training, expertise, administrative support, and capacity-building through regionalized or combined efforts, which were previously provided by the boards of education. Without the opportunity to combine funding or resources to achieve shared outcomes in areas like book publishing, training initiatives, and developing study units, DEA activity and involvement varies significantly from community to community. While the Department of Education did, and still does, conduct widespread consultation on important initiatives with all DEAs, the voices of individual DEAs advocating for change have proven significantly limited compared to that of a regional board. An organization called the Coalition of Nunavut District Education Authorities was created in 2006 in an effort to fill the void of a shared voice. However, this fledgling organization is still in its infancy and while it has spoken on behalf of DEAs in formal consultations with the Department of Education, it has not, thus far, played a substantial, sustainable, or practical supportive role in assisting DEAs to carry out their work.

In 2002 Bill 1, the first education bill created for Nunavut, was presented to the Nunavut Legislative Assembly, at which time the proposed transfer of several responsibilities from the district education authorities to the minister of education was cause for public concern.[28] Members of the Legislative Assembly rejected Bill 1, and the second attempt to draft education legislation was in process from 2004 to 2007, during which time the Department of Education conducted community consultations with school staff, district education authorities, regional Inuit organizations, and the public, as well as with other organizations.[29]

Here again, in response to the draft legislation – now Bill 21 – the role of local control in Nunavut's education system was identified as unclear and underdeveloped. The Coalition of Nunavut DEAs argued:

> Many parent representatives voiced the observation that our schools were better governed 10 years ago than they are today. Ten years ago, the schools were governed by elected boards who were there because of one issue: education. Our MLAs in the Legislature have far too many important issues to be on top of – education concerns are lost in a sea of debates on bad gas, quotas, and devolution. If you need evidence of this, look at the scanty debate on the education budget when it was introduced earlier this year.[30]

In August 2007, in an editorial in *Nunatsiaq News* prior to a visit to Nunavut by Prime Minister Stephen Harper, the chairperson of the Coalition of Nunavut DEAs, Jeeteeta Merkosak, noted the neglect of education and loss of local control:

> [This is] one of the issues that parents feel needs serious re-examination in the life of our young government. In 2000, our Government eliminated regional boards of education and with this decision abolished local governance of the schools. In a stroke, what had been working as an Inuit way of governance of our schools, with decisions made by a council of parents, disappeared for a system where most decisions on schools are made by bureaucrats working outside of our communities.[31]

Merkosak reiterated that local control is the principle that underlies the education systems across Canada and that this principle has been supported by the federal government for First Nations and Inuit communities since 1971. She asked, "If local control is the principle being argued for with devolution [of mineral and gas development rights], why does the same principle not apply to our schools?"[32] In October 2007 the minister of education, Ed Picco, responded to DEA demands for re-establishment of the divisional school boards in Nunavut by saying, "That's not on at all."[33]

There is further evidence that Bill 21 remained controversial in the public's view and that Merkosak and the DEAs were not alone in calling for increased local control. For example, since abolishment of the school boards in 1999, Nunavut Tunngavik Incorporated (NTI) has held the position that the re-establishment of boards would benefit Nunavut.[34] In 2007 NTI released a report on the state of education in Nunavut and its relationship to Inuit culture, in which the reinstatement of regional school boards is one of nine major recommendations.[35] Among a number of arguments in favour of the reinstatement of school boards, NTI states, "While abolishing boards may make administrative and economic sense to a bureaucrat, the boards represented a political point of view that was independent of government, and they could have been relied on to be advocates for parental and community concerns about education."[36]

Bill 21, the result of this long legislative development process, was presented in November 2007. Yet, the Department of Education's proposed rearrangement of responsibilities was hindered further by the Legislative Assembly, which prescribed public consultations in order to ensure public consent for the changes proposed.[37] The bill was immediately sent to the Standing Committee on Health and Education for review and improvement, including further public hearings and acceptance of written reports from various parties. It seemed at the time that Nunavut might well enter its tenth year without its own education legislation.

Local control is certainly not the only criticism of the current education system with which the Department of Education has to contend: language programs, incorporation of *IQ*, disciplinary protocols, and adequate student support are all contentious issues in the public dialogue on Nunavut's education.[38] The department recently issued a new curriculum framework based entirely on the values and principles of *IQ* as well as on the traditional Inuit view of learning and development.[39] It is an impressive and exciting effort. However, as Ann Vick-Westgate points out with reference to Aboriginal education systems in general, the incorporation of Inuit education into Nunavut's education system requires greater examination of pedagogical issues. The Inuit of Nunavut must determine whether education is being delivered in accordance with Inuit ways of doing: "One of the greatest challenges facing communities, educators and researchers in the Arctic is that of developing genuinely Inuit, Dene and other approaches to education, not just sprinkling cultural materials into approaches designed for southern systems. Native and other Northern educators, most of them trained in southern systems, will have to think outside the boundaries of those systems."[40] The evidence thus far is that schools continue to rely on the methods and structure of schooling established by Qallunaat education, whereas learning opportunities that reflect traditional Inuit methods are exceptional. Insofar as education is about knowing, being, and doing as an Inuk, being is perhaps the most challenging component to replicate since it is largely dependent on the employment of Inuit teachers and Inuit Elders who can provide role models for youth. These are the challenges that are critical to the future of a territory that honours its past and looks eagerly toward its future. These are issues that should be turned over to students, parents, and other members of Nunavut communities so that they can seek solutions that meet the local vision of Inuit education.

Casting our Eyes Forward

Since the first sustained contacts between Inuit and Qallunaat and the change in northern resource usage, which gave rise to the colonial period, the relationship between Inuit, their land, and their Qallunaat colonizers has continued to change dramatically. Indeed, since as recently as the early 1970s, when the land claim process was first conceived, social, economic, cultural, and especially technological changes have been drastic. The ways of living pursued by most Inuit no longer necessitate environmental knowledge and a close relationship with the land and sea for survival, as was the case for their ancestors. Instead, formal Qallunaat schooling has become a compulsory aspect of every Inuk's childhood and increasingly determines the direction of their adulthood. Yet Inuit continue to insist that the practice of their cultural traditions, most of which are essentially connected to the environment, are crucial to their sense of identity, to their understanding of their history, and to their capability to pursue successful and happy lives. Therefore, although the formal education system may have been erected with a different set of priorities, it should now assist in the pursuit of an Inuit education that reflects the *IQ* principles. This work demonstrates that up until 1999 this is increasingly what the formal education system did. However, the prioritization of cultural sustainability and *IQ* through education was not included in the land claim agreement or in any other large-scale initiative associated with Inuit rights and benefits. The founders of Nunavut did not address how future generations would have access to *Inuit Qaujimajatuqangit*.

No one can foresee the challenges that arise in circumstances of change such as the settlement of a land claim and creation of a territory. When the negotiations began in the mid-1970s, I do not believe the Inuit of the Eastern Arctic foresaw the threat to their language and way of life posed by increasing integration with the ways of the Qallunaat – a threat that is now, arguably, also posed by environmental changes linked to climate change. Perhaps it was their view at the time that Elders and hunters, acting as historians, linguists, environmental specialists, and spiritual and social guides, would continue to be the real Inuit teachers. The Qallunaat schools would continue to teach English and to provide the skills needed for success in the jobs that would come with Nunavut. It was deemed unnecessary to spend time and energy in negotiations about an education system that was already on the path toward operating according to the wishes of Inuit, guided by boards of education and already moving toward cultural a strong cultural foundation.

Now there are fewer Elders who were alive in traditional times to act as role models to youth. There is greater influence from music, television, video games, and other sources that diminish the use of Inuktitut between family members in the home. Inuktitut is not used as frequently in the workplace as territorial legislation prescribes. Inuit are not hunting as frequently and, indeed, are prevented from doing so by the great costs and, in some cases, by the unpredictability of the weather due to climate change. They are finding fewer opportunities to connect with their past and the identity linked to it. In a film about the land claim, one young Inuit spokesperson expresses his feelings after interviewing Elders: "It all seems so far away, living only on the land under their own laws, being truly nomadic people on their own. Without Qallunaat. We meet Elders that are still alive and talking about those times. What they did and what they think, it's almost foreign to us, our society is so different today."[41] Young Inuit are not satisfied with the school system either; only 25 to 30 percent of students are graduating from high school.[42] This low level of education is preventing them from filling jobs with the Government of Nunavut, the major employer in the territory. Given that there is also a lack of industrial- or wage-employment opportunities, many Inuit remain economically dependent. Mary Simon, a national Inuit leader and spokesperson, has said: "A lot of kids aren't going to school in the northern communities because their parents aren't making them go to school. They're not getting educated academically, so their future is very limited in what they can do. So that's where the things start to fall apart and they don't see the benefits of the land claim agreement."[43]

Only now, with the recent coming into force of Nunavut's Education Act after a decade of negotiation and waiting, with the federal government and Nunavut Tunngavik Incorporated continuing to face substantial challenges in negotiations regarding the future implementation of the Nunavut Land Claims Agreement, and with suicide rates among youth at their highest recorded levels, are Inuit parents and leaders asking why the education system was not taken more seriously earlier.

The history of education in the Eastern Arctic reveals a weakness in the negotiation of the land claim and creation of Nunavut Territory that continues to have significant consequences for the education of Nunavummiut. Although

Inuit political activism and economic development in the Eastern Arctic were gaining momentum in anticipation of the establishment of Nunavut, education was taken for granted. The land claim negotiators did not specifically secure funding, policy, or legislation with regard to the Eastern Arctic's education system. The Government of Nunavut adopted the legislation of the Government of the Northwest Territories as a temporary solution at the time of Nunavut's inception, but it chose to permanently abandon the regional boards of education as a mechanism for decision making. Nunavut existed for ten years without its own educational legislation. One could argue that the resulting legislation is stronger because of that time, work, and public discussion. Or, one might point to the challenges of a young and inexperienced government embarking on complex legislative development and chalk the delays up to growing pains. Indeed, there is no doubt that the Act includes groundbreaking and ambitious requirements. As stated, the work of integrating Inuit education into the formal school system in the interim was not abandoned, but it suffered without clarity, consensus, and leadership during those years. Even with the content of the Education Act now settled, the Department of Education faces some major challenges: limited funding and human resources to pursue the legal mandate of bilingual education within ten years – in addition to the many other requirements on the system and parents who are increasingly disengaged from involvement in educational decision making.

The formal education system has not yet achieved its potential to reflect the vision of Nunavut, a place where Inuit can realize self-determination, sustain their culture, and continue their relationship with the Arctic environment. It was not bitterness, but more likely short-sightedness, that resulted in negligence by Inuit representatives toward the education system during the years of negotiation with the federal government. Great efforts were made by educators and administrators in the late 1980s and the 1990s to make the education system reflective of and responsive to local needs, Inuit culture, and the preservation of Inuktitut. Nonetheless, the history of cultural assimilation in schools, the significant variation between Inuit and Qallunaat societies in the content and knowledge that each considers valuable, and the structural and methodological differences between their systems of education contributed to the underestimation of the role of schools as a necessary mechanism by which to protect and sustain *IQ* and the Inuit relationship with the environment.

During the local period, parents, educators, and even students had the opportunity to grapple with these challenges and to effect change through the mechanism of regional school boards, which helped to empower local education authorities. The result was locally driven education, which was increasingly reflective of Inuit culture and Inuit ways of knowing, being, and doing. When

Nunavut was created in 1999, this system was still reaching toward higher graduation rates and improved alignment with employment opportunities, but in comparison to the assimilative school system of the colonial period and to the Qallunaat-controlled educational change of the territorial period, the approach of the Baffin Divisional Board of Education proved most successful in integrating Inuit education into the schools. This history has brought to light a number of important ingredients of schooling in the Eastern Arctic but none more important than local control. Until parents, community members, and local educational leaders, with access to an appropriate framework of support and resources to implement local decisions and goals, are meaningfully re-engaged and in control of education, the Inuit of the Eastern Arctic will be hindered in their efforts to deliver education that manifests an Inuit vision of the past and future.

Afterword

Bill 21 was passed unanimously by the Nunavut Legislative Assembly and became the Education Act on 18 September 2008.[1] Major changes to the education system included in this legislation, as highlighted by the Government of Nunavut, are summarized as:

- *Inuit Qaujimajatuqangit* must form the foundation for education, with responsibility for that work shared by the Minister of Education, DEAs, and school staff
- dedication to bilingual education in Inuktitut (or another Inuit language) and English or French
- more responsibility for DEAs in policy development, direction of principals, and administration of school activities
- more support for students through inclusive education, counselors in every school, attendance programs, improved behaviour management programs, and a guaranteed student-educator ratio
- legislated recognition of the DEA Coalition to support DEAs and participate in Department of Education planning.

Although I am not able to enter into a fulsome analysis of the Education Act here, these changes demonstrate that a number of aspects of Inuit education, primarily the foundation of *Inuit Qaujimajatuqangit* and dedication to bilingual education, have been legally reinforced by the Education Act. In fact, another piece of legislation that came into force in Nunavut on 1 July 2009 – the Inuit Language Protection Act – also mandates that education must be offered in both Inuktitut and English or French for all grade levels by the school year 2019-20. This goal of a fully bilingual education system within ten years is both very important and very ambitious.

As outlined above, district education authorities have been given increased responsibility in comparison to the 1999-2009 interval, such as for directly supervising principals and for local policy making in relation to issues that have been identified as particularly important to parents. A remaining and considerable concern is whether DEAs will have the capacity to leverage their powers and responsibilities into effective action and implementation without the support of school boards, or if the challenges currently existing – such as lack of access to coordinated capacity-building – will be perpetuated.

Despite the enhanced role of DEAs incorporated into Bill 21, Nunavut Tunngavik Incorporated (NTI) made one last attempt to prevent it from receiving a third reading by the Legislative Assembly, pending further consideration of concerns such as the need to reintroduce school boards. *Nunatsiaq News* reported that on 16 September 2008: "NTI issued a joint press release with all three regional Inuit associations demanding that MLAs [members of the Legislative Assembly] not pass Bill 21 'in its current state' because it still doesn't give enough power to district education authorities, takes too long to implement full Inuktitut-language instruction through Grade 12, and shortchanges special needs students."[2] Ed Picco, the minister of education, fired back at NTI, claiming that the bill had been partially amended in response to NTI's concerns and that the Department of Education had secured the endorsement of the district education authorities to proceed. He was reported to have said that "no legislation will please everyone, but a so-called 'made-in-Nunavut' act is better than what's in place now." Indeed, the Canadian Broadcasting Corporation reported that the legislation passed "to the delight of teachers and education officials, all of whom endorsed the new law enthusiastically."[3]

What conclusions can be drawn about school boards in this context, with the Nunavut government having finally closed the door on them through this legislation? Given the prospect of a territorial election in October 2008 and the expectation that Nunavut's new crop of MLAs would have to restart the process of passing the education legislation, one must recognize the pressure under which this bill was passed. The embarrassment of further delays would have been crushing to those involved in the consultations and legislative development as well as to the government more broadly.

On the one hand, the Education Act includes dozens, if not hundreds, of critical stipulations that the Department of Education badly needed to implement and that were only peripherally related or completely unrelated to the issue of the perceived need for school boards. It is certainly preferable, and entirely overdue, that the Department of Education be operating under legislation developed in Nunavut that reflects many of the wishes of its constituents. It also appears that further delaying the Act to fight for the reintroduction of school boards would have been fruitless because throughout the consultation process the Department of Education never formally considered or discussed the issue.

On the other hand, as NTI pointed out, one wonders how much more successfully many stipulations of the legislation, and many aspects of the vision for education in Nunavut, could be implemented with the support of boards of education? Since it appears that there are still strong voices in Nunavut for whom the role of district education authorities is not satisfactory in facilitating parental and local control of education, it remains in their hands to be advocates for change.

As is the case with any new legislation, it is impossible to anticipate the full implications of the Education Act, particularly as it operates in practice. Nunavummiut now have the obligation to engage with the district education authorities in their newly legislated form and they must work together to implement the many "made-in-Nunavut" directives for the education system, with the aim to discover how effective the DEAs can be in supporting Inuit education in schools.

Appendix: *Inuit Qaujimajatuqangit (IQ)* Guiding Principles

There are eight official *Inuit Qaujimajatuqangit* (*IQ*) principles recognized and widely applied for various purposes by the Government of Nunavut. The definitions of these principles included here were agreed on through consensus decision making by a group of respected Inuit Elders in the context of curriculum development for the Department of Education. These are the (*IQ*) principles as they are presented to Inuit children in schools.

1 ***Inuuqatigiitsiarniq:* The concept of respecting others, building positive relationships, and caring for others**
Inuuqatigiitsiarniq is showing respect and a caring attitude for others. When each person considers their relationships to people and behaves in ways that build these relationships, they build strength both in themselves and in others and together as a community. This is foundational to Inuit ways of being.

2 ***Tunnganarniq:* The concept of fostering good spirit by being open, welcoming, and inclusive**
Tunnganarniq is being welcoming to others, being open in communications, and being inclusive in interactions with people. Demonstrating this attitude is essential in building positive relationships with others.

3 ***Piliriqatigiingniq:* To develop a collaborative relationship and work together for the common good**
The essential Inuit belief that stresses the importance of the group over the individual should pervade all teaching. Expectations for students reflect working for the common good, collaboration, shared leadership, and service. *Piliriqatigiingniq* also sets expectations for supportive behaviour development, strong relationship-building, and consensus-building.

4 ***Avatimik Kamattiarniq:* To show environmental stewardship**
Inuit support and maintain environmental wellness through their respect for, and the importance they place on, relationship-building. Students are expected to articulate respect for mutally interdependent relationships and to demonstrate responsible behaviours that seek to improve and protect these relationships in ways that meet global challenges to environmental wellness and sustainable futures.

5 ***Pilimmaksarniq:* To be empowered and build capacity through knowledge and skills acquisition**
Building personal capacity in Inuit ways of knowing and doing are key expectations for students. Demonstrating empowerment to lead a successful and productive life, that is respectful of all, is a powerful end goal of the education system.

6 ***Qanuqtuurungnarniq:* To be resourceful and seek solutions through creativity, adapability, and flexibility**
The ability to be resourceful, seek solutions, use resources innovatively and creatively, and to demonstrate adaptability and flexibility in response to a rapidly changing world, are strengths all students should develop. Resourcefulness should be demonstrated in all learning and also thinking that seeks to improve the context in which Inuit live.

7 ***Aajiiqatigiingniq:* Consensus decision-making**
The concept of consensus decision making relies on strong communication skills and a strong belief in shared goals. All students are expected to become contributing members of their community and to participate actively in building the strength of the Inuit of Nunavut. Across all curriculum areas, students are expected to think and act collaboratively, to assist with the development of shared understandings, to resolve conflict in consensus-building ways, and to enter into consultation respecting various perspectives and worldviews.

8 ***Pijitsirarniq:* To contribute to the common good through serving and leadership**
The concept of serving is central to the style of leadership and is the measure of the maturity and wisdom of an Inuk. Key here is the understanding that each person has a contribution to make and is a valued contributor to his/her community. Students will be expected to demonstrate this kind of leadership and commitment to serving the common good.

Source: Nunavut Department of Education, *Inuit Qaujimajatuqangit: Education Framework for Nunavut Curriculum,* Nunavut Department of Education, Curriculum and School Services Division, 2007.

Notes

Preface

1 Shelagh D. Grant, "Inuit History in the New Millennium: Challenges and Rewards," in *Northern Visions,* ed. Kerry M. Abel and Ken Coates, 92 (Peterborough, ON: Broadview Press, 2001).

2 Linda Tuhiwai Smith, *Decolonizing Methodologies: Research and Indigenous Peoples* (New York: St. Martin's Press, 1999), 28.

3 Grant, "Inuit History in the New Millennium," 92.

4 For an explanation of the important role of Elders in Inuit society, see Rachel A. Qitsualik, "What, Exactly, Is an Elder?" *Nunatsiaq News,* 25 June 1998, http://www.nunatsiaq.com/archives/nunavut980630/columns.html.

5 This relationship between scholarship, specifically history, and power is discussed further in the Introduction.

6 The term "liminality," more commonly used in academic contexts than in colloquial speech, connotes my position and perspective as "betwixt and between," or as occupying the space between two cultures, two languages, two ways of life, two histories, and so on. I have chosen this word, rather than "marginality" or "outsider," to illustrate that there is a middle ground that offers its own set of experiences, advantages, and challenges.

7 See Introduction note 3 for a definition of Qallunaaq.

8 The transcripts of these discussions were recorded and translated into English by the Department of Education for its own purposes.

9 Smith, *Decolonizing Methodologies,* 1.

Introduction

1 Thomas R. Berger, *Conciliator's Final Report: The Nunavut Project,* Nunavut Land Claims Agreement Implementation Contract Negotiations for the Second Planning Period 2003-2013, 1 March 2006, i.

2 There is a dialect spoken in the Kitikmeot region, written in Roman orthography, called *Inuinnaqtun,* which is now recognized as an official language in Nunavut. There is also the modern term *Inuktut Uqausiit,* or *Inuit Uqausiit,* meaning "Inuit languages," now being used to refer to all dialects and forms of Inuktitut that exist in Alaska, Canada, and Greenland. I have continued to use the word *Inuktitut,* consistent with my sources, in this context.

3 Alex Spalding and Thomas Kusugaq, *Inuktitut: A Multi-Dialectical Outline Dictionary* (Iqaluit: Nunavut Arctic College, 1998), 7.

4 Minnie Aodla Freeman, *Life among the Qallunaat* (Edmonton: Hurtig, 1978), 13.

5 N.C. Bhattacharya, "Education in the Northwest Territories," *The Alberta Journal of Educational Research* 19, 3 (September 1973): 243-54; Robert E. Johns, "History of Administration of Schools, N.W.T.," *Musk-Ox* 18 (1976): 42-57.

6 R. Quinn Duffy, "Providing an Education," in *The Road to Nunavut: The Progress of the Eastern Arctic Inuit since the Second World War,* 95-130 (Montreal and Kingston: McGill-Queen's University Press, 1988); David Damas, *Arctic Migrants/Arctic Villagers: The*

Transformation of Inuit Settlement in the Central Arctic, Native and Northern Series no. 32 (Montreal and Kingston: McGill-Queen's University Press, 2002); Frank James Tester and Peter Kulchyski, *Tammarniit (Mistakes): Inuit Relocation in the Eastern Arctic, 1939-63* (Vancouver: UBC Press, 1994).

7 Frank Darnell, ed., *Education in the North: The First International Conference on Cross-Cultural Education in the Circumpolar Nations* (Fairbanks: University of Alaska Press and the Arctic Institute of North America, 1972).

8 Frank Darnell and Anton Hoem, *Taken to Extremes: Education in the Far North* (Oslo, Norway: Scandinavian University Press, 1996).

9 Mary A. Van Meenan, "Government Policies of Education for the Native Peoples of Siberia and the Canadian Northwest Territories, 1900-90: A Historical Examination" (PhD diss., Department of History, Dalhousie University, 1994).

10 Ann Vick-Westgate, *Nunavik: Inuit-Controlled Education in Arctic Quebec* (Calgary: University of Calgary Press, 2002).

11 J.D. Wilson, "The Visions of Ordinary Participants: Teachers' Views of Rural Schooling in British Columbia in the 1920s," in *A History of British Columbia: Selected Readings,* ed. Pat Roy, 239-55 (Toronto: Copp Clark Pitman, 1989).

12 Neil Sutherland, "I Can't Recall When I Didn't Help: The Working Lives of Pioneering Children in Twentieth Century British Columbia," *Histoire Sociale/Social History* 23, 48 (November 1991): 263-88.

13 Mike Corbett, "A Protracted Struggle: Rural Resistance and Normalization in Canadian Educational History," *Historical Studies in Education/Revue d'histoire de l'éducation* 12, 1 (2001): 19-48.

14 For discussion of the problems of anthropological methodology in the comparative study of cultures, see Jan Vansina, *Paths in the Rainforests: Toward a History of Political Tradition in Equatorial Africa* (Madison: University of Wisconsin Press, 1990), 260-62.

15 For discussion of the role of anthropologists in establishing popular notions of Indianness and "authenticity," see Paige Raibmon, *Authentic Indians: Episodes of Encounter from the Late-Nineteenth-Century Northwest Coast* (Durham, NC, and London: Duke University Press, 2005), 5.

16 Knud Rasmussen, *Intellectual Life of the Iglulik Eskimos,* Report of the Fifth Thule Expedition, 1921-24, vol. 6, no. 1 (Copenhagen, Denmark: Gyldendalske Boghandel, 1929); Franz Boas, *The Central Eskimo,* Annual Report of the Bureau of American Ethnology for the Years 1884-1885, vol. 6 (Washington, DC: Smithsonian Institution, 1988); Diamond Jenness, *Eskimo Administration: II Canada,* Arctic Institute of North America Technical Paper no. 14, 1964.

17 John J. Honigmann and Irma Honigmann, *Eskimo Townsmen* (Ottawa: Canadian Research Centre for Anthropology, University of Ottawa, 1965).

18 Jean L. Briggs, *Never in Anger: A Portrait of an Eskimo Family* (Cambridge, MA: Harvard University Press, 1970).

19 Hugh Brody, *The People's Land: Eskimos and Whites in the Eastern Arctic* (Markham, ON: Penguin Books Canada, 1975); Hugh Brody, *The Other Side of Eden* (Vancouver: Douglas and McIntyre, 2000).

20 Arlene Stairs, "Self-Image, World-Image: Speculations on Identity from Experiences with Inuit," *Ethos* 20, 1 (March 1992): 116-26.

21 Fiona O'Donoghue now goes by the name Fiona Walton.

22 Fiona O'Donoghue, "The Hunger for Professional Learning in Nunavut Schools" (EdD diss., Department of Curriculum, Teaching and Learning, Ontario Institute for Studies in Education of the University of Toronto, 1998); Joanne Marie Tompkins, "Critical and

Shared: Conceptions of Inuit Educational Leadership" (EdD diss., Department of Curriculum, Teaching and Learning, Ontario Institute for Studies in Education of the University of Toronto, 2006); M. Lynn Aylward, "Discourses of Cultural Relevance in Nunavut Schooling," *Journal of Research in Rural Education* 22, 7 (2007): 3, http://www.umaine.edu/jrre/22-7.pdf (accessed 7 September 2007).

23 Fiona O'Donoghue, Joannie Tompkins, Sandy McAuley, Lena Metuq, Nunia Qanatsiaq, and Elizabeth Fortes, *Pursuing a Dream: Inuit Education in the Qikiqtani Region of Nunavut from 1980-1999*, report on the Iqaluit Meetings of 25 May to 1 June 2005 to the Social Sciences and Humanities Research Council – Northern Development Grant, 5 October 2005, 16.

24 Darnell and Hoem, *Taken to Extremes*, 10.

25 Ibid., 11.

26 Linda Tuhiwai Smith, *Decolonizing Methodologies: Research and Indigenous Peoples* (New York: St. Martin's Press, 1999), 34.

27 Kerry Abel and Ken Coates refer to this as "northern mythology" and argue that most history has demonstrated how Canada has impacted the Inuit and the North but not how the North and the Inuit have in turn influenced Canada. See Kerry M. Abel and Ken S. Coates, eds., *Northern Visions: New Perspectives on the North in Canadian History* (Peterborough, ON: Broadview Press, 2001), 9.

28 Smith, *Decolonizing Methodologies*, 39.

29 For an important discussion of the role of historians as "experts" offering "evidence" in legal proceedings to determine the rights of Native peoples in Canada, see Arthur J. Ray, "Native History on Trial: Confessions of an Expert Witness," *Canadian Historical Review* 84, 2 (June 2003): 253-73.

30 Mary-Ellen Kelm, "Desperately Seeking Absolution: Native Agency as Colonialist Alibi?" *Canadian Historical Review* 75, 4 (1994): 545.

31 It is necessary to point out that life in Iqaluit, which has long been the biggest community in the Eastern Arctic, is somewhat different from life in most communities. It supports a much higher Qallunaat population and more English speakers than do other communities, and it is commonly perceived by Inuit as less "traditional." The example from my childhood in Iqaluit would likely have been experienced many times over and in a more exaggerated way for Qallunaat students in other communities.

32 *Qarmaq:* sod house. Spalding and Kusugaq, *Inuktitut*, 110.

33 *Kamik(s):* boot, shoe, footwear. Spalding and Kusugaq, *Inuktitut*, 38.

34 Smith, *Decolonizing Methodologies*, 39.

35 See the discussion of "tradition" in Heidi Bohaker, "*Nindoodemag:* Anishinaabe Identities in the Eastern Great Lakes Region, 1600-1900" (PhD diss., Department of History, University of Toronto, 2006), 22-27.

Chapter 1: History of the Eastern Arctic

1 Heather Myers, "Changing Environment, Changing Times," *Environment* 43, 6 (2001): 35.

2 John Amagoalik, "A Different Place – My Little Corner of Canada Column," *Nunatsiaq News*, 22 October 1999, http://www.nunatsiaq.com/archives/nunavut991030/ corner.html (accessed 3 February 2005).

3 Environment Canada, "Plants of the Arctic Cordillera Ecozone," http://www.ec.gc.ca/soer-ree/English/vignettes/Terrestrial /ac/plants.cfm (accessed 7 July 2007).

4 Environment Canada, "Canadian Climate Normals, 1971-2000: Pond Inlet, Nunavut," http://climate.weatheroffice.ec.gc.ca /climate_normals/index_e.html (accessed 6 January 2008).

5 Environment Canada, "Wildlife of the Northern Arctic Ecozone," http://www.ec.gc.ca/soer-ree/English/vignettes/Terrestrial/ na/wildlife.cfm (accessed 7 July 2007).

6 For information on the species of plants that occur in Nunavut and their traditional uses, see Carolyn Mallory and Susan Aiken, *Common Plants of Nunavut,* published in collaboration with the Nunavut Department of Education, Nunavut Wildlife Management Board, Canadian Museum of Nature (Nepean, ON: National Printers, 2004).

7 Robert McGhee, *Ancient People of the Arctic* (Vancouver: UBC Press, 1996), 9.

8 Richard Harrington, *The Inuit: Life as It Was* (Edmonton: Hurtig, 1981), 90.

9 Renée Fossett, *In Order to Live Untroubled: Inuit of the Central Arctic, 1550 to 1940* (Winnipeg: University of Manitoba Press, 2001), 201.

10 George Wenzel, "Inuit Subsistence and Hunter Support in Nunavut," in *Nunavut: Inuit Regain Control of Their Lands and Their Lives,* ed. Jens Dahl, Jack Hicks, and Peter Jull (Copenhagen, Denmark: International Working Group for Indigenous Affairs, 2000), 181.

11 For commentary by Inuit about leadership, see John Bennett and Susan Rowley, eds., *Uqalurait: An Oral History of Nunavut* (Montreal and Kingston: McGill-Queen's University Press, 2004), 95-98.

12 See Marshall Sahlins, "Notes on the Original Affluent Society," in *Man the Hunter,* ed. Richard B. Lee and Irven DeVore (Chicago: Aldine, 1968), 89. This argument was made at a conference in 1966, and commentary was later published in 1968. Sahlins said: "Rather than anxiety, it would seem the hunters have a confidence born of affluence, of a condition in which all the people's wants (such as they are) are generally easily satisfied."

13 Hugh Brody, *The Other Side of Eden* (Vancouver: Douglas and McIntyre, 2000), 306.

14 Jose Kusugak, "The Tide Has Shifted: Nunavut Works for Us, and It Offers a Lesson to the Broader Global Community," in *Nunavut: Inuit Regain Control of Their Lands and Their Lives,* ed. Jens Dahl, Jack Hicks, and Peter Jull (Copenhagen, Denmark: International Work Group for Indigenous Affairs, 2000), 20.

15 Alex Spalding, quoted in John MacDonald, *The Arctic Sky: Inuit Astronomy, Star Lore, and Legend* (Toronto/Iqaluit: Royal Ontario Museum/Nunavut Research Institute, 1998), 35.

16 For the history of the creation of *sila,* the the weather spirit, see Bennett and Rowley, eds., *Uqalurait,* 174-75.

17 Inuit Tapiriit Kanatami, "Traditional Ecological Knowledge," http://www.itk.ca/environment/tek-ecological.php (accessed 7 July 2007).

18 John Amagoalik, "What Is This Land?" in *The Voice of the Natives: The Canadian North and Alaska,* ed. Hans Blohm (Toronto: Penumbra Press, 2001), 9.

19 Peter Jull, "Politics, Development and Conservation in the International North," *Conservation and the North in a Decade of Uncertainty,* Canadian Arctic Resources Committee Policy Paper no. 2, March 1986, 4.

20 McGhee, *Ancient People,* 571.

21 For more on disease, see Liza Piper and John Sandlos, "A Broken Frontier: Ecological Imperialism in the Canadian North," *Environmental History* 12, 4 (October 2007): 759-95.

22 W. Gillies Ross, "Whaling, Inuit and the Arctic Islands," in *Interpreting Canada's North: Selected Readings,* ed. Kenneth S. Coates and William R. Morrison (Toronto: Copp Clark, 1989), 241. For more information, see W. Gillies Ross, *Whaling and Eskimos: Hudson Bay, 1860-1915,* National Museum of Man Publications in Ethnology no. 10 (Ottawa: National Museums of Canada, 1975). Commercial whaling was permitted in the Eastern Arctic until 1915.

23 Philip Goldring, "Inuit Economic Responses to Euro-American Contacts," in *Interpreting Canada's North: Selected Readings,* ed. Kenneth S. Coates and William R. Morrison (Toronto: Copp Clark, 1989), 264.

24 Fossett, *In Order to Live Untroubled,* 176.
25 Robert Paine, ed., *The White Arctic* (St. John's/Toronto: Institute of Social and Economic Research, Memorial University of Newfoundland/University of Toronto Press, 1977), 8.
26 Fossett, *In Order to Live Untroubled,* 192.
27 Paine, ed., *White Arctic,* 8.
28 N.J. Macpherson, *Dreams and Visions: Education in the Northwest Territories from Early Days to 1984* (Yellowknife: Government of the Northwest Territories, 1991), 27, 31. See also Frédéric Laugrand, Jarich Oosten, and François Trudel, eds., *Apostle to the Inuit: The Journals and Ethnographic Notes of Edmund James Peck, the Baffin Years, 1894-1905* (Toronto: University of Toronto Press, 2006).
29 Macpherson, *Dreams and Visions,* 32. However, Peck's system did not reach the Central Arctic (Kugluktuk and Cambridge Bay), where Roman orthography has always been used.
30 Donald B. Marsh, *Echoes from a Frozen Land,* ed. Winifred Marsh (Edmonton: Hurtig, 1987), 31.
31 Residential schooling is discussed further in Chapter 3.
32 For more on the influence of Inuktitut literacy on Inuit identity and intergenerational dynamics (in a more modern context), see Perry Shearwood, "Inuit Identity and Literacy in a Nunavut Community," *Études/Inuit/Studies* 25, 1-2 (2001): 295-307.
33 For an analysis of the different types of literacy ("taxonomy of literacy") possessed and practised by Inuit in the North, such as biblical, vernacular, schooled, and so on, see Perry Shearwood, "Literacy among the Aboriginal Peoples of the Northwest Territories," *Canadian Modern Language Review/La Revue Canadienne des Langues Vivantes* 43, 4 (May 1987): 630-42.
34 Diamond Jenness, *Eskimo Administration: II Canada,* Arctic Institute of North America Technical Paper no. 14, 1964, 50.
35 Paine, ed., *White Arctic,* 10.
36 See, for example, Jean Barman, "Schooled for Inequality: The Education of British Columbia Aboriginal Children," in *Children, Teachers and Schools in the History of British Columbia,* ed. Jean Barman, Neil Sutherland, and J.D. Wilson, 57-80 (Calgary: Detsilig, 1995); Jean Barman, "Separate and Unequal: Indian and White Girls at All Hallows School," in *Children, Teachers and Schools in the History of British Columbia,* ed. Jean Barman, Neil Sutherland, and J.D. Wilson, 337-58 (Calgary: Detsilig, 1995); and J.R. Miller, *Shingwauk's Vision: A History of Native Residential Schools* (Toronto: University of Toronto Press, 1996).
37 Royal Commission on Aboriginal Peoples (RCAP), "Residential Schools," in *Report of the Royal Commission on Aboriginal Peoples,* vol. 1, part 2, ch. 10, (Ottawa: Indian and Northern Affairs Canada), http://www.ainc-inac.gc.ca/ch/rcap/sg/cg10_e.pdf (accessed 31 October 2007).
38 Marie Battiste, "Introduction," in *First Nations Education in Canada: The Circle Unfolds,* ed. Marie Battiste and Jean Barman (Vancouver: UBC Press, 1995), viii.
39 M. Lynn Aylward, "Discourses of Cultural Relevance in Nunavut Schooling," *Journal of Research in Rural Education* 22, 7 (2007): 3, http://www.umaine.edu/jrre/22-7.pdf (accessed 7 September 2007).
40 National Indian Brotherhood/Assembly of First Nations, *Indian Control of Indian Education* (Ottawa: Assembly of First Nations, 1972),http://web.uvic.ca/ablo/documents/IndianControlofIndianEducation.pdf (accessed 31 October 2007).
41 Ibid., 3.
42 Battiste, "Introduction," viii-ix.
43 RCAP, "Education," in *Report of the Royal Commission on Aboriginal Peoples,* vol. 3, ch. 5, (Ottawa: Indian and Northern Affairs Canada), http://www.ainc-inac.gc.ca/ch/rcap/sg/ci5_e.pdf (accessed 28 January 2008).

44 Battiste, "Introduction," xi.
45 Marlene Brant Castellano, Lynne Davis, and Louise Lahache, eds., *Aboriginal Education: Fulfilling the Promise* (Vancouver: UBC Press, 2000), xiv.
46 Castellano, Davis, and Lahache, "Part 3 – Innovations in Education Practice: Renewing the Promise," in *Aboriginal Education,* 97.
47 RCAP, "Education," 126.
48 Constitution Act of 1867, Section 91(24). See also David W. Elliott, *Law and Aboriginal Peoples in Canada,* 4th ed. (North York, ON: Captus Press, 2000), 13. This lack of reference to the Inuit in the Constitution Act of 1867 is due to the fact that Canada was not in possession of the Arctic at the time; however, when ownership was transferred in 1880, no effort was made to refer to the Inuit in law.
49 Frank James Tester and Peter Kulchyski explain that the federal government argued that the Inuit were a different race from the Indians, that they did not belong to Canada at the time of the Constitution Act of 1867, and that they had been treated differently from Indians (as they had no reservations, treaties, etc.), all of which meant they should be exempt from special status and considered regular Canadians. However, Quebec, supported by noted anthropologist Franz Boas, convinced the justices that the term "Indian" had regularly been applied to the Inuit, and based on that historical precedent they ruled against the federal government. See Frank James Tester and Peter Kulchyski, *Tammarniit (Mistakes): Inuit Relocation in the Eastern Arctic, 1939-63* (Vancouver: UBC Press, 1994), 32-34.
50 Elliott, *Law and Aboriginal Peoples,* 14.
51 Natalia Loukacheva, "Autonomy and Indigenous Peoples of the Arctic: Legal Status of Inuit (Case Study of Greenland and Nunavut)" (PhD diss., Department of Law, University of Toronto, 2004), 74.
52 This was Peter Freuchen Ittinuar, elected as a member of Parliament for the New Democratic Party in the riding of Nunatsiaq. See Government of Canada, "Members of Parliament," *Federal Election Trivia,* http://www2.parl.gc.ca/ParlInfo/Compilations/ElectionsAndRidings/TriviaMembersOfParliament.aspx?Language=E#12 (accessed 16 April 2007).
53 Government of Canada, "Rights of the Aboriginal Peoples of Canada," *Constitution Act* R.S.C., 1982.
54 Bradford W. Morse, ed., *Aboriginal Peoples and the Law: Indian, Métis and Inuit Rights in Canada,* rev. 1st ed. (Ottawa: Carleton University Press, 1989), 783.
55 Elliott, *Law and Aboriginal Peoples,* 13-20.
56 Loukacheva, "Autonomy and Indigenous Peoples," 64.
57 The main difficulties resulting from this oversight are experienced by Inuit residing outside of Nunavut or other land claim regions of Canada. See Zacharias Kunuk, dir., *Kiviaq vs. Canada,* film (Isuma Productions, 2006).
58 Jack Hicks and Graham White, "Nunavut: Inuit Self-Determination through a Land Claim and Public Government?" in *Nunavut: Inuit Regain Control of Their Lands and Their Lives,* ed. Jens Dahl, Jack Hicks, and Peter Jull (Copenhagen, Denmark: International Work Group for Indigenous Affairs, 2000), 51.
59 "Tapirisat" means "association" in Inuktitut. ITC's name was changed to Inuit Tapiriit Kanatami (ITK) in 2001. ITK represents various Inuit groups nationally, including those in Inuvialuit, Nunavut, Nunavik, and Nunatsiavut; however, the Inuit of Nunavut were a leading force in the creation of ITK.
60 Inuit Tapiriit Kanatami, "ITC Founding Conference: August, 1971," in *About ITK/History,* http://www.itk.ca/corporate/history-founding-conference.php (accessed 14 April 2007).

61 Inuit Tapiriit Kanatami, "Transcript of First ITC Meeting," in *The Origin of ITK*, http://www.itk.ca/corporate/history-origin-transcript-first-meeting.php (accessed 14 April 2007).
62 For more on land-use studies, see Rick Riewe, "Inuit Land Use Studies and the Native Claims Process," in *Aboriginal Resource Use in Canada: Historical and Legal Aspects*, ed. Kerry Abel and Jean Friesen, 287-99 (Winnipeg: University of Manitoba Press, 1991).
63 See Alice French, *The Restless Nomad* (Winnipeg: Pemmican, 1992), 69: "To the people of the north the land belonged to everyone who adhered to her rules. It was not to be bought and sold because it belonged to all of us."
64 Loukacheva, "Autonomy and Indigenous Peoples," 86.
65 This document was called "Agreement-in-Principle as to the Settlement of Inuit Land Claims in the Northwest Territories and the Yukon Territory between the Government of Canada and Inuit Tapirisat of Canada." See R. Quinn Duffy, *The Road to Nunavut: The Progress of the Eastern Arctic Inuit since the Second World War* (Montreal and Kingston: McGill-Queen's University Press, 1988), 236.
66 Ibid., 236-37.
67 Ibid., 240.
68 For a list of "formidable obstacles" faced by Inuit negotiators, as well as the approaches they took in overcoming those obstacles, see John Merritt, "Nunavut: Preparing for Self-Government," *Northern Perspectives* 21, 1 (1993): http://www.carc.org/pubs/v21no1/nunavut1.htm (accessed 18 April 2007).
69 Duffy, *Road to Nunavut*, 245.
70 I could not access a copy of the document *Parnagujuk: "A Plan for Progress,"* so my comments on it are based on secondary sources. However, I think it is reasonable to speculate that because the shape of this plan provided the basis for most negotiations throughout the late 1980s, it also represents a first step in conceding individual Inuit rights.
71 In response to a plebiscite that asked, "Do you think the Northwest Territories should be divided? Yes or No?" the Inuit of the western Arctic communities, where the populations are more substantially Euro-Canadian, recorded solid opposition. However, the response of the Inuit communities won out, with more than 60 per cent voting in favour of division.
72 The reason for this change is not explained in any resources I could find. I would speculate that it was necessary to create an organization to represent solely those Inuit of the Nunavut region.
73 Hicks and White, "Nunavut," 57.
74 Kusugak, "The Tide Has Shifted," 21. The training trust fund was earmarked specifically for preparations for the implementation of Nunavut Territory, but it was not extended beyond 1999.
75 Nunavut Tunngavik Incorporated, "History and Overview," *About Nunavut Tunngavik Incorporated*, http://www.tunngavik.com/ english/about.html (accessed 14 April 2007).
76 Peter Jull, "Negotiating Nationhood, Renegotiating Nationhood: Canada's Nunavut and Nunavut's Canada," *Balayi: Culture, Law and Colonialism* 3 (2001): 78.
77 Hicks and White, "Nunavut," 31.
78 Frank Tester, in Kunuk, dir., *Kiviaq vs. Canada*.
79 Loukacheva, "Autonomy and Indigenous Peoples," 94.
80 Paul Quassa, quoted in Loukacheva, "Autonomy and Indigenous Peoples," 95.
81 Jose Kusugak, in Kunuk, dir., *Kiviaq vs. Canada*.
82 Frank Tester, in ibid. He proceeds to discuss the example of universal family allowances, which were automatically handed out to the Inuit starting at mid-century in Canada

regardless of whether they required support or were capable of supporting themselves. His point is that the Inuit were treated like children in a way that Euro-Canadian citizens would never have been. See also Tester and Kulchyski, *Tammarniit,* 43-101.

83 Shepard Krech III provides a critique of the image and mythology of the "Noble Savage," or "Ecological Indian," which he argues has stereotyped Native peoples and their relationship with the environment, diminishing Native agency, dismissing cultural diversity, and overlooking evidence to the contrary. See Shepard Krech III, *The Ecological Indian: Myth and History* (New York: Norton, 2000).

84 Nancy M. Williams and Graham Baines, eds., *Traditional Ecological Knowledge* (Canberra: Centre for Resource and Environmental Studies, Australian National University, 1993), 9.

85 Julie Cruikshank, *Do Glaciers Listen? Local Knowledge, Colonial Encounters, and Social Imagination* (Vancouver: UBC Press, 2005), 256.

86 Krech, *Ecological Indian;* Shepard Krech III, "Reflections on Conservation, Sustainability, and Environmentalism in Indigenous North America," *American Anthropologist* 107 (2005): 78-86.

87 Krech, "Reflections on Conservation," 79.

88 Cruikshank, *Do Glaciers Listen?,* 256.

89 Krech, "Reflections on Conservation," 79.

90 Derek Rasmussen, "Qallunology: A Pedagogy for the Oppressor," *Canadian Journal of Native Education* 25, 2 (2001): 107.

91 George W. Wenzel, "Traditional Ecological Knowledge and Inuit: Reflections on TEK Research and Ethics," *Arctic* 51, 2 (June 1999): 119.

92 Bennett and Rowley, eds., *Uqalurait,* xxi.

93 Hugh Brody, *The People's Land: Eskimos and Whites in the Eastern Arctic* (Markham, ON: Penguin Books Canada, 1975), 125.

94 Ibid., 126.

95 Nunavut Social Development Council, *Report on the Nunavut Traditional Knowledge Conference* (Igloolik: Nunavut Tunngavik Incorporated, 22-24 March 1998).

96 As noted in the Appendix, eight principles of *IQ* are now recognized by the Department of Education and the Government of Nunavut more broadly. Six of these were originally prioritized and defined specifically for use in schools by the Elders of the Nunavut Department of Education during curriculum development workshops conducted in 2000. Two additional principles were later added by the Government of Nunavut in 2004. For the purposes of this book, I have chosen to work from the version of the IQ principles currently used; however, it should not be considered the only version or description of the *IQ* principles, which are defined and applied for numerous purposes within the Government of Nunavut.

97 Jaypetee Arnakak, "Commentary: What Is Inuit Qaujimajatuqangit?" *Nunatsiaq News,* 25 August 2000, http://www.nunatsiaq.com/archives /nunavut000831/nvt20825_17.html (accessed 10 January 2008).

98 Jeannette C. Armstrong, "Traditional Indigenous Education: A Natural Process," *Canadian Journal of Native Education* 14, 3 (1987): 15.

99 Ibid., 16.

100 Ibid., 17.

101 George Wenzel, "'I Was Once Independent': The Southern Seal Protest and Inuit," *Anthropologica* 29, 2 (1987): 205.

102 Arlene Stairs, "Self-Image, World-Image: Speculations on Identity from Experiences with Inuit," *Ethos* 20, 1 (March 1992): 122. A personal communication with a linguist at the Nunavut Department of Education resulted in somewhat alternate spellings for these

words (perhaps due to the dialect differences) but confirmed that they represent "traditional ways of teaching" versus "classroom-style formal teaching."

103 Brody, *Other Side of Eden,* 64.

Chapter 2: Living and Learning on the Land

Epigraphs: Ivan W. Mouat, "Education in the Arctic District," *Musk-Ox* 7 (1970): 8. His reference to "Kabloona" is an older spelling of Qallunaat; Joe Karetak, *The Inuit Version of Where Our Thoughts Are Believed to Be Generated* (Arviat: Department of Education, Government of Nunavut, n.d.). This text is a reflection paper resulting from a meeting of the Elders' Advisory Committee.

1 "Survival" here can be understood literally; finding oneself on the land without knowledge can quickly result in accidental death or death by exposure and/or starvation. In the context of a modern, settlement lifestyle, which involves greater protection from the elements, another connotation of "survival" takes on importance.

2 For the *IQ* principles, refer to the Appendix.

3 For discussion of the meaning of *sila,* see Chapter 1.

4 Lyle Dick, *Muskoxland: Ellesmere Island in the Age of Contact* (Calgary: University of Calgary Press, 2001), 105-6.

5 For an excellent account by an Inuit Elder of the educational relationship between children and parents, and of the differences between what young girls and boys were taught, see Barnabus Pirjuaq, "Before the Qallunaat Came," in *The Voice of the Natives: The Canadian North and Alaska,* ed. Hans Blohm (Toronto: Penumbra Press, 2001), 154-61.

6 Renée Fossett, *In Order to Live Untroubled: Inuit of the Central Arctic, 1550 to 1940* (Winnipeg: University of Manitoba Press, 2001), 199.

7 Alootook Ipellie, "People of the Good Land," in *The Voice of the Natives: The Canadian North and Alaska,* ed. Hans Blohm (Toronto: Penumbra Press, 2001), 20.

8 For an excellent narrative on the birth and rearing of an Inuit child, see Hugh Brody, *The Other Side of Eden* (Vancouver: Douglas and McIntyre, 2000), 9-64.

9 John Bennett and Susan Rowley, eds., *Uqalurait: An Oral History of Nunavut* (Montreal and Kingston: McGill-Queen's University Press, 2004), 37.

10 Bernard Iquugaqtuq, quoted in ibid., 24.

11 Lee Guemple, "Men and Women, Husbands and Wives: The Role of Gender in Traditional Inuit Society," *Études/Inuit/Studies* 10, 1-2 (1986): 13.

12 Qaida, quoted in Janet Mancini Bilson, "New Choices for a New Era," in *Gossip: A Spoken History of Women in the North,* ed. Mary Crnkovich (Ottawa: Canadian Arctic Resources Committee, 1990), 46.

13 *Amauti:* hood of woman's parka. Alex Spalding and Thomas Kusugaq, *Inuktitut: A Multi-Dialectical Outline Dictionary* (Iqaluit: Nunavut Arctic College, 1998), 7.

14 Anna, quoted in Bilson, "New Choices," 46.

15 Apphia Awa, quoted in Nancy Wachowich, *Saqiyuq: Stories from the Lives of Three Inuit Women* (Montreal and Kingston: McGill-Queen's University Press, 1999), 19.

16 Pauktuutit, Inuit Women's Association, *Arnait: The Views of Inuit Women on Contemporary Issues* (Ottawa: Pauktuutit 1991), 10.

17 Rachel A. Qitsualik, "Baby Thief, Part One," *Nunatsiaq News,* 18 July 2003, http://www.nunatsiaq.com/archives/30725/news/editorial/columns.html (accessed 24 August 2007).

18 *Isuma:* thought; sense; intelligence; feeling; inspiration; imagination. Spalding and Kusugak, *Inuktitut,* 33.

19 Jean L. Briggs, "Expecting the Unexpected: Canadian Inuit Training for an Experimental Lifestyle," *Ethos* 19, 3 (September 1991): 267.

20 Brody, *Other Side of Eden,* 31.
21 Pamela R. Stern, "Learning to Be Smart: An Exploration of the Culture of Intelligence in a Canadian Inuit Community," *American Anthropologist* 101, 3 (1999): 505.
22 See the Appendix.
23 Gideon Qitsualik, quoted in *Elders' Advisory Committee Meeting Transcript* (Arviat: Department of Education, Government of Nunavut, 1-3 June 2004), 56.
24 Brody, *The Other Side of Eden,* 89.
25 Fossett, *In Order to Live Untroubled,* 197-98.
26 Dick, *Muskoxland,* 145.
27 Philip Lange, "Some Qualities of Inuit Social Interaction," in *The White Arctic,* ed. Robert Paine (St. John's/Toronto: Institute of Social and Economic Research, Memorial University of Newfoundland/University of Toronto Press, 1977), 107.
28 Eber Hampton, "Towards a Redefinition of Indian Education," in *First Nations Education in Canada: The Circle Unfolds,* ed. Marie Battiste and Jean Barman (Vancouver: UBC Press, 1995), 8.
29 See the Appendix.
30 Mark Kalluak, in *Elders' Advisory Committee Meeting Transcript,* 28-29.
31 Moses Koihok, in ibid., 35.
32 John Amagoalik, "What Is This Land?" in *The Voice of the Natives: The Canadian North and Alaska,* ed. Hans Blohm (Toronto: Penumbra Press, 2001), 9.
33 Jacopie Kokseak, quoted in Bennett and Rowley, eds., *Uqalurait,* 29.
34 Jean L. Briggs, *Never in Anger: A Portrait of an Eskimo Family* (Cambridge, MA: Harvard University Press, 1970), 269.
35 Ibid., 267; Stern, "Learning to Be Smart," 511.
36 Pirjuaq, "Before the Qallunaat Came," 155.
37 Fossett, *In Order to Live Untroubled,* 7.
38 Pudlo Pudlat, quoted in Bennett and Rowley, eds., *Uqalurait,* 32.
39 Peter Paniloo, in Barry Greenwald, dir., *Life in the Settlements: Between Two Worlds,* film, In Celebration of Nunavut Series vol. 7 (National Film Board of Canada, 1990).
40 Mark Kalluak, quoted in Department of Education, Culture and Employment, *Innuqatigiit: The Curriculum from the Inuit Perspective* (Yellowknife: Government of the Northwest Territories, August 1996), 19.
41 Zacharias Kunuk's 2006 feature film, *The Journals of Knud Rasmussen,* effectively demonstrates the intense sensory experience of the igloo gatherings and shamanism as well as the importance of those events for the reinforcement of values, beliefs, and identity.
42 Sherry Farrell-Racette, quoted in Kathy L. Hodgson-Smith, "Issues of Pedagogy in Aboriginal Education," in *Aboriginal Education: Fulfilling the Promise,* ed. Marlene Brant Castellano, Lynne Davis, and Louise Lahache (Vancouver: UBC Press, 2000), 163.
43 Bennett and Rowley, eds., *Uqalurait,* 11.
44 Emil Imaruittuq, quoted in ibid., 29.
45 Apphia Awa, quoted in Wachowich, *Saqiyuq,* 27.
46 Pauktuutit, Inuit Women of Canada, *The Inuit Way: A Guide to Inuit Culture* (Ottawa: Pauktuutit, 2006), 10.
47 Alice Ayalik, in *Elders' Advisory Committee Meeting Transcript,* 30.
48 Bennett and Rowley, eds., *Uqalurait,* 13.
49 Qitsualik, "Baby Thief, Part One."
50 Mariano Aupilardjuk, in *Elders' Advisory Committee Meeting Transcript,* 67.
51 Quoted from Knud Rasmussen's fifth Thule expedition report, in Fossett, *In Order to Live Untroubled,* 7-8.

52 For supplementary information on early encounters, see Gillian Robertson, ed., *Isuma: Inuit Studies Reader* (Montreal: Isuma, 2004).
53 John S. Matthiasson, *Living on the Land: Change among the Inuit of Baffin Island* (Peterborough, ON: Broadview Press, 1992), 86.
54 Ibid., 54.
55 Taqtu, quoted in Susan Cowan, ed., *We Don't Live in Snow Houses Now: Reflections of Arctic Bay* (Ottawa: Canadian Arctic Producers, 1976), 97.

Chapter 3: Qallunaat Schooling

Epigraphs: Alootook Ipellie, "People of the Good Land," in *The Voice of the Natives: The Canadian North and Alaska,* ed. Hans Blohm (Toronto: Penumbra Press, 2001), 23; Robert McAlpine, "Kablunait and Innuit: The Effect of the White Man upon the Eskimo Minority," *North* 8, 1 (1961): 32.

1 Duane Champagne, "A Multidimensional Theory of Colonialism: The Native North American Experience," in *Social Change and Cultural Continuity among Native Nations* (Lanham, MD: Altamira Press, 2007), 131-43.
2 Ibid., 134.
3 Ibid., 141.
4 For a convincing argument against the "virgin soil" theory (i.e., lack of biological resistance among Aboriginal peoples in the New World) in favour of a more complex analysis that considers socio-economic aspects of colonialism as factors in the spread of disease, see David S. Jones, "Virgin Soils Revisited," *William and Mary Quarterly* 60, 4 (2003): 703-42.
5 Alootook Ipellie, "The Colonization of the Arctic," in *Indigena: Contemporary Native Perspectives,* ed. Gerald McMaster and Lee-Ann Martin, exhibition catalogue (Vancouver: Douglas and McIntyre, 1992), 7.
6 The year 1971 marks the advent of the Inuit representative organization, Inuit Tapirisat of Canada.
7 Malachi Arreak, quoted in Janet Mancini Bilson and Kyra Mancini, *Inuit Women: Their Powerful Spirit in a Century of Change* (Toronto, New York, and Plymouth, MA: Rowman and Littlefield, 2007), 5.
8 Frank James Tester and Peter Kulchyski, *Tammarniit (Mistakes): Inuit Relocation in the Eastern Arctic, 1939-63* (Vancouver: UBC Press, 1994), 4.
9 These policies include, but are not limited to: the relocation of Inuit families from their traditional seasonal subsistence camps scattered throughout the land to the communities of the Eastern Arctic that exist today; the slaughter of Inuit dogs, crucial for transportation and subsistence survival; the coerced relocation of Inuit from Northern Quebec to the High Arctic; removal of individuals with various illnesses to sanitoria in southern Canada, where they had limited communications with their families and where they often died and were buried in unmarked graves; and, the creation of religiously affiliated residential schools, which were a primary – and overwhelmingly negative – force of assimilation for Inuit children.
10 Tester and Kulchyski, *Tamarniit,* 6.
11 Zebedee Nungak, "Life among the Qallunaat: Three Lifetimes in One," in *The Voice of the Natives: The Canadian North and Alaska,* ed. Hans Blohm (Toronto: Penumbra Press, 2001), 163.
12 George Wenzel, "Inuit Subsistence and Hunter Support in Nunavut," in *Nunavut: Inuit Regain Control of Their Lands and Their Lives,* ed. Jens Dahl, Jack Hicks, and Peter Jull (Copenhagen, Denmark: International Working Group for Indigenous Affairs, 2000), 183.

13 John S. Matthiasson, *Living on the Land: Change among the Inuit of Baffin Island* (Peterborough, ON: Broadview Press, 1992), 54.
14 Wenzel, "Inuit Subsistence," 183.
15 Barry Greenwald, dir., *Life in the Settlements: Between Two Worlds,* film, In Celebration of Nunavut Series vol. 7 (National Film Board of Canada, 1990).
16 Qallunaat brought to Inuit epidemics of tuberculosis, polio, and smallpox, to name the most virulent. Persons with the worst cases were often removed from the North to live in hospices in Hamilton or Montreal. See Diamond Jenness, "Eskimo Health," in *Eskimo Administration: II Canada,* 139-49, Arctic Institute of North America Technical Paper no. 14, 1964; and Pat Sandiford Grygier, *A Long Way from Home: The Tuberculosis Epidemic among the Inuit* (Monreal and Kingston: McGill-Queen's University Press, 1994).
17 David Damas, *Arctic Migrants/Arctic Villagers: The Transformation of Inuit Settlement in the Central Arctic,* Native and Northern Series no. 32 (Montreal and Kingston: McGill-Queen's University Press, 2002), 191.
18 Peter Irniq, "Mending the Past: Memory and the Politics of Forgiveness," paper presented at the K.C. Irving Centre, Acadia University, Wolfville, Nova Scotia, 19 October 2004, 3.
19 Paul McNicoll, Frank Tester, and Peter Kulchyski, "Arctic Abstersion: *The Book of Wisdom for Eskimo,* Modernism and Inuit Assimilation," *Études/Inuit/Studies* 23, 1-2 (1999): 218.
20 Ibid., 208.
21 Ibid., 204.
22 Tunu Napartuk, "Youth Perspective (Inuit Health Information Initiative Conference)," *Inuktitut* 91 (2002): 64-72.
23 Hugh Brody, *The Other Side of Eden* (Vancouver: Douglas and McIntyre, 2000), 43.
24 Mariano Aupilardjuk, quoted in Mark Kalluak, ed., *Qaujimatait Meeting Transcript* (Arviat: Department of Education, Government of Nunavut, 8 June 2001), 35.
25 Alootook Ipellie, *Arctic Dreams and Nightmares* (Penticton, BC: Theytus Books, 1993), xi.
26 Alice French, *The Restless Nomad* (Winnipeg: Pemmican, 1992), 69.
27 Matthiasson, *Living on the Land,* 159.
28 Alootook Ipellie, "People of the Good Land," in *The Voice of the Natives: The Canadian North and Alaska,* ed. Hans Blohm (Toronto: Penumbra Press, 2001), 26.
29 Diamond Jenness, *Eskimo Administration: II Canada,* Arctic Institute of North America Technical Paper no. 14 (1964), 21.
30 Damas, *Arctic Migrants/Arctic Villagers,* 195, refers to this as the "Policy of Dispersal."
31 Peter Jull, "Inuit and Nunavut: Renewing the New World," in *Nunavut: Inuit Regain Control of Their Lands and Their Lives,* ed. Jens Dahl, Jack Hicks, and Peter Jull (Copenhagen, Denmark: International Working Group for Indigenous Affairs, 2000), 123.
32 Jenness, *Eskimo Administration,* 76.
33 Shelagh D. Grant, *Sovereignty or Security? Government Policy in the Canadian North, 1936-1950* (Vancouver: UBC Press, 1988), 242.
34 Ibid., 249.
35 Damas, *Arctic Migrants/Arctic Villagers,* 26.
36 Peter Clancy, "The Making of Eskimo Policy in Canada, 1952-62: The Life and Times of the Eskimo Affairs Committee," *Arctic* 40, 3 (September 1987): 192.
37 Grant, *Sovereignty or Security?* 188.
38 Alan Rudolph Marcus, *Relocating Eden: The Image and Politics of Inuit Exile in the Canadian Arctic* (Hanover, NH: University Press of New England, 1995), 27.
39 Grant, *Sovereignty or Security?* 199-200.
40 Jenness, *Eskimo Administration,* 79.

41 Jean Lesage, quoted in Mary A. Van Meenan, "Government Policies of Education for the Native Peoples of Siberia and the Canadian Northwest Territories, 1900-90: A Historical Examination" (PhD diss., Department of History, Dalhousie University, 1994), 196.

42 Royal Commission on Aboriginal Peoples (RCAP), "Residential Schools," in *Report of the Royal Commission on Aboriginal Peoples,* vol. 1, part 2, ch. 10 (Ottawa: Indian and Northern Affairs Canada), http://www.ainc-inac.gc.ca/ch/rcap/sg/cg10_e.pdf (accessed 31 October 2007).

43 Jean Barman, "Schooled for Inequality: The Education of British Columbia Aboriginal Children," in *Children, Teachers and Schools in the History of British Columbia,* ed. Jean Barman, Neil Sutherland, and J.D. Wilson, 57-80 (Calgary: Detsilig, 1995); Jean Barman, "Separate and Unequal: Indian and White Girls at All Hallows School," in *Children, Teachers and Schools in the History of British Columbia,* ed. Jean Barman, Neil Sutherland, and J.D. Wilson, 337-58 (Calgary: Detsilig, 1995).

44 In 1960 Jean Chrétien, then minister of Indian affairs, declared that education of the Inuit should result in "equal status, opportunity and responsibility, a role they share with all other Canadians"; quoted in Robert E. Johns, "History of Administration of Schools, N.W.T.," *Musk-Ox* 18 (1976): 43.

45 Donald B. Marsh, *Echoes from a Frozen Land,* ed. Winifred Marsh (Edmonton: Hurtig, 1987), 31.

46 Jenness, *Eskimo Administration,* 42.

47 John S. Milloy, *A National Crime: The Canadian Government and the Residential School System, 1879-1986* (Winnipeg: University of Manitoba Press, 1999), 254.

48 Maata Pudlat, "Boy Have Things Changed," in *Gossip: A Spoken History of Women in the North,* ed. Mary Crnkovich (Ottawa: Canadian Arctic Resources Committee, 1990), 18.

49 Irniq, "Mending the Past," 1.

50 In July 2008 a lawsuit was filed by seven former students in the Nunavut Court of Justice, seeking damages from the Canadian government for denying them the right to communicate with their families, for forbidding them to practise their culture, and for contributing to their loss of both cultural identity and a sense of belonging with their community. See Chris Windeyer, "'Eskimo Experiment' Claimants Seek Cash, Apology," *Nunatsiaq News,* 4 July 2008, http://www.nunatsiaqnews.com/archives/2008/807/80704/news/nunavut/80704_1350.html (accessed 12 July 2008).

51 Peter Freuchen Ittinuar, *Teach an Eskimo How to Read,* ed. Thierry Rodon, Life Stories of Northern Leaders Series (Iqaluit: Nunavut Arctic College, 2008), 59.

52 Milloy, *National Crime,* 254.

53 Bishop Reynald Rouleau, quoted in Todd Phillips, "RC Bishop Apologizes for Abuses against Inuit Students," *Nunatsiaq News,* 1 March 1996, http://www.nunanet.com/~nunat/week/60301.html#3 (accessed 29 July 2007).

54 Ipellie, "Colonization of the Arctic," 10.

55 French, *Restless Nomad,* 4.

56 Ibid., 19.

57 Apphia Awa, quoted in Nancy Wachowich, *Saqiyuq: Stories from the Lives of Three Inuit Women* (Montreal and Kingston: McGill-Queen's University Press, 1999), 107.

58 French, *Restless Nomad,* 96.

59 Margery Hinds, *School-House in the Arctic* (London: Geoffrey Bles, 1958), 107.

60 Irniq, "Mending the Past," 5.

61 Taqtu, quoted in Susan Cowan, ed., *We Don't Live in Snowhouses Now: Reflections of Arctic Bay* (Ottawa: Canadian Arctic Producers, 1976), 97.

62 Paul Welsman, "Education of Native Peoples in the Northwest Territories: A Northern Model," in *The North in Transition,* ed. Nils Orvik and Kirk Patterson (Kingston: Centre for International Relations, Queen's University, 1976), 27.
63 Johns, "History of Administration," 47.
64 Ibid.
65 N.J. Macpherson, *Dreams and Visions: Education in the Northwest Territories from Early Days to 1984* (Yellowknife: Government of the Northwest Territories, 1991), 17.
66 Ibid., 18
67 Ibid.
68 Ronald Dalby, "Twentieth Century School," *North* 9, 2 (1962): 15.
69 R. Quinn Duffy, "Providing an Education," in *The Road to Nunavut: The Progress of the Eastern Arctic Inuit since the Second World War* (Montreal and Kingston: McGill-Queen's University Press, 1988), 106.
70 Macpherson, *Dreams and Visions,* 19.
71 Ibid., 269.
72 Ibid., 270.
73 Gordon Robertson, quoted in ibid., 287.
74 Dalby, "Twentieth Century School," 16.
75 John J. Honigmann and Irma Honigmann, *Eskimo Townsmen* (Ottawa: Canadian Research Centre for Anthropology, University of Ottawa, 1965), 177-78.
76 Dalby, "Twentieth Century School," 16.
77 David Wilson, quoted in Macpherson, *Dreams and Visions,* 190.
78 Duffy, "Providing an Education," 106.
79 Ivan W. Mouat, "Education in the Arctic District," *Musk-Ox* 7 (1970): 6.
80 Van Meenan, "Government Policies," 260.
81 Department of Education, *Survey of Education,* ed. B.C. Gillie (Yellowknife: Government of the Northwest Territories, 29 February 1972), 117.
82 Dorothy L. Robinson, quoted in Macpherson, *Dreams and Visions,* 65.
83 These expectations echo the jack-of-all-trades demands on teachers in rural British Columbia during the early phases of school system development; see J.D. Wilson, "The Visions of Ordinary Participants: Teachers' Views of Rural Schooling in British Columbia in the 1920s," in *A History of British Columbia: Selected Readings,* ed. Pat Roy, 239-55 (Toronto: Copp Clark Pitman, 1989).
84 Dave Webster, quoted in Macpherson, *Dreams and Visions,* 224.
85 For an interesting discussion of the attitudes and behaviours of Qallunaat toward Inuit that can be construed as patronizing or fall under the rubric of "tutelage," see Robert Paine, "The Nursery Game: Colonizers and the Colonized," in *The White Arctic,* ed. Robert Paine (St. John's/Toronto: Institute of Social and Economic Research, Memorial University of Newfoundland/University of Toronto Press, 1977), 78-106.
86 Welsman, "Education of Native Peoples," 31.
87 As was the case for rural farming families in British Columbia, children's development of hunting skills and help in procuring food could be vital to the economic viability of the family, so they were expected to juggle the demands of school and work at home. See Neil Sutherland, "I Can't Recall When I Didn't Help: The Working Lives of Pioneering Children in Twentieth Century British Columbia," *Histoire Sociale/Social History* 23, 48 (November 1991): 263-88.
88 Honigmann and Honigmann, *Eskimo Townsmen,* 178.
89 Hinds, *School-House in the Arctic,* 103.
90 Kenn Harper, quoted in Macpherson, *Dreams and Visions,* 216-17.

91 R.A.J. Phillips, "The Opening Door," *North* 7, 6 (1960): 4.

92 The NWT Teacher Education Program operated out of Yellowknife and then Fort Smith until 1979, when a branch of the program was added in Frobisher Bay to better accommodate Inuit students and differences between the priorities of the eastern and western Northwest Territories. See Macpherson, *Dreams and Visions,* 200-4.

93 Colin Irwin, "Lords of the Arctic, Wards of the State: The Growing Inuit Population, Arctic Resettlement and Their Effects on Social and Economic Change," *Northern Perspectives* 17, 1 (1989): 1, http://www.carc.org/pubs/v17no1/2.htm (accessed 2 August 2007).

94 Ipellie, "Colonization of the Arctic," 12.

95 Irwin, "Lords of the Arctic."

96 Frank G. Vallee, "Eskimos of Canada as a Minority Group: Social and Cultural Perspectives," in *Education in the North: The First International Conference on Cross-Cultural Education in the Circumpolar Nations,* ed. Frank Darnell (Fairbanks: University of Alaska and the Arctic Institute of North America, 1972), 29.

97 Mouat, "Education in the Arctic District," 8.

98 For more information on the effectiveness of the first generation to emerge from government high schools in negotiating with the federal government, see Peter Jull, "Redefining Aboriginal-White Relations: Canada's Inuit," *International Journal of Canadian Studies/ Revue internationale d'études canadiennes,* 3 (1991): 11-25.

99 Irniq, "Mending the Past," 4.

Chapter 4: Educational Change

Epigraphs: Ivan W. Mouat, "Education in the Arctic District," *Musk-Ox* 7 (1970): 9; Markusie Inuaaluk, letter, *Inuit Today* 5, 8 (September 1976): 10.

1 In this chapter, I broaden my scope of reference to include the entire Northwest Territories and, when necessary, refer to the Inuit under the category of Aboriginal or Native, the terms typically used during this period to refer to the various First Nations and Inuit groups. This period involved an ongoing dialogue between the Inuit of the Eastern Arctic, as well as other Native groups in the Mackenzie District, and the Government of the Northwest Territories, culminating in the division of the territory in 1999.

2 Robert E. Johns, "History of Administration of Schools, N.W.T.," *Musk-Ox* 18 (1976): 52.

3 Government of the Northwest Territories, Office of the Commissioner of the Northwest Territories, "Past Commissioners," http://www.commissioner.gov.nt.ca/history (accessed 18 September 2007). In 1986 the position was reformed to resemble that of a provincial lieutenant governor, and all responsibility for matters of the NWT Legislative Assembly was handed to elected officials.

4 Mary A. Van Meenan, "Government Policies of Education for the Native Peoples of Siberia and the Canadian Northwest Territories, 1900-90: A Historical Examination" (PhD diss., Department of History, Dalhousie University, 1994), 269-70.

5 R.A.J. Phillips, "The Opening Door," *North* 7, 6 (1960): 5.

6 Frances Abele, Carolyn Dittburner, and Katherine A. Graham, "Towards a Shared Understanding in the Policy Discussion about Aboriginal Education," in *Aboriginal Education: Fulfilling the Promise,* ed. Marlene Brant Castellano, Lynne Davis, and Louise Lahache (Vancouver: UBC Press, 2000), 5.

7 Ibid., 8.

8 J.R. Mallea, "Introduction: Cultural Diversity and Canadian Education," in *Cultural Diversity and Canadian Education,* ed. J.R. Mallea and Jonathan D. Young, 1-16 (Ottawa: Carleton University Press, 1984).

9 Harold Troper and Morton Weinfeld, "Diversity in Canada," in *Ethnicity, Politics, and Public Policy*, ed. Harold Troper and Morton Weinfeld (Toronto: University of Toronto Press, 1999), 5.

10 Mallea, "Introduction," 12. See also, Cornelius Jaenen, "Mutilated Multiculturalism," in *Canadian Education in the 1980s*, ed. J. Donald Wilson (Calgary: Detsilig, 1981), 79-96.

11 Karen R. Mock, "25 Years of Multiculturalism – Past, Present and Future, Part I," *Canadian Social Studies* 31 (Spring 1997): 123.

12 N.J. Macpherson, *Dreams and Visions: Education in the Northwest Territories from Early Days to 1984* (Yellowknife: Government of the Northwest Territories, 1991), 280.

13 Ibid., 20.

14 Department of Education, *Survey of Education*, ed. B.C. Gillie (Yellowknife: Government of the Northwest Territories, 29 February 1972). Except in the case of direct quotations, specific page numbers are not cited for subsequent references to the *Survey* in this chapter. B.C. Gillie was one of the only federal bureaucrats from Ottawa to move to Yellowknife and participate in the transfer of the education system to the Northwest Territories.

15 Department of Education, *Survey*, 2.

16 Both Nunavut and the Northwest Territories presently rely on the Alberta curriculum for structuring grades 10 to 12 and providing high school leaving exams.

17 Department of Education, *Survey*, 2-3.

18 See comments by Taqtu and Lew Philip in Susan Cowan, ed., *We Don't Live in Snowhouses Now: Reflections of Arctic Bay* (Ottawa: Canadian Arctic Producers, 1976), 97 and 179, respectively.

19 Department of Education, *Survey*, 8.

20 Ibid., 9.

21 Ibid., 36.

22 Ibid., 17.

23 Ibid., 105.

24 Northwest Territories Executive Committee, *Report of the Special Committee of the Council of the Northwest Territories to Study the "Survey of Education – Northwest Territories"* (Yellowknife: Council of the Northwest Territories, January 1973). Except in the case of direct quotations, specific page numbers are not cited for subsequent references to the *Report* in this chapter.

25 None of these representatives was Inuit.

26 Northwest Territories Executive Committee, *Report*, 2.

27 Ibid.

28 Ibid.

29 Ibid., 4.

30 Ibid., 28.

31 Ibid., Appendix B.

32 Macpherson, *Dreams and Visions*, 183.

33 Ibid.

34 Ibid., 186.

35 John D. Lee, quoted in Macpherson, *Dreams and Visions*, 200.

36 Ibid.

37 Department of Education, Curriculum Division, *Elementary Education in the Northwest Territories: A Handbook for Curriculum Development* (Yellowknife: Government of the Northwest Territories, 1972).

38 Department of Education, Programme Development Division, *Learning in the Middle Years: A Handbook for Curriculum Development* (Yellowknife: Government of the Northwest Territories, 1973).

39 B.C. Gillie, quoted in Macpherson, *Dreams and Visions,* 291.
40 Department of Education, Curriculum Division, *Elementary Education,* 10.
41 Ibid., 13.
42 Ibid., 7.
43 Ibid., 8.
44 Department of Education, Programme Development Division, *Learning in the Middle Years,* 4.
45 See "Curriculum Development and an Angry Young Man," in Macpherson, *Dreams and Visions,* 288.
46 Department of Education, Curriculum Division, *Elementary Education,* 3.
47 Ibid., 9.
48 This letter appears in Macpherson, *Dreams and Visions,* 290.
49 Ibid.
50 B.C. Gillie, quoted in ibid., 22.
51 According to Macpherson, *Dreams and Visions,* 290, "A number of more traditional teachers left the employ of the department in June, 1972."
52 B.C. Gillie, quoted in Macpherson, *Dreams and Visions,* 22.
53 In a 1974 newspaper, the NWT Teacher's Association angrily defended itself against Robinson's "change or get out" approach. Before explaining the high demands on teachers in the North, the association wrote, "In defense of teachers who, in fact, innovated much of the philosophy of the Department of Education while attempting to teach children, and develop a curriculum for the school programs, our Association must speak out!" See "The Teachers' Reply," in Macpherson, *Dreams and Visions,* 299.
54 Department of Education, Programme Development Division, *Piksaaq* (Yellowknife, Ottawa, and Winnipeg: Government of the Northwest Territories, 1974).
55 Government of the Northwest Territories (GNWT), *An Ordinance Respecting Education in the Northwest Territories [Chapter 2],* (Yellowknife: Council of the Northwest Territories, 1977).
56 Macpherson, *Dreams and Visions,* 280.
57 Stipulation 57(2) reads: "The school staff shall utilize aspects of the local cultures in the curriculum, curriculum material and teaching methods of the schools, and the principal shall consult with and be guided by the local education authority in planning such utilization." GNWT, *Ordinance Respecting Education,* 48.
58 Ibid., 49.
59 Stipulation 54(1) reads: "The local education authority shall prescribe the language of instruction to be used for kindergarten, where a kindergarten program is offered, and for the first two years of the school program following kindergarten." GNWT, *Ordinance Respecting Education,* 47.
60 Ibid., 22.
61 Ibid., 30-33.
62 Department of Education, Education Programs and Evaluation Division, *Philosophy of Education in the Northwest Territories* (Yellowknife: Government of the Northwest Territories, 1978).
63 Ibid., i.
64 Ibid.
65 Ibid., 5.
66 Ibid., 6.
67 M. Lynn Aylward, "Discourses of Cultural Relevance in Nunavut Schooling," *Journal of Research in Rural Education* 22, 7 (2007): 3, http://www.umaine.edu/jrre/22-7.pdf (accessed 7 September 2007).

68 Paul Welsman, "Education of Native Peoples in the Northwest Territories: A Northern Model," in *The North in Transition,* ed. Nils Orvik and Kirk Patterson (Kingston: Centre for International Relations, Queen's University, 1976), 37.
69 Macpherson, *Dreams and Visions,* 20.
70 Ibid., 21.
71 Van Meenan, "Government Policies of Education," 230.
72 David Omar Born, *Eskimo Education and the Trauma of Social Change,* Northern Science Research Group Report (Ottawa: Department of Indian Affairs and Northern Development, 15 January 1970). Born conducted this study in the community now known as Sanikiluaq, located in the Belcher Islands of Hudson Bay. He informally interviewed (using an interpreter) each child and at least one adult from each household about their attitudes toward the school. Although this study cannot represent the entire population of Inuit in the Eastern Arctic, it is one of the only collections of opinions of children and parents from this time period.
73 Ibid., 2.
74 Ibid., 14.
75 Ibid., 11.
76 Ibid., 13.
77 Ibid., 18.
78 Ibid.
79 Ibid., 22.
80 Ibid., 33.
81 Ibid., 23.
82 Ibid., 32.
83 Ibid., 41.
84 Desmond Sparham, "Education at Cape Dorset: An Evaluation," *Eskimo* 6 (Spring-Summer 1974): 13.
85 John J. Honigmann and Irma Honigmann, *Eskimo Townsmen* (Ottawa: Canadian Research Centre for Anthropology, University of Ottawa, 1965), 179.
86 John Amagoalik, *Changing the Face of Canada,* ed. Louis McComber, Life Stories of Northern Leaders Series (Iqaluit: Nunavut Arctic College, 2007), 43; James Arvaluk, *That's My Vision,* ed. Noel McDermott, Life Stories of Northern Leaders Series (Iqaluit: Nunavut Arctic College, 2007), 32-39.
87 Arvaluk, *That's My Vision,* 39.
88 Amagoalik, *Changing the Face of Canada,* 44.
89 Ibid., 45.
90 Ibid.
91 Arvaluk, *That's My Vision,* 39.
92 Inuit-Eskimo Association of Canada, "Coppermine Conference Report July 14-18, 1970," ed. Norman R. Dunne, partially reproduced in *Nunavut Sivuniksavut Course Readings: Inuit-Government Relations* (Ottawa: Nunavut Sivuniksavut, n.d.), 55-115. A note to the report points out that it is primarily a word-for-word transcript of the discussions, taken from audiotapes, and it also includes appendixes of the meeting's resolutions and of responses to those resolutions by a number of government sources.
93 The Inuit Cultural Institute, dissolved in the 1980s, was an organization run by Inuit to record their culture through various means.
94 "The Inuit Educational Concept," ed. Rachel Qitsualik, special issue of *Ajurnarmat,* 4 (Inuit Cultural Institute, November 1979): 1. The pages of this publication are not numbered, so I have applied my own page numbers.

95 Ibid., 2.
96 Ibid., 5.
97 Ibid., 6.
98 Ibid., 8.
99 Ibid., 10.
100 Johns, "History of Administration," 43. The 5,943 students categorized as "other" is attributed by the author of this article to the rapid influx of population from southern Canada due to projects such as the pipeline construction and other resource initiatives. This growth would have been concentrated in the western regions of the NWT at this time.
101 Frank Vallee, quoted in Darnell, ed., *Education in the North,* 39.

Chapter 5: Reclaiming the Schools

Epigraphs: Frank Darnell, "Education and the Circumpolar Nativistic Movement: Twenty Years of Change for the Better," in *Self-Determination in Native Education in the Circumpolar North: Proceedings of the Seminar Inuit Control of Inuit Education,* ed. Malcolm Farrow and David Wilman (Yellowknife: Department of Education, Government of the Northwest Territories, August 1989), 41; Baffin Divisional Board of Education (BDBE), *Our Future Is Now: Directions for Education in the Baffin* (Iqaluit: Baffin Divisional Board of Education, 1987), 2.

1 These three regional boards are the Baffin Divisional Board of Education, incorporated in 1985 (later referred to as the Qikiqtani Divisional Board of Education); the Keewatin Divisional Board of Education, incorporated in 1988 (later referred to as the Kivalliq Divisional Board of Education); and the Kitikmeot Board of Education, incorporated in 1989.
2 Iqaluit has historically been the "hub" of the Eastern Arctic, through which most people travel on their way to other Nunavut communities. It is the site of the Gordon Robertson Education Centre (later called Inuksuk High School), which most Inuit students in the Eastern Arctic would have attended prior to the mid-1990s, as well as the home of Arctic College Teacher Education Program), and in 1999 Iqaluit became the capital of Nunavut. Where appropriate in this chapter, Iqaluit is referred to by its former name of Frobisher Bay.
3 As is the case with governments everywhere, department names change as portfolios are shifted over the years. Although the NWT Department of Education was sometimes officially called the Department of Education, Culture and Employment, for consistency's sake I refer to it simply as the Department of Education.
4 Northwest Territories Legislative Assembly, "History of the Legislative Assembly," http://www.assembly.gov.nt.ca/_live/pages/wpPages/factshistoryofthelegislativeassembly.aspx (accessed 2 December 2007).
5 Frank Darnell and Anton Hoem, *Taken to Extremes: Education in the Far North* (Oslo, Norway: Scandinavian University Press, 1996), 167.
6 Although within this chapter I cannot fully discuss the evolving political movement toward self-determination, which was shaped primarily by an Inuit land claim in the Northwest Territories, I make further reference to it in the Conclusion.
7 Department of Education, *Survey of Education,* ed. B.C. Gillie (Yellowknife: Government of the Northwest Territories, 29 February 1972).
8 Northwest Territories Legislative Assembly, Special Committee on Education (hereafter Special Committee), *Learning, Tradition and Change in the Northwest Territories* (Yellowknife: Northwest Territories Legislative Assembly, 1982), 10.

9 Robert E. Johns, "History of Administration of Schools, N.W.T.," *Musk-Ox* 18 (1976): 56.
10 Darnell and Hoem, *Taken to Extremes,* 158.
11 Special Committee, *Learning, Tradition and Change,* 17.
12 The Department of Education in Yellowknife officially retained responsibility for defining the curriculum outcomes that were to determine the boards' development of classroom programs. This distinction becomes blurred in the history of the Baffin Divisional Board of Education, which introduced a number of initiatives that were not consistent with the mandate set by the Department of Education. I have used the terms programs or programming and curriculum fairly interchangeably in this case study, but it should be noted that the BDBE and the other boards were not entirely independent of curriculum standards established centrally.
13 Special Committee, *Learning, Tradition and Change,* 10.
14 Ibid., 17.
15 See Ann Vick-Westgate, *Nunavik: Inuit-Controlled Education in Arctic Quebec* (Calgary: University of Calgary Press, 2002).
16 Frances Abele, Carolyn Dittburner, and Katherine A. Graham, "Towards a Shared Understanding in the Policy Discussion about Aboriginal Education," in *Aboriginal Education: Fulfilling the Promise,* ed. Marlene Brant Castellano, Lynne Davis, and Louise Lahache (Vancouver: UBC Press, 2000), 9.
17 Mary Cousins, "Educational Opportunities for the Native Canadian," in *Indigenous Peoples and Education in the Circumpolar North,* ed. William G. Demmert Jr. (Juneau: Alaska State Department of Education, 1987), 46-47.
18 Geoffrey B. Isherwood, Knute Sorensen, and Eric Colbourne, "Educational Development in the North: Preparing Inuit Leaders for School Board Control," *Education Canada* 26, 3 (1986): 10.
19 Ibid., 10-11.
20 Ibid., 14.
21 Northwest Territories Legislative Assembly, *An Ordinance to Amend the Education Ordinance* (Yellowknife: Government of the Northwest Territories, 1982).
22 BDBE, "Education in the Baffin," paid insert, *Nunatsiaq News,* 1 October 1993, 2.
23 Darnell and Hoem, *Taken to Extremes,* 167.
24 BDBE, *Our Future Is Now: Directions for Education in the Baffin,* 2.
25 Ibid., 4.
26 BDBE, *Piniaqtavut: Integrated Program* (Iqaluit: BDBE, 1989). The Introduction to *Piniaqtavut* specifies that it is a "program," not a curriculum, in that it suggests learning experiences, resources, and materials rather than describing the outcomes that students should acquire through schooling. For my purposes, the difference between curriculum and program is negligible in that they both describe what educational administration – in this case, locally driven administration – mandated teachers to achieve in the classroom.
27 Ibid., i.
28 Ibid.
29 BDBE, *Our Future is Now ... Implementing Inuuqatigiit* (Iqaluit: BDBE, 1996), 2.
30 BDBE, *Piniaqtavut,* iii.
31 Ibid., i.
32 Ibid.
33 Ibid., ii.
34 Ibid., v.
35 Ibid., 1.
36 Ibid.

37 The BDBE references the "interactive/experiential" model detailed in Jim Cummins, *Empowering Minority Students* (Sacramento, CA: California Association for Bilingual Education, 1989).
38 BDBE, *Piniaqtavut,* ii.
39 Ibid., iii.
40 BDBE, *Annual Report 1989-1990* (Iqaluit: BDBE, 1990), A7.
41 Although some of these pedagogical approaches can be directly attributed to Inuit culture, others relate to trends that had for some time been promoted in education and schooling across the country. An example is the "progressive" practices that were widely publicized by the 1968 Hall-Dennis report, titled *Living and Learning,* introduced in Ontario. See Nadeem A. Memon, *Contextualizing Hall-Dennis: The Rise of Progressive Educational Practices in Ontario, 1968-1972* (MA thesis, Department of Theory and Policy Studies, Ontario Institute of Studies in Education of the University of Toronto, 2006).
42 Department of Education, *Education in the NWT* (Yellowknife: Government of the Northwest Territories, 1988), 3.
43 Department of Education, *Our Students, Our Future: An Educational Framework* (Yellowknife: Government of the Northwest Territories, March 1991), 12.
44 Department of Education, *Our Students, Our Future,* 16-18.
45 Ibid., 18.
46 Ibid., 13.
47 Ibid., 5.
48 Department of Education, Culture and Employment (DECE), *Inuuqatigiit: The Curriculum from the Inuit Perspective* (Yellowknife: Government of the Northwest Territories, August 1996), 3: "The name of the curriculum, *Inuuqatigiit,* means Inuit to Inuit, people to people, living together, or family to family. It implies togetherness and family unity between people. This is the foundation of the curriculum: a unity of Inuit philosophy for the benefit of children, teachers, schools and communities."
49 Ibid., 2.
50 Ibid., 5.
51 Ibid., 11.
52 Ibid., 129.
53 Ibid.
54 Ibid., 15.
55 Ibid., 5.
56 Ibid., 19. I have not made the pursuit of bilingual education a major focus of this analysis. However, in terms of achieving the reintegration of Inuit education into schools, a crucial component is opportunities to teach and learn in the original language in which the activities were pursued.
57 BDBE, *Our Future Is Now ... Implementing Inuuqatigiit,* 3.
58 Ibid.
59 BDBE, *Our Future is Now ... Implementing Inuuqatigiit: Goals, Strategies and Actions 1995-2000* (Iqaluit: BDBE, 1996).
60 M. Lynn Aylward, "Discourses of Cultural Relevance in Nunavut Schooling," *Journal of Research in Rural Education* 22, 7 (2007): 6, http://www.umaine.edu/jrre/22-7.pdf (accessed 7 September 2007).
61 BDBE, "Education: Preparing for Nunavut," paid insert, *Nunatsiaq News,* 30 September 1994.
62 Personal communication from Cathy McGregor, director of the BDBE from 1992 to 1999, 17 December 2008.

63 Dawn Loney, *Working Together – Your Community and Your School: A Piniaqtavut/ Inuuqatigiit Strategy Book* (Iqaluit: BDBE, 1997), 1.
64 Ibid., 10.
65 Caleb Apak, "*Inuktitut* Asks about Education," *Inuktitut Magazine* 48 (July 1981): 9.
66 Ibid.
67 BDBE, *Module Development Part 1 – Traditional Skills – Career and Technology Studies* (Iqaluit: Department of Education, Culture and Employment, Government of Northwest Territories, 1995-96).
68 *Qamutiik:* sled. Alex Spalding and Thomas Kusugaq, *Inuktitut: A Multi-Dialectical Outline Dictionary* (Iqaluit: Nunavut Arctic College, 1998), 108.
69 M. Alexander Tufts, "Pisukvigijait – Where You Walk: Inuit Students' Perceptions of Connections between Their Culture and School Science" (MEd diss., Department of Curriculum and Instruction, University of New Brunswick, 1998), 2-3.
70 Ibid., 3.
71 Ibid., 9.
72 Ibid., 18.
73 Ibid., 18-32.
74 Ibid., 39.
75 Meeka Arnakaq quoted in: Leena Evic-Twerdin and Mary Wilman, "Elders' Discussion on Inuktitut Education," in *Self-Determination in Native Education in the Circumpolar North: Proceedings of the Seminar Inuit Control of Inuit Education Iqaluit,* ed. Malcolm Farrow and David Wilman (Yellowknife: Department of Education, Government of the Northwest Territories, August 1989), 16.
76 David Serkoak, "Community Control in Native Education: A Sense of Ownership, Responsibility, and Commitment," in *Self-Determination in Native Education in the Circumpolar North: Proceedings of the Seminar Inuit Control of Inuit Education,* ed. Malcolm Farrow and David Wilman (Yellowknife: Department of Education, Government of the Northwest Territories, August 1989), 59.
77 Fiona O'Donoghue, Joanne Tompkins, Sandy McAuley, Lena Metuq, Nunia Qanatsiaq, and Elizabeth Fortes, *Pursuing a Dream: Inuit Educaiton in the Qikiqtani Region of Nunavut from 1980-1999,* report on the Iqaluit Meetings of 25 May to 1 June 2005 to the Social Sciences and Humanities Research Council – Northern Development Grant, 5 October 2005, 2.
78 Ibid., 6.
79 Ibid.
80 Ibid.
81 Ibid., 7.
82 Ibid., 14.
83 BDBE *Annual Report 1993-94* (Iqaluit: BDBE, 1995), 3.
84 BDBE, *Annual Report 1996-97* (Iqaluit: BDBE, 1997), 2.
85 BDBE, *Annual Report 1990-1991* (Iqaluit: Baffin Divisional Board of Education, 1991), A16.
86 BDBE, *Annual Report 1996-97,* 2.
87 Statistics Canada cites a national high school graduation rate of 75 percent in 2001. See Statistics Canada, *Education Indicators in Canada: Report of the Pan-Canadian Education Indicators Program* (Ottawa: Statistics Canada, 2005).
88 The NWT Department of Education and the Nunavut Department of Education have not yet been able to replace the Alberta curriculum for grades 10 to 12.
89 Aylward, "Discourses of Cultural Relevance," 4.

90 Frank Pearce, "NWT Grade 12 Not a Real Grade 12?" *Nunatsiaq News,* 30 September 1994, 7, 38.

91 Nunavut Implementation Commission, *Footprints in New Snow: A Comprehensive Report from the Nunavut Implementation Commission to the Department of Indian Affairs and Northern Development, Government of the Northwest Territories and Nunavut Tunngavik Incorporated Concerning the Establishment of the Nunavut Government* (Ottawa: Bradda Printing Services, 1995), 26.

92 Ibid., 26-27.

93 Ibid.

94 Ibid., 27.

95 The Department did create three "Regional School Operations" offices to oversee operational and administrative support to schools and district education authorities. Staff primarily include program and student support specialists, and Superintendents of Schools overseen by an Executive Director. However, these offices do not officially have policy making or curriculum development powers independent of the Department of Education Headquarters. While practices do vary between the regions, they are not legally invested with powers to change education at the regional or local level.

96 Consulting Audit Canada, "Executive Summary," in *Accountability and Structural Options for Nunavut's Education, Health and Social Services Boards,* April 1999, 14.

97 Government of Nunavut, "Government of Nunavut to Phase Out Health and Education Boards," news release, 22 April 1999.

98 Government of Nunavut, "Nunavut Boards of Health and Social Services and Education," backgrounder, 22 April 1999.

99 Personal communication from Cathy McGregor, director of the BDBE from 1992 to 1999, 12 December 2007.

100 John Thomas, quoted in Marion Rahn, "Iqaluit Education Authority Wants School Board Reform," *Special Report on Education. Nunatsiaq News.* 9 October 1998, http://www.nunatsiaqnews.com/archives/nunavut981031/nvt81009_17.html (accessed 10 January 2008).

101 John Maurice, quoted in ibid.

102 Ibid.

Conclusion: Lessons Learned

Epigraph: Tagak Curley, in Kath Clarida-Fry, dir., *Staking the Claim: Dreams, Democracy and Canadian Inuit,* film (Ottawa: Entheos Films, 1 March 2007); P.J. Akeeagok, in Kath Clarida-Fry, dir., *Staking the Claim,* 2007.

1 Mark Salber Phillips and Gordon Schochet, eds., *Questions of Tradition* (Toronto: University of Toronto Press, 2004), x, emphasis in original.

2 Jan Vansina, *Paths in the Rainforests: Toward a History of Political Tradition in Equatorial Africa* (Madison: University of Wisconsin Press, 1990), 257-58.

3 Heidi Bohaker, "*Nindoodemag:* Anishinaabe Identities in the Eastern Great Lakes Region, 1600-1900" (PhD diss., Department of History, University of Toronto, 2006), 23.

4 Ibid.

5 Vansina, *Paths in the Rainforests,* 260.

6 Ibid.

7 Paige Raibmon, *Authentic Indians: Episodes of Encounter from the Late-Nineteenth-Century Northwest Coast* (Durham, NC, and London: Duke University Press, 2005), 202.

8 Ibid., 201.

9 Ibid., 13.

10 Ibid., 207.

11 Janet McGrath, (Tamalk), "Elder's Perspective: Mariano Aupilaarjuk," *Inuktitut* 92 (2002): 54-67.

12 For an analysis of educational change in one Nunavut community (including the post-1999 period) that focuses on the integration of *IQ* and the balance between educational needs identified by the school and those identified by the community, see Adam Pulpan, "The Relationship of School, Inuit Qaujimajatuqangit and Elders in the Education of Youth within a Nunavut Community" (MEd thesis, Department of Education, York University, 2006).

13 Thomas Suluk, quoted in "Negotiators Reach Wildlife Agreement-in-Principle," *Nunatsiaq News,* 30 October 1981, http://www.nunatsiaq.com/archives/april0199/nvt90401_14.html (accessed 17 November 2007).

14 Ann Vick-Westgate, *Nunavik: Inuit-Controlled Education in Arctic Quebec* (Calgary: University of Calgary Press, 2002), 2.

15 Government of Quebec, *James Bay and Northern Quebec Agreement and Complementary Agreements,* new ed. (Sainte-Foy, QC: Les Publications du Québec, 1998), Section 17.0.1., http://www.ainc-inac.gc.ca/pr/agr/que/jbnq9_e.PDF (accessed 17 November 2007).

16 Ibid., Section 17.0.85.

17 Thomas R. Berger, *Conciliator's Final Report: The Nunavut Project,* Nunavut Land Claims Agreement Implementation Contract Negotiations for the Second Planning Period 2003-2013, 1 March 2006, i.

18 Nunavut Tunngavik Incorporated was created to oversee the implementation of the NLCA and the ongoing management of Inuit benefits.

19 Berger, *Conciliator's Final Report,* 2.

20 Ibid., 14.

21 Ibid., iii.

22 Ibid., iv.

23 Ibid., 25.

24 Ibid., 31-32. See also John Thompson, "News Analysis: The Vanishing Inuit Teacher in Nunavut," *Nunatsiaq News,* 19 October 2007, http://www.nunatsiaq.com/archives/2007/710/7 1019/news/nunavut/71019_614.html (accessed 10 January 2008).

25 In 2000 the rate of infant mortality in Nunavut was three times the national average, of tuberculosis more than eight times, of sexually transmitted disease fifteen to twenty times, and of suicide six times. See Jack Hicks and Graham White, "Nunavut: Inuit Self-Determination through a Land Claim and Public Government?" in *Nunavut: Inuit Regain Control of Their Lands and Their Lives,* ed. Jens Dahl, Jack Hicks, and Peter Jull (Copenhagen, Denmark: International Work Group for Indigenous Affairs, 2000), 89.

26 Ibid., 87.

27 Ibid.

28 Jim Bell, "Government Should Withdraw *Education Act,*" *Nunatsiaq News,* 18 October 2002, http://www.nunatsiaq.com/archives/nunavut 021004/news/editorial/editorial.html#oct18 (accessed 15 March 2008). See also Patricia D'Souza, "Tootoo Blasts New *Education Act,*" *Nunatsiaq News,* 26 April 2002, http://www.nunatsiaq.com/archives/nunavut020426/news/nunavut/20426_5.html (accessed 15 March 2008).

29 The report by Berger is also said to have been taken into consideration in development of the updated bill. See Government of Nunavut, "Nunavut's New *Education Act,*" backgrounder, 18 September 2008.

30 Jeeteeta Merkosak and Christa Kunuk, "DEA Coalition Explains Their Demands," *Nunatsiaq News,* 22 September 2006, http://www.nunatsiaq.com/archives/60929/opinionEditorial/ letters.html (accessed 10 January 2008).

31 Jeeteeta Merkosak, "Education and the Prime Minister's Visit," *Nunatsiaq News,* 10 August 2007, http://www.nunatsiaq.com/opinionEditorial/opinions.html (accessed 19 August 2007).
32 Ibid.
33 Ed Picco, quoted in John Thompson, "New *Education Act* Will Still Have Critics, Minister Admits," *Nunatsiaq News,* 5 October 2007, http://www.nunatsiaq.com/test/archives/2007/710/71005/news/nunavut/ 71005_566.html (accessed 12 January 2008).
34 Jim Bell, "Entrench Inuit Education Rights, NTI Says," *Nunatsiaq News,* 24 November 2006, http://www.nunatsiaq.com/archives/61124/news/nunavut/61124_05.html (accessed 10 January 2008).
35 Nunavut Tunngavik Incorporated, *Saqqiqpuq: Annual Report on the State of Inuit Culture and Society – Kindergarten to Grade 12 Education in Nunavut* (Iqaluit: Nunavut Tunngavik Incorporated, 2007).
36 Ibid., 28.
37 "In the Legislative Assembly: Language Laws, *Education Act* under Review," *Nunatsiaq News,* 7 March 2008, http://www.nunatsiaq.com/news/nunavut/80314_1014.html (accessed 15 March 2008).
38 Sara Minogue, "IDEA Slams *Education Act* Omissions," *Nunatsiaq News,* 6 January 2006, http://www.nunatsiaq.com/archives/60106/ news/nunavut/60106_05.html (accessed 10 January 2008).
39 Nunavut Department of Education, *Inuit Qaujimajatuqangit: Education Framework for Nunavut Curriculum* (Iqaluit: Nunavut Department of Education, Curriculum and School Services Division, 2007).
40 Vick-Westgate, *Nunavik,* 15.
41 P.J. Akeeagok, in Kath Clarida-Fry, dir., *Staking the Claim.*
42 The figure 25 percent is often used (by Berger, the Canadian Broadcasting Corporation, and *Nunatsiaq News*), but the Nunavut Department of Education currently reports it is closer to 30 percent.
43 Mary Simon, in Kath Clarida-Fry, dir., *Staking the Claim.*

Afterword

1 Government of Nunavut, "Nunavut's New *Education Act,*" backgrounder, 18 September 2008.
2 Chris Windeyer, "NTI Lobbies MLAs to Delay *Education Act,*" *Nunatsiaq News,* 19 September 2008, http://www.nunatsiaq.com/archives/2008/809/80919/news/nunavut/80919_1531.html (accessed 24 October 2008).
3 "Nunavut Legislature Dissolves for Election; Inuit Language Act Becomes Law," CBC News, 19 September 2008, http://www.cbc.ca/canada/north/story/2008/09/19/nunavut-laws.html (accessed 24 October 2008).

Bibliography

Government and Education/Curriculum Documents

Baffin Divisional Board of Education (BDBE). *Annual Report 1989-1990*. Iqaluit: BDBE, 1990.

–. *Annual Report 1990-1991*. Iqaluit: BDBE, 1991.

–. *Annual Report 1993-94*. Iqaluit: BDBE, 1995.

–. *Annual Report 1996-97*. Iqaluit: BDBE, 1997.

–. "Education in the Baffin." Paid insert, *Nunatsiaq News*. 1 October 1993.

–. "Education: Preparing for Nunavut." Paid insert, *Nunatsiaq News*, 30 September 1994.

–. *Module Development Part 1 – Traditional Skills – Career and Technology Studies*. Iqaluit: Department of Education, Culture and Employment, Government of the Northwest Territories, 1995-96.

–. *Our Future Is Now: Directions for Education in the Baffin*. Iqaluit: BDBE, 1987.

–. *Our Future Is Now ... Implementing Inuuqatigiit*. Iqaluit: BDBE, 1996.

–. *Our Future Is Now ... Implementing Inuuqatigiit: Goals, Strategies and Actions 1995-2000*. Iqaluit: BDBE, 1996.

–. *Piniaqtavut: Integrated Program*. Iqaluit: BDBE, 1989.

Berger, Thomas R. *Conciliator's Final Report: The Nunavut Project*. Nunavut Land Claims Agreement Implementation Contract Negotiations for the Second Planning Period 2003-2013. 1 March 2006.

Consulting Audit Canada. "Executive Summary." In *Accountability and Structural Options for Nunavut's Education, Health and Social Services Boards*, April 1999.

Department of Education. *Education in the NWT*. Yellowknife: Government of the Northwest Territories, 1988.

–. *Our Students, Our Future: An Educational Framework*. Yellowknife: Government of the Northwest Territories, March 1991.

–. *Survey of Education*. Ed. B.C. Gillie. Yellowknife: Government of the Northwest Territories, 29 February 1972.

Department of Education, Culture and Employment. *Inuuqatigiit: The Curriculum from the Inuit Perspective*. Yellowknife: Government of the Northwest Territories, August 1996.

Department of Education, Curriculum Division. *Elementary Education in the Northwest Territories: A Handbook for Curriculum Development*. Yellowknife: Government of the Northwest Territories, 1972.

Department of Education, Education Programs and Evaluation Division. *Philosophy of Education in the Northwest Territories*. Yellowknife: Government of the Northwest Territories, 1978.

Department of Education, Programme Development Division. *Learning in the Middle Years: A Handbook for Curriculum Development*. Yellowknife: Government of the Northwest Territories, 1973.

–. *Piksaaq*. Yellowknife, Ottawa, and Winnipeg: Government of the Northwest Territories, 1974.

Government of Canada. "Rights of the Aboriginal Peoples of Canada." *Constitution Act* R.S.C., 1982.

Government of the Northwest Territories. *An Ordinance Respecting Education in the Northwest Territories [Chapter 2]*. Yellowknife: Council of the Northwest Territories, 1977.

Government of Nunavut. "Government of Nunavut to Phase Out Health and Education Boards." News release. 22 April 1999.

–. "Nunavut Boards of Health and Social Services and Education." Backgrounder. 22 April 1999.

–. "Nunavut's New *Education Act.*" Backgrounder. 18 September 2008.

Loney, Dawn. *Working Together – Your Community and Your School: A Piniaqtavut/ Inuuqatigiit Strategy Book*. Iqaluit: BDBE, 1997.

Northwest Territories Executive Committee. *Report of the Special Committee of the Council of the Northwest Territories to Study the "Survey of Education – Northwest Territories."* Yellowknife: Council of the Northwest Territories, January 1973.

Northwest Territories Legislative Assembly. *An Ordinance to Amend the Education Ordinance.* Yellowknife: Government of the Northwest Territories, 1982.

Northwest Territories Legislative Assembly, Special Committee on Education. *Learning, Tradition and Change in the Northwest Territories.* Yellowknife: Northwest Territories Legislative Assembly, 1982.

Nunavut Department of Education. *Inuit Qaujimajatuqangit: Education Framework for Nunavut Curriculum.* Iqaluit: Nunavut Department of Education, Curriculum and School Services Division, 2007.

Nunavut Implementation Commission. *Footprints in New Snow: A Comprehensive Report from the Nunavut Implementation Commission to the Department of Indian Affairs and Northern Development, Government of the Northwest Territories and Nunavut Tunngavik Incorporated Concerning the Establishment of the Nunavut Government.* Ottawa: Bradda Printing Services, 1995.

Statistics Canada. *Education Indicators in Canada: Report of the Pan-Canadian Education Indicators Program.* Ottawa: Statistics Canada, 2005.

Films

Clarida-Fry, Kath, dir. *Staking the Claim: Dreams, Democracy and Canadian Inuit.* Ottawa: Entheos Films, 1 March 2007.

Greenwald, Barry, dir. *Life in the Settlements: Between Two Worlds.* In Celebration of Nunavut Series vol. 7. National Film Board of Canada, 1990.

Zacharias Kunuk, dir. *Kiviaq vs. Canada.* Isuma Productions, 2006.

–. *The Journals of Knud Rasmussen.* Isuma Productions, 2006.

Internet Sources

CBC News."Nunavut Legislature Dissolves for Election; Inuit Language Act Becomes Law." 19 September 2008, http://www.cbc.ca/canada/north/story/2008/09/19/nunavut-laws.html (accessed 24 October 2008).

Environment Canada. "Plants of the Arctic Cordillera Ecozone." http://www.ec.gc.ca/soerree/English/vignettes/Terrestrial/ac/plants.cfm (accessed 7 July 2007).

–. "Canadian Climate Normals, 1971-2000: Pond Inlet, Nunavut." http://climate.weatheroffice.ec.gc.ca/climate_normals/index_e.html (accessed 6 January 2008).

–. "Wildlife of the Northern Arctic Ecozone." http://www.ec.gc.ca/soerree/English/vignettes/Terrestrial/na/wildlife.cfm (accessed 7 July 2007).

Government of Canada. "Members of Parliament." *Federal Election Trivia.* http://www2.parl.gc.ca/ParlInfo/Compilations/ElectionsAndRidings/TriviaMembersOfParliament.aspx?Language=E#12. (accessed 16 April 2007).

–. "Rights of the Aboriginal Peoples of Canada." Part II, *Constitution Act* R.S.C. 1982. http://www.canlii.org/eliisa/highlight.do?text=Charter+of+Rights+and+Freedoms&language=en&searchTitle=Federal&path=/en/ca/const/const1982.html (accessed 17 April 2007).

Government of the Northwest Territories. "Past Commissioners." *Office of the Commissioner of the NWT.* http://www.commissioner.gov.nt.ca/history/ (accessed: 18 September 2007).

–. "History of the Legislative Assembly." *The Legislative Assembly of the Northwest Territories.* http://www.assembly.gov.nt.ca/live/pages/wpPages/factshistoryofthelegislativeassembly.aspxlive/pages/wpPages/factshistoryofthelegislativeassembly.aspx (accessed 2 December 2007).

Government of Quebec. Section 17.0.1. *James Bay and Northern Quebec Agreement and Complementary Agreements.* 1998 Edition. Sainte-Foy, Québec: Les Publications du Québec, 1998. http://www.ainc-inac.gc.ca/pr/agr/que/jbnq9_e.PDF (accessed 17 November 2007).

Inuit Tapiriit Kanatami. "ITC Founding Conference: August, 1971." About ITK/History. http://www.itk.ca/ corporate/history-founding-conference.php (accessed 14 April 2007).

–. "Transcript of First ITC Meeting." The Origin of ITK. http://www.itk.ca/corporate/history-origin-transcript-first-meeting.php (accessed 14 April 2007).

–. "Traditional Ecological Knowledge." http://www.itk.ca/environment/tek-ecological.php (accessed 7 July 2007).

National Indian Brotherhood/Assembly of First Nations. *Indian Control of Indian Education.* Ottawa: Assembly of First Nations, 1972. http://web.uvic.ca/ablo/documents/IndianControlofIndianEducation.pdf (accessed 31 Oct 2007).

Nunavut Tunngavik Incorporated. "History and Overview." *About Nunavut Tunngavik Incorporated.* http://www.tunngavik.com/english/about.html (accessed 14 April 2007).

Royal Commission on Aboriginal Peoples (RCAP). "Residential Schools." *Report of the Royal Commission on Aboriginal Peoples.* Volume 1; Part 2; Chapter 10, Indian and Northern Affairs Canada. http://www.aincinac.gc.ca/ch/rcap/sg/cg10_e.pdf (accessed 31 Oct 2007).

–. "Education." *Report of the Royal Commission on Aboriginal Peoples.* Volume 3; Chapter 5, Indian and Northern Affairs Canada. http://www.ainc-inac.gc.ca/ch/rcap/sg/ci5_ e.pdf (accessed 28 Jan 2008).

Newspaper Articles

Nunatsiaq News

Amagoalik, John. "A Different Place – My Little Corner of Canada Column." 22 October 1999, http://www.nunatsiaq.com/archives/nunavut991030/ corner.html (accessed 3 February 2005).

Arnakak, Jaypetee. "Commentary: What Is Inuit Qaujimajatuqangit?" 25 August 2000, http://www.nunatsiaq.com/archives/nunavut000831/nvt20825_17.html (accessed 10 January 2008).

Bell, Jim. "Entrench Inuit Education Rights, NTI Says." 24 November 2006, http://www.nunatsiaq.com/archives/61124/news/nunavut/61124_05.html (accessed 10 January 2008).

–. "Government Should Withdraw *Education Act*." 18 October 2002, http://www.nunatsiaq.com/archives/nunavut021004/news/editorial/editorial.html#oct18 (accessed 15 March 2008).

D'Souza, Patricia. "Tootoo Blasts New *Education Act*." 26 April 2002, http://www.nunatsiaq.com/archives/nunavut020426/news/nunavut/20426_5.html (accessed 15 March 2008).

"In the Legislative Assembly: Language Laws, *Education Act* under Review." 7 March 2008, http://www.nunatsiaq.com/news/nunavut/80314_1014.html (accessed 15 March 2008).

Merkosak, Jeeteeta. "Education and the Prime Minister's Visit." 10 August 2007, http://www.nunatsiaq.com/opinionEditorial/opinions.html (accessed 19 August 2007).

Merkosak, Jeeteeta, and Christa Kunuk. "DEA Coalition Explains Their Demands." 22 September 2006, http://www.nunatsiaq.com/archives/60929/opinionEditorial/letters.html (accessed 10 January 2008).

Minogue, Sara. "IDEA Slams *Education Act* Omissions." 6 January 2006, http://www.nunatsiaq.com/archives/60106/news/nunavut/60106_05.html (accessed 10 January 2008).

"Negotiators Reach Wildlife Agreement-in-Principle." 30 October 1981, http://www.nunatsiaq.com/archives/april0199/nvt90401_14.html (accessed 17 November 2007).

Pearce, Frank. "NWT Grade 12 Not a Real Grade 12?" 30 September 1994, 7, 38.

Phillips, Todd. "RC Bishop Apologizes for Abuses against Inuit Students." 1 March 1996, http://www.nunanet.com/~nunat/week/60301.html#3 (accessed 29 July 2007).

Qitsualik, Rachel A. "Baby Thief, Part One." 18 July 2003, http://www.nunatsiaq.com/archives/30725/news/editorial/columns.html (accessed 24 August 2007).

–. "What, Exactly, Is an Elder?" 25 June 1998, http://www.nunatsiaq.com/archives/nunavut980630/columns.html (accessed 10 January 2008).

Rahn, Marion. "Iqaluit Education Authority Wants School Board Reform." *Special Report on Education*. 9 October 1998, http://www.nunatsiaqnews.com/archives/nunavut981031/nvt81009_17.html (accessed 10 January 2008).

Thompson, John. "New *Education Act* Will Still Have Critics, Minister Admits." 5 October 2007, http://www.nunatsiaq.com/test/archives/2007/710/71005/news/nunavut/71005_566.html (accessed 12 January 2008).

–. "News Analysis: The Vanishing Inuit Teacher in Nunavut." 19 October 2007, http://www.nunatsiaq.com/archives/2007/710/71019/news/nunavut/71019_614.html (accessed 10 January 2008).

Windeyer, Chris. "'Eskimo Experiment' Claimants Seek Cash, Apology." 4 July 2008, 9. http://www.nunatsiaqnews.com/archives/2008/807/80704/news/nunavut/80704_1350.html (accessed 12 July 2008).

–. "NTI Lobbies MLAs to Delay *Education Act*." 19 September 2008, http://www.nunatsiaq.com/archives/2008/809/80919/news/nunavut/80919_1531.html (accessed 24 October 2008).

Published Sources: Books and Articles

Abel, Kerry M., and Ken S. Coates, eds. *Northern Visions: New Perspectives on the North in Canadian History*. Peterborough, ON: Broadview Press, 2001.

Abele, Frances, Carolyn Dittburner, and Katherine A. Graham. "Towards a Shared Understanding in the Policy Discussion about Aboriginal Education." In *Aboriginal Education: Fulfilling the Promise*, ed. Marlene Brant Castellano, Lynne Davis, and Louise Lahache, 3-24. Vancouver and Toronto: UBC Press, 2000.

Amagoalik, John. *Changing the Face of Canada*. Ed. Louis McComber. Life Stories of Northern Leaders Series. Iqaluit: Nunavut Arctic College, 2007.

–. "What Is This Land?" In *The Voice of the Natives: The Canadian North and Alaska,* ed. Hans Blohm, 9-10. Toronto: Penumbra Press, 2001.

Apak, Caleb. "*Inuktitut* Asks about Education." *Inuktitut Magazine* 48 (July 1981): 6-15.

Armstrong, Jeannette C. "Traditional Indigneous Education: A Natural Process." *Canadian Journal of Native Education* 14, 3 (1987): 14-19.

Arvaluk, James. *That's My Vision.* Ed. Noel McDermott. Life Stories of Northern Leaders Series. Iqaluit: Nunavut Arctic College, 2007.

Aylward, M. Lynn. "Discourses of Cultural Relevance in Nunavut Schooling." *Journal of Research in Rural Education* 22, 7 (2007): 1-9. http://www.jrre.psu.edu/articles/22-7.pdf (accessed 7 September 2007).

Barman, Jean. "Schooled for Inequality: The Education of British Columbia Aboriginal Children." In *Children, Teachers and Schools in the History of British Columbia,* ed. Jean Barman, Neil Sutherland, and J.D. Wilson, 57-80. Calgary: Detsilig, 1995.

–. "Separate and Unequal: Indian and White Girls at All Hallows School." In *Children, Teachers and Schools in the History of British Columbia,* ed. Jean Barman, Neil Sutherland, and J.D. Wilson, 337-58. Calgary: Detsilig, 1995.

Battiste, Marie. "Introduction." In *First Nations Education in Canada: The Circle Unfolds,* ed. Marie Battiste and Jean Barman, vii-xx. Vancouver: UBC Press, 1995.

Battiste, Marie, and Jean Barman, eds. *First Nations Education in Canada: The Circle Unfolds.* Vancouver: UBC Press, 1995.

Bennett, John, and Susan Rowley, eds. *Uqalurait: An Oral History of Nunavut.* Montreal and Kingston: McGill-Queen's University Press, 2004.

Bhattacharya, N.C. "Education in the Northwest Territories." *The Alberta Journal of Educational Research* 19, 3 (September 1973): 243-54.

Bilson, Janet Mancini. "New Choices for a New Era." In *Gossip: A Spoken History of Women in the North,* ed. Mary Crnkovich, 43-59. Ottawa: Canadian Arctic Resources Committee, 1990.

Bilson, Janet Mancini, and Kyra Mancini. *Inuit Women: Their Powerful Spirit in a Century of Change.* Toronto, New York, and Plymouth, MA: Rowman and Littlefield, 2007.

Boas, Franz. *The Central Eskimo.* Annual Report of the Bureau of American Ethnology for the Years 1884-1885, vol. 6. Washington, DC: Smithsonian Institution, 1988.

Briggs, Jean L. "Expecting the Unexpected: Canadian Inuit Training for an Experimental Lifestyle." *Ethos* 19, 3 (September 1991): 259-87.

–. *Never in Anger: A Portrait of an Eskimo Family.* Cambridge, MA: Harvard University Press, 1970.

Brody, Hugh. *The Other Side of Eden.* Vancouver and Toronto: Douglas and McIntyre, 2000.

–. *The People's Land: Eskimos and Whites in the Eastern Arctic.* Markham, ON: Penguin Books Canada, 1975.

Castellano, Marlene Brant, Lynne Davis, and Louise Lahache, eds. *Aboriginal Education: Fulfilling the Promise.* Vancouver and Toronto: UBC Press, 2000.

–. "Part 3 – Innovations in Education Practice: Renewing the Promise." In *Aboriginal Education: Fulfilling the Promise,* ed. Marlene Brant Castellano, Lynne Davis, and Louise Lahache, 97-100. Vancouver: UBC Press, 2000.

Champagne, Duane. "A Multidimensional Theory of Colonialism: The Native North American Experience." In *Social Change and Cultural Continuity among Native Nations,* ed. Duane Champagne, 131-43. Lanham, MD: Altamira Press, 2007.

Clancy, Peter. "The Making of Eskimo Policy in Canada, 1952-62: The Life and Times of the Eskimo Affairs Committee." *Arctic* 40, 3 (September 1987): 191-97.

Corbett, Mike. "A Protracted Struggle: Rural Resistance and Normalization in Canadian Educational History." *Historical Studies in Education/Revue d'histoire de l'éducation* 12, 1 (2001): 19-48.

Cousins, Mary. "Educational Opportunities for the Native Canadian." In *Indigenous Peoples and Education in the Circumpolar North,* ed. William G. Demmert Jr., 40-47. Juneau: Alaska State Department of Education, 1987.

Cowan, Susan, ed. *We Don't Live in Snow Houses Now: Reflections of Arctic Bay.* Ottawa: Canadian Arctic Producers, 1976.

Cruikshank, Julie. *Do Glaciers Listen? Local Knowledge, Colonial Encounters, and Social Imagination.* Vancouver: UBC Press, 2005.

Cummins, Jim. *Empowering Minority Students.* Sacramento, CA: California Association for Bilingual Education, 1989.

Dalby, Ronald. "Twentieth Century School." *North* 9, 2 (1962): 14-16.

Damas, David. *Arctic Migrants/Arctic Villagers: The Transformation of Inuit Settlement in the Central Arctic.* Native and Northern Series no. 32. Montreal and Kingston: McGill-Queen's University Press, 2002.

Darnell, Frank, ed. *Education in the North: The First International Conference on Cross-Cultural Education in the Circumpolar Nations.* Fairbanks: University of Alaska and the Arctic Institute of North America, 1972.

–. "Education and the Circumpolar Nativistic Movement: Twenty Years of Change for the Better." In *Self-Determination in Native Education in the Circumpolar North: Proceedings of the Seminar Inuit Control of Inuit Education.* ed. Malcolm Farrow and David Wilman, 24-42. Yellowknife: Department of Education, Government of the Northwest Territories, August 1989.

Darnell, Frank, and Anton Hoem. *Taken to Extremes: Education in the Far North.* Oslo, Norway: Scandinavian University Press, 1996.

Dick, Lyle. *Muskoxland: Ellesmere Island in the Age of Contact.* Calgary: University of Calgary Press, 2001.

Duffy, R. Quinn. "Providing an Education." In *The Road to Nunavut: The Progress of the Eastern Arctic Inuit since the Second World War,* ed. R. Quinn Duffy, 95-130. Montreal and Kingston: McGill-Queen's University Press, 1988.

–. *The Road to Nunavut: The Progress of the Eastern Arctic Inuit Since the Second World War.* Montreal and Kingston: McGill-Queen's University Press, 1988.

Evic-Twerdin, Leena, and Mary Wilman. "Elders' Discussion on Inuktitut Education." In *Self-Determination in Native Education in the Circumpolar North: Proceedings of the Seminar Inuit Control of Inuit Education Iqaluit,* ed. Malcolm Farrow and David Wilman, 13-23. Yellowknife: Department of Education, Government of the Northwest Territories, August 1989.

Elliott, David W. *Law and Aboriginal Peoples in Canada.* 4th ed. North York, ON: Captus Press, 2000.

Freeman, Minnie Aodla. *Life among the Qallunaat.* Edmonton: Hurtig, 1978.

French, Alice. *The Restless Nomad.* Winnipeg: Pemmican, 1992.

Fossett, Renée. *In Order to Live Untroubled: Inuit of the Central Arctic, 1550-1940.* Winnipeg: University of Manitoba Press, 2001.

Goldring, Philip. "Inuit Economic Responses to Euro-American Contacts." In *Interpreting Canada's North: Selected Readings,* ed. Kenneth S. Coates and William R. Morrison, 252-77. Toronto: Copp Clark, 1989.

Grant, Shelagh D. "Inuit History in the New Millennium: Challenges and Rewards." In *Northern Visions,* ed. Kerry M. Abel and Ken Coates, 91-106. Peterborough, ON: Broadview Press, 2001.

–. *Sovereignty or Security? Government Policy in the Canadian North, 1936-1950.* Vancouver: UBC Press, 1988.

Grygier, Pat Sandiford. *A Long Way from Home: The Tuberculosis Epidemic among the Inuit.* Montreal and Kingston: McGill-Queen's University Press, 1994.

Guemple, Lee. "Men and Women, Husbands and Wives: The Role of Gender in Traditional Inuit Society." *Études/Inuit/Studies* 10, 1-2 (1982): 9-24.

Hampton, Eber. "Towards a Redefinition of Indian Education." In *First Nations Education in Canada: The Circle Unfolds,* ed. Marie Battiste and Jean Barman, 5-46. Vancouver: University of British Columbia Press, 1995.

Harrington, Richard. *The Inuit: Life as It Was.* Edmonton: Hurtig, 1981.

Hicks, Jack, and Graham White. "Nunavut: Inuit Self-Determination through a Land Claim and Public Government?" In *Nunavut: Inuit Regain Control of Their Lands and Their Lives,* ed. Jens Dahl, Jack Hicks, and Peter Jull, 30-117. Copenhagen, Denmark: International Work Group for Indigenous Affairs, 2000.

Hinds, Margery. *School-House in the Arctic.* London: Geoffrey Bles, 1958.

Hodgson-Smith, Kathy L. "Issues of Pedagogy in Aboriginal Education." In *Aboriginal Education: Fulfilling the Promise,* ed. Marlene Brant Castellano, Lynne Davis, and Louise Lahache, 156-70. Vancouver and Toronto: UBC Press, 2000.

Honigmann, John J., and Irma Honigmann. *Eskimo Townsmen.* Ottawa: Canadian Research Centre for Anthropology, University of Ottawa, 1965.

Inuaaluk, Markusie. "Letter." *Inuit Today* 5, 8 (September 1976): 10.

Ipellie, Alootook. *Arctic Dreams and Nightmares.* Penticton, BC: Theytus Books, 1993.

–. "The Colonization of the Arctic." In *Indigena: Contemporary Native Perspectives,* ed. Gerald McMaster and Lee-Ann Martin, 1-17. Exhibition catalogue. Vancouver: Douglas and McIntyre, 1992.

–. "People of the Good Land." In *The Voice of the Natives: The Canadian North and Alaska,* ed. Hans Blohm, 19-33. Toronto: Penumbra Press, 2001.

Irwin, Colin. "Lords of the Arctic, Wards of the State: The Growing Inuit Population, Arctic Resettlement and Their Effects on Social and Economic Change." *Northern Perspectives* 17, 1 (1989): http://www.carc.org/pubs/v17no1/2.htm (accessed 2 August 2007).

Isherwood, Geoffrey B., Knute Sorensen, and Eric Colbourne. "Educational Development in the North: Preparing Inuit Leaders for School Board Control." *Education Canada* 26, 3 (1986): 9-15.

Ittinuar, Peter Freuchen. *Teach an Eskimo How to Read ...* Ed. Thierry Rodon. Life Stories of Northern Leaders Series. Iqaluit: Nunavut Arctic College, 2008.

Jaenen, Cornelius. "Mutilated Multiculturalism." In *Canadian Education in the 1980s,* ed. J. Donald Wilson, 79-96. Calgary: Detsilig, 1981.

Jenness, Diamond. *Eskimo Administration: II Canada.* Arctic Institute of North America Technical Paper no. 14. 1964.

–. "Eskimo Health." In *Eskimo Administration: II Canada,* 139-49. Arctic Institute of North America Technical Paper no. 14. 1964.

Johns, Robert E. "History of Administration of Schools, N.W.T." *Musk-Ox* 18 (1976): 42-57.

Jones, David S. "Virgin Soils Revisited." *William and Mary Quarterly* 60, 4 (2003): 703-42.

Jull, Peter. "Redefining Aboriginal-White Relations: Canada's Inuit." *International Journal of Canadian Studies/Revue internationale d'etudes canadiennes* 3 (1991): 11-25.

–. "Inuit and Nunavut: Renewing the New World." In *Nunavut: Inuit Regain Control of Their Lands and Their Lives,* ed. Jens Dahl, Jack Hicks, and Peter Jull, 118-37. Copenhagen, Denmark: International Working Group for Indigenous Affairs, 2000.

–. "Negotiating Nationhood, Renegotiating Nationhood: Canada's Nunavut and Nunavut's Canada." *Balayi: Culture, Law and Colonialism* 3 (2001): 67-86.

Kelm, Mary-Ellen. "Desperately Seeking Absolution: Native Agency as Colonialist Alibi?" *Canadian Historical Review* 75, 4 (1994): 543-56.

Krech III, Shepard. *The Ecological Indian: Myth and History.* New York: Norton, 2000.

–. "Reflections on Conservation, Sustainability, and Environmentalism in Indigenous North America." *American Anthropologist* 107 (2005): 78-86.

Kusugak, Jose. "The Tide Has Shifted: Nunavut Works for Us, and It Offers a Lesson to the Broader Global Community." In *Nunavut: Inuit Regain Control of Their Lands and Their Lives,* ed. Jens Dahl, Jack Hicks, and Peter Jull, 20-30. Copenhagen, Denmark: International Work Group for Indigenous Affairs, 2000.

Lange, Philip. "Some Qualities of Inuit Social Interaction." In *The White Arctic,* ed. Robert Paine, 107-28. St. John's/Toronto: Institute of Social and Economic Research, Memorial University of Newfoundland/University of Toronto Press, 1977.

Laugrand, Frédéric, Jarich Oosten, and François Trudel, eds. *Apostle to the Inuit: The Journals and Ethnographic Notes of Edmund James Peck, the Baffin Years, 1894-1905.* Toronto: University of Toronto Press, 2006.

MacDonald, John. *The Arctic Sky: Inuit Astronomy, Star Lore, and Legend.* Toronto/Iqaluit: Royal Ontario Museum/Nunavut Research Institute, 1998.

Macpherson, N.J. *Dreams and Visions: Education in the Northwest Territories from Early Days to 1984.* Yellowknife: Government of the Northwest Territories, 1991.

Mallea, J.R. "Introduction: Cultural Diversity and Canadian Education." In *Cultural Diversity and Canadian Education,* ed. J.R. Mallea and Jonathan D. Young, 1-16. Ottawa: Carleton University Press, 1984.

Mallory, Carolyn, and Susan Aiken. *Common Plants of Nunavut.* Published in collaboration with the Nunavut Department of Education, Nunavut Wildlife Management Board and Canadian Museum of Nature. Nepean, ON: National Printers, 2004.

Marcus, Alan Rudolph. *Relocating Eden: The Image and Politics of Inuit Exile in the Canadian Arctic.* Hanover, NH: University Press of New England, 1995.

Marsh, Donald B. *Echoes from a Frozen Land.* Ed. Winifred Marsh. Edmonton: Hurtig, 1987.

Matthiasson, John S. *Living on the Land: Change among the Inuit of Baffin Island.* Peterborough, ON: Broadview Press, 1992.

McAlpine, Robert. "Kablunait and Innuit: The Effect of the White Man upon the Eskimo Minority." *North* 8, 1 (1961): 26-32.

McGhee, Robert. *Ancient People of the Arctic.* Vancouver: UBC Press, 1996.

McGrath, Janet (Tamalk). "Elder's Perspective: Mariano Aupilaarjuk." *Inuktitut* 92 (2002): 54-67.

McNicoll, Paul, Frank Tester, and Peter Kulchyski. "Arctic Abstersion: *The Book of Wisdom for Eskimo,* Modernism and Inuit Assimilation." *Études/Inuit/Studies* 23, 1-2 (1999): 199-219.

Merritt, John. "Nunavut: Preparing for Self-Government." *Northern Perspectives* 21, 1 (1993): http://www.carc.org/pubs/v21no1/nunavut1.htm (accessed 18 April 2007).

Miller, J.R. *Shingwauk's Vision: A History of Native Residential Schools.* Toronto: University of Toronto Press, 1996.

Milloy, John S. *A National Crime: The Canadian Government and the Residential School System, 1879-1986.* Winnipeg: University of Manitoba Press, 1999.

Mock, Karen R. "25 Years of Multiculturalism – Past, Present and Future, Part I." *Canadian Social Studies* 31 (Spring 1997): 123-24.

Morse, Bradford W., ed. *Aboriginal Peoples and the Law: Indian, Métis and Inuit Rights in Canada.* Rev. 1st ed. Ottawa: Carleton University Press, 1989.

Mouat, W. Ivan. "Education in the Arctic District." *Musk-Ox* 7 (1970): 1-9.

Myers, Heather. "Changing Environment, Changing Times." *Environment* 43, 6 (2001): 32-45.

Napartuk, Tunu. "Youth Perspective (Inuit Health Information Initiative Conference)," *Inuktitut* 91 (2002): 64-72.

Nunavut Tunngavik Incorporated. *Saqqiqpuq: Annual Report on the State of Inuit Culture and Society – Kindergarten to Grade 12 Education in Nunavut.* Iqaluit: Nunavut Tunngavik Incorporated, 2007.

Nungak, Zebedee. "Life among the Qallunaat: Three Lifetimes in One." In *The Voice of the Natives: The Canadian North and Alaska,* ed. Hans Blohm, 163-64. Toronto: Penumbra Press, 2001.

Paine, Robert. "The Nursery Game: Colonizers and the Colonized." In *The White Arctic,* ed. Robert Paine, 78-106. St. John's/Toronto: Institute of Social and Economic Research, Memorial University of Newfoundland/University of Toronto Press, 1977.

–, ed. *The White Arctic.* St. John's/Toronto: Institute of Social and Economic Research, Memorial University of Newfoundland/University of Toronto Press, 1977.

Pauktuutit, Inuit Women of Canada. *The Inuit Way: A Guide to Inuit Culture.* Ottawa: Pauktuutit, 2006.

Pauktuutit, Inuit Women's Association. *Arnait: The Views of Inuit Women on Contemporary Issues.* Ottawa: Pauktuutit, 1991.

Phillips, Mark Salber, and Gordon Schochet, eds. *Questions of Tradition.* Toronto: University of Toronto Press, 2004.

Phillips, R.A.J. "The Opening Door." *North* 7, 6 (1960): 1-9.

Piper, Liza, and John Sandlos. "A Broken Frontier: Ecological Imperialism in the Canadian North." *Environmental History* 12, 4 (October 2007): 759-95.

Pirjuaq, Barnabus. "Before the Qallunaat Came." In *The Voice of the Natives: The Canadian North and Alaska,* ed. Hans Blohm, 154-61. Toronto: Penumbra Press, 2001.

Pudlat, Maata. "Boy Have Things Changed." In *Gossip: A Spoken History of Women in the North,* ed. Mary Crnkovich, 17-20. Ottawa: Canadian Arctic Resources Committee, 1990.

Qitsualik, Rachel, ed. "The Inuit Educational Concept." Special issue of *Ajurnarmat* no. 4. Inuit Cultural Institute, November 1979.

Raibmon, Paige. *Authentic Indians: Episodes of Encounter from the Late-Nineteenth-Century Northwest Coast.* Durham, NC, and London: Duke University Press, 2005.

Rasmussen, Derek. "Qallunology: A Pedagogy for the Oppressor." *Canadian Journal of Native Education* 25, 2 (2001): 105-212.

Rasmussen, Knud. *Intellectual Life of the Iglulik Eskimos.* Report of the Fifth Thule Expedition, 1921-24, vol. 6, no. 1. Copenhagen, Denmark: Gyldendalske Boghandel, 1929.

Ray, Arthur J. "Native History on Trial: Confessions of an Expert Witness." *Canadian Historical Review* 84, 2 (June 2003): 253-73.

Riewe, Rick. "Inuit Land Use Studies and the Native Claims Process." In *Aboriginal Resource Use in Canada: Historical and Legal Aspects,* ed. Kerry Abel and Jean Friesen, 287-99. Winnipeg: University of Manitoba Press, 1991.

Robertson, Gillian, ed. *Isuma: Inuit Studies Reader.* Montreal: Isuma, 2004.

Ross, W. Gillies. *Whaling and Eskimoes: Hudson Bay, 1860-1915.* National Museum of Man Publications in Ethnology no. 10. Ottawa: National Museums of Canada, 1975.

–. "Whaling, Inuit and the Arctic Islands." In *Interpreting Canada's North: Selected Readings,* ed. Kenneth S. Coates and William R. Morrison, 235-51. Toronto: Copp Clark, 1989.

Sahlins, Marshall. "Notes on the Original Affluent Society." In *Man the Hunter*, ed. Richard B. Lee and Irven DeVore, 85-89. Chicago: Aldine, 1968.

Serkoak, David. "Community Control in Native Education: A Sense of Ownership, Responsibility, and Commitment." In *Self-Determination in Native Education in the Circumpolar North: Proceedings of the Seminar Inuit Control of Inuit Education.* ed. Malcolm Farrow and David Wilman, 53-63. Yellowknife: Department of Education, Government of the Northwest Territories, August 1989.

Shearwood, Perry. "Inuit Identity and Literacy in a Nunavut Community." *Études/Inuit/Studies* 25, 1-2 (2001): 295-307.

–. "Literacy among the Aboriginal Peoples of the Northwest Territories." *Canadian Modern Language Review/La Revue canadienne des langues vivantes* 43, 4 (May 1987): 630-42.

Smith, Linda Tuhiwai. *Decolonizing Methodologies: Research and Indigenous Peoples.* New York: St. Martin's Press, 1999.

Spalding, Alex, and Thomas Kusugaq. *Inuktitut: A Multi-Dialectical Outline Dictionary.* Iqaluit: Nunavut Arctic College, 1998.

Sparham, Desmond. "Education at Cape Dorset: An Evaluation." *Eskimo* (Spring-Summer 1974): 12-13.

Stairs, Arlene. "Self-Image, World-Image: Speculations on Identity from Experiences with Inuit." *Ethos* 20, 1 (March 1992): 116-26.

Stern, Pamela R. "Learning to Be Smart: An Exploration of the Culture of Intelligence in a Canadian Inuit Community." *American Anthropologist* 101, 3 (1999): 502-14.

Sutherland, Neil. "I Can't Recall When I Didn't Help: The Working Lives of Pioneering Children in Twentieth Century British Columbia." *Histoire sociale/Social History* 23, 48 (November 1991): 263-88.

Tester, Frank James, and Peter Kulchyski. *Tammarniit (Mistakes): Inuit Relocation in the Eastern Arctic, 1939-63.* Vancouver: UBC Press, 1994.

Troper, Harold, and Morton Weinfeld. "Diversity in Canada." In *Ethnicity, Politics, and Public Policy,* ed. Harold Troper and Morton Weinfeld, 3-25. Toronto: University of Toronto Press, 1999.

Vallee, Frank G. "Eskimos of Canada as a Minority Group: Social and Cultural Perspectives." In *Education in the North: The First International Conference on Cross-Cultural Education in the Circumpolar Nations,* ed. Frank Darnell, 24-42. Fairbanks: University of Alaska Press and the Arctic Institute of North America, 1972.

Vansina, Jan. *Paths in the Rainforests: Toward a History of Political Tradition in Equatorial Africa.* Madison: University of Wisconsin Press, 1990.

Vick-Westgate, Ann. *Nunavik: Inuit-Controlled Education in Arctic Quebec.* Calgary, AB: University of Calgary Press, 2002.

Wachowich, Nancy. *Saqiyuq: Stories from the Lives of Three Inuit Women.* Montreal and Kingston: McGill-Queen's University Press, 1999.

Welsman, Paul. "Education of Native Peoples in the Northwest Territories: A Northern Model." In *The North in Transition,* ed. Nils Orvik and Kirk Patterson, 21-47. Kingston: Centre for International Relations, Queen's University, 1976.

Wenzel, George. "Inuit Subsistence and Hunter Support in Nunavut." In *Nunavut: Inuit Regain Control of Their Lands and Their Lives,* ed. Jens Dahl, Jack Hicks, and Peter Jull, 180-93. Copenhagen, Denmark: International Work Group for Indigenous Affairs, 2000.

– "'I Was Once Independent': The Southern Seal Protest and Inuit." *Anthropologica* 29, 2 (1987): 195-210.

–. "Traditional Ecological Knowledge and Inuit: Reflections on TEK Research and Ethics." *Arctic* 51, 2 (June 1999): 113-24.

Williams, Nancy M., and Graham Baines, eds. *Traditional Ecological Knowledge.* Canberra: Centre for Resource and Environmental Studies, Australian National University, 1993.

Wilson, J.D. "The Visions of Ordinary Participants: Teachers' Views of Rural Schooling in British Columbia in the 1920s." In *A History of British Columbia: Selected Readings,* ed. Pat Roy, 239-55. Toronto: Copp Clark Pitman, 1989.

Unpublished Sources (Reports, Theses)

Bohaker, Heidi. "*Nindoodemag:* Anishinaabe Identities in the Eastern Great Lakes Region, 1600-1900." PhD diss., Department of History, University of Toronto, 2006.

Born, David Omar. *Eskimo Education and the Trauma of Social Change.* Northern Science Research Group Report. Ottawa: Department of Indian Affairs and Northern Development, 15 January 1970.

Elders' Advisory Committee Meeting Transcript. Arviat: Department of Education, Government of Nunavut, 1-3 June 2004.

Inuit-Eskimo Association of Canada. "Coppermine Conference Report, July 14-18, 1970." Ed. Norman R. Dunne. Partially reproduced in *Nunavut Sivuniksavut Course Readings: Inuit-Government Relations,* 55-115 (Ottawa: Nunavut Sivuniksavut, n.d.).

Irniq, Peter. "Mending the Past: Memory and the Politics of Forgiveness." Paper presented at the K.C. Irving Centre, Acadia University, Wolfville, Nova Scotia, 19 October 2004.

Jull, Peter. "Politics, Development and Conservation in the International North." *Conservation and the North in a Decade of Uncertainty.* Canadian Arctic Resources Committee Policy Paper no. 2. March 1986.

Kalluak, Mark, ed. *Qaujimatait Meeting Transcript.* Arviat: Department of Education, Government of Nunavut, 8 June 2001.

Karetak, Joe. *The Inuit Version of Where Our Thoughts Are Believed to Be Generated.* Arviat: Department of Education, Government of Nunavut, n.d.

Loukacheva, Natalia. "Autonomy and Indigenous Peoples of the Arctic: Legal Status of Inuit (Case Study of Greenland and Nunavut)." PhD diss., Department of Law, University of Toronto, 2004.

Memon, Nadeem A. "Contextualizing Hall-Dennis: The Rise of Progressive Educational Practices in Ontario, 1968-1972." MA thesis, Department of Theory and Policy Studies, Ontario Institute for Studies in Education of the University of Toronto, 2006.

Nunavut Social Development Council. *Report on the Nunavut Traditional Knowledge Conference.* Igloolik: Nunavut Tunngavik Incorporated, 22-24 March 1998.

O'Donoghue, Fiona. "The Hunger for Professional Learning in Nunavut Schools." EdD diss., Department of Curriculum, Teaching and Learning, Ontario Institute for Studies in Education of the University of Toronto, 1998.

O'Donoghue, Fiona, Joannie Tompkins, Sandy McAuley, Lena Metuq, Nunia Qanatsiaq, and Elizabeth Fortes. *Pursuing a Dream: Inuit Educaiton in the Qikiqtani Region of Nunavut from 1980-1999.* Report on the Iqaluit Meetings of 25 May to 1 June 2005 to the Social Sciences and Humanities Research Council – Northern Development Grant, 5 October 2005.

Pulpan, Adam. "The Relationship of School, Inuit Qaujimajatuqangit and Elders in the Education of Youth within a Nunavut Community." MEd thesis, Department of Education, York University, 2006.

Tompkins, Joanne Marie. "Critical and Shared: Conceptions of Inuit Educational Leadership." EdD diss., Department of Curriculum, Teaching and Learning, Ontario Institute for Studies in Education of the University of Toronto, 2006.

Tufts, M. Alexander. "Pisukvigijait – Where You Walk: Inuit Students' Perceptions of Connections between Their Culture and School Science." MEd diss., Department of Curriculum and Instruction, University of New Brunswick, 1998.

Van Meenan, Mary A. "Government Policies of Education for the Native Peoples of Siberia and the Canadian Northwest Territories, 1900-90: A Historical Examination." PhD diss., Department of History, Dalhousie University, 1994.

Index

Printed and bound in Canada by Friesens
Set in Minion and Helvetica Condensed by Artegraphica Design Co. Ltd.
Copy editor: Robert Lewis
Proofreader: Jean Wilson
Cartographer: Eric Leinberger